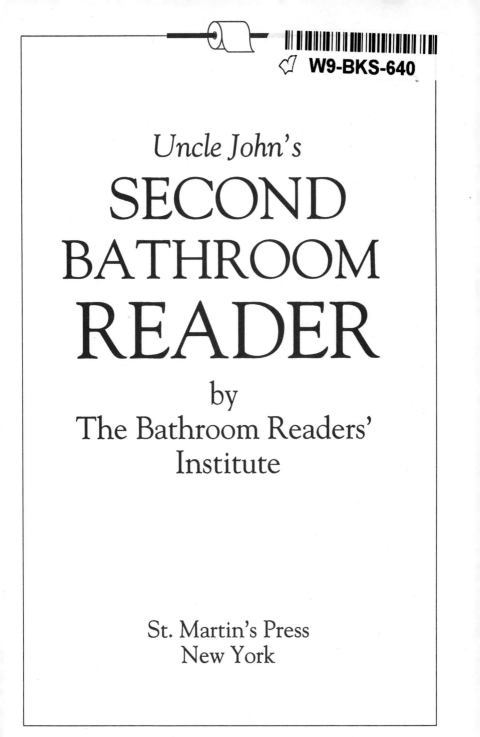

Uncle John's
SECOND BATHROOM READER

by
The Bathroom Readers'
Institute

St. Martin's Press
New York

Produced and Packaged by Javnarama
Design by Javnarama
Cover directed by Michael Brunsfeld, executed by Richard Kizu-Blair

Library of Congress Cataloging-in-Publication Data

Uncle John's second bathroom reader / the Bathroom Readers' Institute.
    p.   cm.
  ISBN 0-312-03446-6
  1. Wit and humor.   2. American wit and humor.   I. Bathroom Readers' Institute (Berkeley, Calif.)   II. Title: Second bathroom reader.
PN6153.U45   1989
818'.5407—dc20   89-10332
                                                          CIP

THANK YOU

The Bathroom Readers' Institute sincerely thanks the people whose advice and assistance made this book possible.

Michael Brunsfeld
Richard Kizu-Blair
John Javna
Gordon Javna
Bob Shannon
Stuart Moore
Rachel Blau
Andrea Sohn
Gordon Van Gelder
Fifth Street Computers
Eric Lefcowitz
Mike Wilkins
Jim Morton
Gene Brissie
Ivan Stang
Northwest EXTRA
Carol Schreiber
Penelope Houston
Fritz von Springmeyer
Gene Sculatti
Pat Mitchell

Steve Gorelick
Leslie Boies
Jack Mingo
Franz Ross
Sam Javna
Charlie Weimer
Stephen Louis
Carla Small
Lorrie Bodger
Gideon Javna
Reddy Kilowatt
Gene Novogrodsky
Bob Migdal
Betsy Joyce
Greg Small
Adrienne Levine
Jay Nitschke
Mike Goldfinger

And all the Bathroom Readers

INTRODUCTION

W hen the Bathroom Readers' Institute put together our first *Uncle John's Bathroom Reader* last year, we urged America's secret readers to come out of the water closet, to "sit down and be counted." And they did, pouring into bookstores around America by the tens of thousands.

Clearly, we've flushed out a new "silent majority"—which is great, because as you might imagine, we really love our work.
- First, it's a challenge to come up with interesting ideas for pieces in the book.
- Second, it's a pleasure to write for an audience we know is going to read every page at least once...and sometimes two or three times.
- And finally, *The Bathroom Reader* gives us a chance to do some throughly enjoyable research; rest assured that everything included here has been tested under actual Bathroom Readers' conditions.

What has the B.R.I. learned about bathroom reading?
- The ideal piece of lavatory lit is a unique blend of light reading and weighty subject matter.
- The topics should be heavy enough to provide food for thought, but avoid clogging the reader's mind wth details.
- The bits of information should be easy to absorb.
- Ideas should flow smoothly from one article to the next.
- A person's mind is more fluid when he or she is in the john, so the best bathroom reading is informative as well as entertaining.

We could go on and on (as we often do), but if you're a bathroom reader, you can already read the writing on the wall.

Go ahead and take the plunge into *Uncle John's Second Bathroom Reader*. And remember: "Go With the Flow."

CONTENTS

NOTE

Because the B.R.I. understands your reading needs, we've divided the contents by length as well as subject.
Short—a quick read
Medium—1 to 3 pages
Long—for those extended visits, when something a little more involved is required.

UNCLE JOHN'S MAILBAG

Our first Uncle John's Bathroom Reader *brought in lots of mail with interesting comments...and suggestions for this second volume. Here's a random sample*

Dear Fellow Bathroom Connoisseurs:
I thoroughly enjoyed your first book....For many years I would search my house for something interesting to read before I would enter my asylum. I have even been known to do my homework while I was in the bathroom. In fact, when I was younger I once watched a whole quarter of the Super Bowl while in the bathroom. It's relaxing and quiet in there, and no one bothers you—except for the few who don't understand, and ask you every few minutes if you've fallen in.

—*Adam B., Richmond Heights, Missouri*

Dear Uncle John,
I am from a long line of Bathroom Readers. At first I thought it was an Italian thing to do crosswords and read for long periods of time in the head, because my father is Italian and my grandfather was straight off the boat....Now I know better.

—*Vinnie B.*

Uncle John,
It was a strain writing, but now that we've started, it's a relief. I'm sure the feeling will pass, so being brief, we'd like to "sit down and be counted"—It's the only way to get a-head in life. We've enjoyed the book—it has really bowled us over! We were unable to flush out any discrepancies....Well, that about wipes it up.

—*Mike and Dan M., Colora, Maryland*

Dear Sirs:
What about the possibility of inserting a picture of a wayside comfort station such as were common in the Roman Empire days? In case you are not familiar with this convenience, let me say that it would normally consist of a group of holes, perhaps 25 in number, in an open location in the main part of an ancient city or town. All

---

The character most often portrayed in films is Sherlock Holmes—193 times since 1900.

seats were side by side without any pretence or privacy. I can imagine that such a citizen convenience was a hub of gossip and activity for both men and women.

—R. Wilfed B., Totonto, Canada

Dear B.R.I.
We really enjoyed Volume I of your book and have a great idea for a few pages in Volume II: Elvis Presley sightings!! They've been rampant this year, most notably in Kalamazoo, Michigan, where the King reportedly frequents all-night grocery stores and Burger Kings.

—Ron and Lisa B., Des Moines, Iowa

Uncle John—
We always kept the Sears Catalog in our outhouse and used the paper. We had already bought what we wanted out of it, of course. Talk about rough—that stuff was worse than corn cobs!

—Dan R., Athens, Georgia

Dear B.R.I.—
All right, I confess! I read your book cover-to-cover on an airplane— not in the bathroom!

—Julie S., Merritt Island, Florida

Gentlemen:
I enjoyed the footnotes immensely. Maybe some of them can be questions next time, such as:
• Why are hot dog buns packed 8 to a package while the hot dogs themselves always come 10 to a package? To even things out, you have to buy 5 packs of buns, and 4 packs of weiners.
• Why are toilet papers and tissues scented? You shouldn't be able to smell tissues if your nose is stuffed up, and you shouldn't be putting toilet paper up to your nose....Should you?

—Andy D., Gainesville, Fla.

Dear Uncle John:
I laughed so hard while reading your book that I dropped it in the toilet. Don't worry—I bought another one.

—Bill D., Tenafly, N.J.

Keep those cards and letters coming—they're great bathroom reading!

THOMAS CRAPPER: MYTH OR HERO?

*If our mail was any gauge, the most controversial tidbit in the first
Bathroom Reader was our comment that the widely accepted
notion that Thomas Crapper invented the toilet is a hoax.
Readers sent all kinds of evidence "proving" that Crapper was
real. But was he? Let's take a closer look.*

FLUSHED WITH PRIDE

The name Thomas Crapper appears to have been unknown among bathroom historians until 1969, when English writer Wallace Reyburn published a 99-page book entitled *Flushed With Pride—The Story of Thomas Crapper.*

This biography (which Reyburn's publisher calls "The Little Classic of the Smallest Room") begins this way:

"Never has the saying 'a prophet is without honor in his own land' been more true than in the case of Thomas Crapper. Here was a man whose foresight, ingenuity, and perseverence brought to perfection one of the great boons to mankind. But is his name revered in the same way as, for example, that of the Earl of Sandwich?"

Of course not. Not, anyway, until Reyburn's book was published.

CRAPPER, THE MAN
According to Reyburn:
• Tom Crapper was born in 1837, and died in 1910.
• He is responsible for many toilet innovations—including, as bathroom-ologist Pat Mitchell puts it, "the toilets that flush in a rush seen in public restrooms today, and the...trap in plumbing that keeps sewer gas from rising into our homes."
• But the most important of Crapper's alleged accomplishments was "Crapper's Valveless Water Waste Preventer," an apparatus that made flushing more efficient. *Cleaning Management* magazine calls it "the forerunner of our present-day flush system."
• For this contribution, Crapper was supposedly appointed the Royal Plumber by King Edward VII.

- Crapper's name was stenciled on all the cisterns—and later, toilets—his company manufactured: "T. Crapper & Co., Chelsea, London." American soldiers stationed in England during World War I began calling a toilet a "crapper."

FACT OR FICTION?

Beats us. But here are a few possibilities to consider:

- The premier bathroom history, an impressive tome called *Clean and Decent*, makes absolutely no mention of Thomas Crapper.

- Reyburn followed up *Flushed With Pride* with another social "history," entitled *Bust Up: The Uplifting Tale of Otto Titzling and the Development of the Bra.*

- Charles Panati, in *Extraordinary Origins of Everyday Things*, notes that "the acclumulation of toilet-humor puns, double-entendres, and astonishing coincidences eventually reveals...Reyburn's hoax." He offers some examples: "He moved to London and eventually settled on Fleet Street, where he perfected the 'Crapper W.C. Cistern after many dry runs.'...The installation of a flushing toilet at the Royal Palace was 'a high-water mark in Crapper's career.'... He was particularly close with his niece, 'Emma Crapper,' and had a friend named 'B.S.' "

- On the other hand, Pat Mitchell sent us this information: "It seems that in recent years, a certain Ken Grabowski, researcher at the Field Museum of Natural History in Chicago, has unselfishly, unswervingly, and unrelentingly sought to uncover the truth. His findings? Indeed, there was a Thomas Crapper (1836-1910). And Crapper founded a London plumbing fixture company in 1861. His efforts did produce many improvements in the fixtures he manufactured. His company's products (with his name upon them) were distributed all over Europe. Military barracks included. These were still there during World War I."

CONCLUSION

The Bathroom Readers Institute is stuck; we can't relieve the tension or wipe away the rumors. The legend of Crapper seems to have survived all the stink people have made about his life. Or, as Pat Mitchell puts it, "I'm not certain the legend can be killed, but if it could, does B.R.I. want to be the executioner?"

It's not polite to stare, but a butterfly probably can't help it—it has 12,000 eyes.

WORD PLAY

In the first Bathroom Reader we supplied the origins of familiar phrases. Here are some more.

STEAL SOMEONE'S THUNDER
Meaning: To pre-empt; to draw attention away from someone else's achievements in favor of your own.
Background: English dramatist John Dennis invented a gadget for imitating the sound of thunder and introduced it in a play in the early 1700s. The play flopped. Soon after, Dennis noted that another play in the same theater was using his sound-effects device. He angrily exclaimed, "That is my thunder, by God; the villains will play my thunder, but not my play." The story got around London, and the phrase grew out of it.

PAY THROUGH THE NOSE
Meaning: To pay a high price; to pay dearly.
Background: Comes from ninth-century Ireland. When the Danes conquered the Irish, they imposed an exorbitant Nose Tax on the island's inhabitants. "They took a census (by counting noses) and levied oppressive sums on their victims, forcing them to pay by threatening to have their noses actually slit." Paying the tax was "paying through the nose."

HAPPY AS A CLAM
Meaning; Blissfully happy; perfectly content.
Background: The original phrase was, "Happy as a clam at high tide." Why at high tide? Because people can't dig clams out then. They're "safe and happy" until low tide, when their breeding grounds are exposed. The saying was shortened through use.

TO LAY AN EGG
Meaning: To fail.
Background: From the British sport of cricket. When you fail to score, you get a zero—which looks like an egg. The term is also taken from baseball, where a zero is a "goose egg."

There are more cars in Southern California than there are cows in India.

SWEET NUTHIN'S

Interesting facts about American candies from
B.R.I. member Jim Morton.

THREE MUSKETEERS. Most people today have no idea where the name for the Three Musketeers bar came from. Advertising in the fifties and sixties suggested the candy bar was so named because it was big enough for three people to share. The truth is, Three Musketeers bars were originally made of three separate nougat sections: vanilla, chocolate and strawberry. Eventually, the strawberry and vanilla nougat sections were eliminated, leaving only chocolate nougat in each Three Musketeers bar.

BLACK CROWS. The Mason Candy Company decided to introduce a new candy treat in 1890. The candy, a licorice-flavored gumdrop, was to be called Black Rose. But the printer misunderstood the instructions and printed the wrappers with the name "Black Crows." The printer refused to reprint the job, claiming it was Mason's mistake. Rather than pay to reprint the wrappers, the folks at Mason decided to change the name of the product. Today, one-hundred years later, Black Crows are still available by that name.

M&Ms. In 1930, Frank Mars, a candy-maker in Chicago, told his son Forrest to get out of the country and not come back. Forrest went to England with a few thousand dollars and the recipe for Milky Ways. He quickly set up shop and began selling his own versions of his father's candy bars. While in England, Forrest discovered "Smarties," a candy-coated chocolate treat that was popular with the Brits. He bought the rights to market "Smarties" in America, where he went into partnership with a business associate named Bruce Murrie. The candies were called M&Ms; short for Mars and Murrie.

HERSHEY'S. Milton Hershey, the inventor of the Hershey Bar, was an unusual man. As a child he was brought up in a strict Mennonite family. Unlike most entrepreneurs, he never sought the usual material wealth that accompanies success. In 1909 he took a large sum of the money he had earned making candy bars, and opened the

Only 53% of Americans have ever been to a dentist.

Milton Hershey School for orphaned boys. Nine years later he donated the candy company to a trust for the school. Today, the Milton Hershey School and School Trust still own 56% of the Hershey Company.

SPARKLERS. Wintergreen LifeSavers, when chewed in the dark, give off sparks. This is due to a chemical process known as triboluminescence.

SUGAR DADDY. Robert O. Welch, the inventor of the Sugar Daddy, is also the founder of the John Birch Society.

MEXICAN HATS. Heide's Mexican Hats candies were originally called "Wetem and Wearems." Kids were supposed to lick the candies and stick them to their foreheads. What possible reason for kids wanting to use the candies in this fashion is unknown.

CRACKER JACKS. The dog on the Cracker Jack package is named Bingo, after the folk song that generations of kids were forced to learn in grade school.

OH HENRY. Every day at about the same time, a young man named Henry would stop in at the Williamson Candy Company in Chicago, and flirt with the girls making the candy. Soon the girls were asking Henry to do things for them. Whenever he came into the store they would start, "Oh Henry, will you do this! Oh Henry, will you do that!" When Williamson introduced a new candy bar in 1920, one of the salesmen suggested that they call the bar "Oh Henry" in honor of the likeable young fellow.

CHARLESTON CHEW. Sometimes the names of candy bars come from fads that are popular when they are introduced. The Charleston Chew was introduced during the roaring twenties when the Charleston dance craze was in full swing.

CLARK BAR. Often candy manufacturers spend hours agonizing over what to call their confections. But David L. Clark wasn't one to waste time on such efforts. When he introduced his candy bar in 1917 he simply named it after himself.

Estimates show that it may take a plastic container 50,000 years to decompose.

THE LAST LAUGH: EPITAPHS

Who collects unusual epitaphs? Lots of people, we're discovering.
Here are some authentic ones, supplied by B.R.I. members.

Seen in Falkirk, Scotland:
Solomon Pease
Here under this sod, and under
   these trees
Is buried the body of Solomon
   Pease
But here in his hole lies only
   the pod,
His soul is shelled out, and
   gone up to God.

Seen in Hatfield, Massachusetts:
Arabella Young, 1771
Here lies as silent clay,
Miss Arabella Young.
Who on the 21st of May,
Began to hold her tongue.

Seen in Bradford, Vermont:
Mary S. Hoyt, 1836
She lived—what more can
   then be said?
She died—and all we know
she's dead.

Seen in Skaneatles, New York:
Sally Briggs
Underneath this pile of stones,
Lies all that's left of Sally
   Jones.
Her name was Briggs, it was
   not Jones,
But Jones was used to rhyme
   with stones.

Seen in Topsfield, Massachusetts:
Mary Lefavour, 1797
Reader pass on and ne'er waste
   your time
On bad biography and bitter
   rhyme.
For what I am this cum'brous
   clay insures
And what I was, is no affair of
   yours.

Seen in Lincoln, Maine:
Sacred to the memory of
   Jared Bates,
Who died Aug. the 6th, 1800.
His widow, aged 24, lives at
   7 Elm Street,
Has every qualification for a
   good wife,
And longs to be comforted.

Seen in Kent, England:
Grim death took me without
   any warning.
I was well at night, and dead
   in the morning.

Seen in Tombstone, Arizona:
Lester Moore
Here lies
Lester Moore
Four slugs from a 44.
No Les
No more.

With the amount of fuel held in a jumbo jet, you could drive around the world in a car 4 times.

ELEMENTARY, MY DEAR STEVE

The famous sleuth, Leslie Boies, and her faithful companion, Steve, have a few simple mysteries for you to solve. Answers on p. 223

The celebrated detective, Leslie Boies, was home working on a case one day when Steve came wandering in.

"I just saw the strangest thing," he mused. "A man walked into Effie's Bar down on Carlotta Street and ordered a glass of water. Suddenly the bartender pulled out a gun and pointed it at him."

"What happened then, Steve?" Leslie looked up, interested.

"That's the strange part—the man said " 'Thank you,' and left"

"Well, I expect he would," Leslie chuckled. "The bartender did him a favor."

What had happened in the bar?

2. Steve was reading the newspaper, and Leslie was combing her hair.

"Here's a story about a guy named Moore," Steve told her, "whose life was saved by a *dream*. Apparently, he owns some sort of factory and commutes into the city every morning at 7:00 A.M.. Then he takes the 5:30 P.M. train home every night.

"One morning last week, he met the night watchman as he arrived at work. The night watchman told him that he'd had a dream the previous night that the 5:30 train would crash that day...and he warned Moore not to take his regular train. Would you believe it—Moore actually waited and took a later train. And afterwards, he heard that the 5:30 P.M. train *did* crash! Now, Moore is trying to figure out how to reward the night watchman. What do you think he should do, Les?"

Leslie looked up and thought for a second.

"Well, Moore should give the him a bonus...and then he should fire the guy."

Steve was startled. "Huh? Why do you say that, Les?"

"Why Steve, I'm surprised at you. It's elementary."

What was Leslie thinking?

Turtles don't have any teeth.

AD TRICKS

Former adman Terry Galanoy once wrote a book called Down
the Tube, *in which he revealed many secrets of
making TV ads, including these:*

BEER ADS

B EER ADS
"For years, static pictures of a glass of beer have been made
with a light-grade motor oil in the bottom of the glass and a
foamy head of whipped-up detergent on top."

SHAMPOO ADS

The models "washing" their hair in shampoo commercials are often
really using something else on their heads. According to Galanoy,
they either use laundry detergent, because "it whips up creamy and
frothy and rich-looking," or "beaten egg whites, which are carefully laid on the hair not by beauticians, but by home economists,
who ice up the lady's head as if they were icing up a cake."

FOOD ADS

"There are a lot of everyday camera tricks for making food look better. Soap chips are sprinkled on cereal because they look more like
sugar than sugar does. Lard is scooped out to make ice cream shapes
in a sundae dish because ice cream melts under hot lights and lard
doesn't. Small stones replace boiled rice because boiled rice goes
out a sticky mess."

HAIR COLOR ADS

"You...can't be sure at whom you are looking. For example, one
commercial for Clairol hair coloring used one girl for the front of
the hair and another for the back. The back of the first girl's hair
wasn't attractive enough, but they wanted her face, so they hired a
back-of-the-head backup for her."

TESTIMONIALS

Those hidden camera commercials?..."Sometimes they have to
shoot 100 women and enough film to make three features in order
to get one 'spontaneous' endorsement."

Until 1796, the state of Tennessee was known as Franklin.

PRIME TIME PROVERBS

TV's comments about everyday life in America, collected by Jack Mingo and John Javna for their book, Prime Time Proverbs—*an excellent supplement for your bathroom library.*

ON REVENGE
Sam: "Let me give you some advice, Carla. I suggest you turn the other cheek."
Carla: "Mooning her isn't enough—I want to hurt her!"
—*Cheers*

ON RELIGION
"Let's leave religion to the televangelists. After all, they're the professionals."
—**Cheviot,**
Max Headroom

"Edith, Sunday's supposed to be the day of rest. How can I rest when I'm going to church?"
—**Archie Bunker**
All in the Family

"I thought I was on my way to Nirvana. All I ended up with was recurrent flashbacks of the original Mouseketeers."
—**Reverend Jim Ignatowski,**
Taxi

ON OPPORTUNITY
"How do you like my luck? Every time opportunity knocks, I ain't got enough money to open the door."
—**Sgt. Ernie Bilko,**
The Phil Silvers Show

ON SINGLE MOTHERS
Blanche: "It says here in this Spock book that it's important to have male role models during your formative years."
Rose: " Well, what does Spock know about raising babies? On Vulcan they're all in pods."
—*The Golden Girls*

ON LIFE
Coach Ernie Pantusso: "How's life, Norm?"
Norm Peterson: "It's a dog-eat-dog world, and I'm wearing Milkbone underwear."
—*Cheers*

Wednesday Addams: "Look, a black widow spider village."
Gomez Addams: "Amazing, just like a tiny human world."
Wednesday: "Yes, all they do is fight."
Morticia Addams: "Well, that's life."
The Addams Family

RUMORS

Here's the second installment of a feature we included in BR #1. Rumors are a special kind of gossip—outrageous stories that, one expert explains, "reveal the desires, fears, and obsessions of a society." They're also a lot of fun. Did you hear the one about...

RUMOR: Proctor & Gamble is secretly owned by the Moonies (Reverend Sun Myung Moon's Unification Church).

HOW IT STARTED: Apparently, it was originally fueled by widespread paranoia about Moon's flower-selling legions. (They're everywhere!) The secret tipoff was supposed to be P&G's logo—the man in the moon. It was "a signal" to other Moonies.

WHAT HAPPENED: Proctor & Gamble executives first got wind of the rumor in 1979 and ignored it...until they got over 1,000 phone inquiries about the matter in a single month. Alarmed, they sent a letter to newspaper editors around the country pointing out that neither the Unification Church nor Rev. Moon owned even one share of stock in the company. Despite this, P&G continued to get 300 inquiries about it every month for several years.

THE RUMOR: A few years ago, three white Midwestern women, visiting New York City for the first time, were on an elevator in their hotel. A large black man with a big dog got on and hissed, "Sit, Lady." The terrified women immediately slid to the floor—whereupon the man informed them he was actually talking to his dog, Lady. The embarrassed women got up and contritely began asking about restaurants. They got the gentleman's recommendation for a good one, went, and enjoyed it. And when it came time to pay the bill, they were informed it had already been taken care of...by Reggie Jackson, the man they'd "met" in the elevator.

HOW IT STARTED: Unknown, but the story was reported as fact all over the country, including stories in newspapers in New York, L.A., Detroit, and Salt Lake City.

WHAT HAPPENED: A New York reporter finally called Jackson and asked him to confirm it. Jackson's reply: "I've heard that story a million times and it's not true. I would never own a dog in New York. It would be cruel."

The word "girl" shows up in the Bible only once.

THE RUMOR: Green M&Ms are an aphrodisiac.
HOW IT STARTED: Unknown.
WHAT HAPPENED: M&M Mars, the company that makes the candy, gets frequent requests for custom-packed bags of green M&Ms. They always refuse.

THE RUMOR: While President Richard Nixon was visiting China, he tried to steal a priceless Chinese teacup by slipping it into his briefcase. The Chinese spotted him. But instead of confronting Nixon directly, they entertained him with a magician who—while performing—surreptitiously retrieved the cup and substituted a worthless replica. Nixon didn't realize it 'til he got back to the U.S.
HOW IT STARTED: The official Chinese news agency released the story.
WHAT HAPPENED: The American government ignored it. Experts explained that the Chinese used it as propaganda to reinforce their self-image: "It symbolized," said one expert, "the victory of the resourceful Chinese over the crafty foreigner, and the ability of the Chinese to know how to act without having anyone lose face."

THE RUMOR: McDonald's owner Ray Kroc contributed a big chunk of his company's profits to the Church of Satan, a devil-worshiping cult in San Francisco.
HOW IT STARTED: Unknown, but a McDonald's manager first heard it in a Georgia fundamentalist church in 1979.
WHAT HAPPENED: Not wanting to give it credibility, McDonald's ignored it until it spread so far that an Ohio minister claimed Kroc had actually admitted it was true on "The Phil Donahue Show," and a few religious groups began calling for a boycott of the food chain. The company's public relations director quickly obtained a transcript of the program to prove Kroc had said nothing of the kind, then made appearances before several fundamentalist groups to explain the situation. It worked—they retracted boycott calls and dropped the matter.

THE RUMOR: When Army brass was planning its 1983 invasion of Grenada, they decided they needed someone who could speak Spanish, to communicate with the Grenadian citizens. So they convinced a Spanish-speaking supply sergeant named Ontiveros to land with the first paratroopers. He jumped, came under fire, and spent the entire invasion morning shouting 'Qué pasa?' at uncomprehending Grenadians. Finally, Sergeant Ontiveros realized that the Army had screwed up—Grenadians speak English, not Spanish.

HOW IT STARTED: It was a popular rumor in the Army, "reflecting," as one source put it, " the feelings of enlisted soldiers toward the officers who had planned the invasion."

WHAT HAPPENED: A reporter checked the names listed on the invasion force, and found there was no one named Ontiveros in it. An Army press officer added: "I don't doubt the story for a minute.... Except that it's not true."

THE RUMOR: Dr. Pepper's secret ingredient is prune juice.

HOW IT STARTED: Unknown, but it's been whispered for about 40 years. The company speculates that the combination of Dr. Pepper's unidentifiable "fruity taste" and their penchant for secrecy about the soft drink's formula stimulates kids' imaginations.

WHAT HAPPENED: The company prepared a pamphlet which they send out to people who ask about the ingredients. It says: "There are 23 flavors and other ingredients (none of which are prunes) that produce the inimitable taste of Dr. Pepper."

THE RUMOR: Mama Cass of the group, "the Mamas and Papas," died by choking on a ham sandwich.

HOW IT STARTED: When the 220-lb. Mama died suddenly in 1974, her doctor issued a quick statement speculating that "she probably choked on a sandwich."

WHAT HAPPENED: The bizarre report was picked up by newspapers, including The New York Times and Rolling Stone magazine, and presented as fact. Actually, when the coroner's report was issued a week later; it gave the cause of death as a heart attack "brought on by obesity." Too late—the rumor was already circulating.

THE RUMOR: Ex-president Jimmy Carter saw a UFO.

HOW IT STARTED: Carter is responsible. He told someone: "I don't laugh at people any more when they say they've seen UFOs, because I've seen one myself." He then described it in detail.

WHAT HAPPENED: The Air Force issued a statement explaining that Carter had mistaken the planet Venus for an alien spacecraft.

Census report: U.S. men live longest in the Pacific states (Ore., Cal., Hawaii, Alaska, Wash.).

TALES OF '60s TV

Weird things happened on TV during the '60s.
Here are a few examples.

T HE SAGA OF ARNOLD ZENKER
On March 29, 1967, television actors went on strike. And
Walter Cronkite—the most popular newscaster in America—decided to walk out with them. CBS was forced to fill his anchor spot with one of their executives—but who could take Cronkite's place? They auditioned seven men for the spot, and all of them seemed too tense.

Finally, in desperation, they picked their 28-year-old manager of programming, Arnold Zenker—without an audition—because he had looked calm on a local newscast that morning. And for no apparent reason, he was an overnight smash. He received 3,000 fan letters. In fact, he was so popular that when Cronkite returned a few weeks later, he opened his first show with, "Good evening. This is Walter Cronkite, sitting in for Arnold Zenker."

"Bring back Zenker" buttons could be seen in TV studios for a while, but the novelty gradually wore off. Zenker, however, was still in shock. "There's nothing like breaking in on the 'Cronkite Show,'" he said in a classic understatement.

LONG GREEN
On January 13, 1965, the irreverent TV host Soupy Sales was suspended from his New York children's program. Why? Because he told young viewers to reach in their fathers' billfolds and send him "those little green pieces of paper." The station manager announced he was afraid the joke might be "misinterpreted" by viewers.

THE WEDDING
One of the most-watched televison events of the decade (and certainly one of the most talked-about) was the marriage of Tiny Tim to Miss Vicky Budinger on "The Tonight Show."

Tiny Tim, the ukelele player who'd been catapulted to fame on "Laugh-In," had mentioned that he was getting married, within earshot of a "Tonight Show" publicist. The PR man suggested to

---

Census results: American women live longest in the South (Ken., Tenn., Miss., Ala.).

Johnny Carson that he offer to let Tim get married right on the program. Tim's response: "Oh, could we?"

NBC went all out. For the man who sang "Tiptoe Through the Tulips," they ordered ten thousand tulips directly from Holland and filled the stage with them. Miss Vicky wore a $2,500 Victorian gown, Tim a black silk frock coat with a top hat. They passed up Carson's champagne toast in favor of a milk-and-honey drink that Tim concocted, and when they were pronounced man and wife, they kissed. "The fifth kiss we ever had," said Tiny.

Then they flew off to their honeymoon and at least three days of celibacy. ("S-E-X is the least important part of marriage," explained Mr. Tim.)

THE NEW NIXON

In 1968 the Republican candidate for president, Richard Nixon, went on "Laugh-In" and said, "Sock It to Me." Believe it or not, this little event might have helped him squeak by Hubert Humphrey in the presidential election. Why? Nixon's image for two decades had been that of a humorless, colorless character. His appearance on a "hip" show lent credibility to his claim that he was a "new" Nixon. Ironically, Hubert Humphrey was also asked to appear, but declined. Rowan and Martin planned to have him say "Sock it to him, not me" right after Nixon went on. When Humphrey realized his mistake, he asked to appear also. But it was too late.

TOURIST BONANZA

"Bonanza" was the #1 TV show in America in 1964 and 1965. It seemed so real to people that they refused to believe the Ponderosa Ranch was an imaginary place. To accommodate them, a special tour was set up near Lake Tahoe, where outdoor scenes for "Bonanza" were filmed. Guides brought tourists to an anonymous old shack in the Lake Tahoe area and told them it was the "real" Ponderosa.

UH-H-H-H

Walter Cronkite was known for his ability to keep talking on the air, no matter what was going on. But one time—and only one time—he was left speechless.

What did it? The moon landing. "I just went blank," Cronkite explained afterward.

The only place you can see the sun rise on the Pacific and set on the Atlantic is Panama.

PHOBIAS

*Are you struck with terror at the thought of wool? If someone
mentions spiders, do you go limp? Maybe you've got a phobia.
See if any of these rings a bell:*

Aulophobia: Fear of flutes
Neophobia: Fear of anything
new
Bogyphobia: Fear of demons
and goblins
Triskaidekaphobia: Fear of
the number 13
Gamophobia: Fear of marriage
Scopophobia: fear of being
stared at
Aurophobia: Fear of gold
Chrematophobia: Fear of
money
Astraphobia: Fear of thunder
and lightning
Blennophobia: Fear of slime
Phasmophobia: Fear of ghosts
Arachnephobia: Fear of
spiders
Hedonophobia: Fear of
pleasure
Chaetophobia: Fear of hair
Catoptrophobia: Fear of
mirrors
Ombrophobia: Fear of rain
Isopterophobia: Fear of
termites
Laliophobia: Fear of talking
Pogonophobia: Fear of beards
Theophobia: Fear of God
Ecclesiophobia: Fear of
churches

Taurophobia: Fear of bulls
Teratophobia: Fear of
monsters
Tapinophobia: Fear of small
things
Homichlophobia: Fear of fog
Geumophobia: Fear of flavors
Hadephobia: Fear of hell
Gymnophobia: Fear of nudity
Levophobia: Fear of things on
the left side of the body
Ichthyophobia: Fear of fish
Mechanophobia: Fear of
machines
Pteronophobia: Fear of
feathers
Politicophobia: Fear of
politicians
Siderodromophobia: Fear of
trains (or traveling on them)
Symmetrophobia: Fear of
things that are symmetrical
Xenophobia: Fear of foreigners
and unfamiliar things
Zoophobia: Fear of animals
Anthrophobia: Fear of people
Ophidiophobia: Fear of snakes
Graphophobia: Fear of writing
in public
Linonophobia: Fear of string
Pantophobia: Fear of
everything

Hear, hear: You'll find a snake's ears in its jaws.

FAMILIAR NAMES

*Some people achieve immortality because their names
become commonly associated with an item or activity.
You already know the names—now here are the people.*

Joel Roberts Poinsett. A lifelong American diplomat, secretary
of war under Martin Van Buren. While ambassador to Mexico,
he brought the first *poinsettia* back to the United States.

Patrick Hooligan. A notorious hoodlum who lived in London
in the mid-1800s. His name became a generic term for "trouble-
maker."

Leopold von Sacher-Masoch. An Austrian novelist. His books
reflected his sexual disorder, a craving which was later dubbed
masochism.

Frederick S. Duesenburg. An automobile manufacturer. His 1930
Duesenburg SJ was the most exquisite vehicle of its time, so
impressive that its nickname—the Duesey—became a slang term
for something really terrific. When someone says, "That's a real
doozey," they're talking about Frederick.

Charles Mason / Jeremiah Dixon. English surveyors. In the 1760s,
they were called in to settle a boundary dispute between two
prominent Colonial families—the Penns of Pennsylvania, and the
Calverts of Maryland. A hundred years later, the line they laid out
became the North/South border.

Arnold Reuben. A New York deli owner in the '40s and '50s.
He put corned beef, sauerkraut, and Russian dressing on a piece of
rye bread and named the whole thing after himself—the Reuben
sandwich.

Alexander Graham Bell. Inventor of the telephone (1876). The
standard measurement of "sound intensity," the *decibel,* was named
in his honor.

Watch out for flying hockey pucks—they travel at up to 100 mph.

Sir Benjamin Hall. The "chief commissioner of works" for the British government in the 1850s, when the tower clock on the Houses of Parliament got its largest bell. Newspapers of the time dubbed it "Big Ben," after Hall.

Pierre Magnol. A French professor of botany in the 1600s. Gave us the flower name *magnolia*.

Alessandro Volta. A celebrated Italian physicist. His experiments with electricity in the late 1700s led to the invention of the dry-cell battery. The *volt* was named for him.

Belinda Blurb. A model portrayed on a book jacket by American illustrator Gelett Burgess. She inspired the common term for a publisher's comments on a book cover.

Samuel A. Maverick. Texas cattle baron in the mid-1800s. Had so many unbranded stray calves that they became known as *mavericks*. Eventually, the term came to include independent-minded people as well.

Franz Anton Mesmer. An Austrian physician. Popularized outrageous medical theories on animal magnetism in Paris in 1780s. He *mesmerized* the public.

Guy Fawkes. English political agitator who tried to blow up Parliament in 1605, but was caught and executed. The British began celebrating November 5 as Guy Fawkes Day, burning effigies of "the old Guy." Since the effigies were dressed in old clothes, the term *guy* came to mean *bum*. In America during Colonial times, its meaning was broadened to mean any male.

William Russell Frisbie. American pie maker. Founded the Frisbie Pie Company in Bridgeport, Connecticut, in 1871. In the early 1900s, students from Yale—located up the road in New Haven, Connecticut—found they could flip the Frisbie pie tins like flying saucers.

Madame de Pompadour. Mistress of King Louis XV of France in the mid-1700s. Popularized the hairstyle that reappeared, in modified form, on the heads of Elvis and James Dean.

Why do flamingoes hold their heads upside down? It's the only way they can eat.

CELLULOID HEROES

Popular films often inspire musicians to write their best songs. Here are a few examples.

THAT'LL BE THE DAY, by Buddy Holly and Jerry Allison (The Crickets).
INSPIRATION: *The Searchers.*
John Wayne's favorite—and maybe his best—cowboy film, *The Searchers*, was released in 1956.

Wayne's character in the movie was a defiant, macho loner, an anti-hero who fit right in with the James Dean/Marlon Brando image of the mid-'50s. Whenever anyone said something he disagreed with, he'd sneer, "That'll be the day." The phrase caught on among teenagers, and two high school musicians from Lubbock, Texas, Buddy Holly and Jerry Allison, used it in a song.

They recorded it with their band, the Crickets, in 1957, and it became the first hit in a series of records that made Holly a rock legend.

THE MIGHTY QUINN, by Bob Dylan.
INSPIRATION: *The Savage Innocents.*
Who—or what—inspired Bob Dylan to write "The Mighty Quinn (Quinn the Eskimo)"? He's not saying, but chances are it was a little-known 1960 film called *The Savage Innocents.*

What does the movie have to do with Quinn the Eskimo? Well, it starred Anthony Quinn. And he played an Eskimo.

NIGHT MOVES, by Bob Seger.
INSPIRATION: *American Graffiti.*
"The song was inspired by *American Graffiti*," Seger says. " I came out of the theater in 1972 thinking, 'Hey, I've got a story to tell, too! Nobody has ever told about how it was to grow up in my neck of the woods.' "

So Seger wrote "Night Moves" about the early '60s, when he and his teenage friends around Ann Arbor, Michigan would drive into farmers' fields to party. "Everybody had their headlights on, so there was light to dance," Seger recalls. "They'd play 45s, and we'd be blasting them out: Ronettes, Crystals...." Seger's personal

---

A queen bee can lay as many as 3,000 eggs in a day.

"American Graffiti" sold over a million copies and became the favorite tune of his career. "I don't know if I'll ever write one as good as that again," he says.

BIG GIRLS DON'T CRY, by Bob Crewe and Bob Gaudio (The Four Seasons).
INSPIRATION: A "B" movie on TV.
This was one of the biggest hits of 1962. According to Bob Crewe, the man who co-wrote it:
"I was up late one night in my apartment, watching a dreadful movie—I think it was with John Payne and some blonde bombshell. I had been drinking...and I was drifting in and out of sleep. I woke up at one point and Payne was smacking the blonde across the face and knocked her on her bottom. He said something like, 'Well, whadda ya think of that, baby?' She gets up, straightens her dress, pushes her hair back, stares at him and says, 'Big girls don't cry,' and storms out the door. I ran and jotted down the line. The next day we turned it into a song."

BEAT IT, by Michael Jackson.
INSPIRATION: *West Side Story.*
There's a distinct similarity between the "Beat It" video and the filmed musical *West Side Story* —which tends to indicate that Michael Jackson was inspired by the award-winning 1961 film. Indeed, he's known to have studied it. "The theme of my song," he said, "is about two gangs coming together to rumble, to fight." Just like the Sharks and the Jets.
But the best evidence is this: The first two words in *West Side Story* —spoken when a member of the Sharks accidentally wanders into Jet territory—are "Beat it!"

SCHOOL'S OUT, by Alice Cooper.
INSPIRATION: A Bowery Boys movie.
From 1937 to 1958, Leo Gorcey, Huntz Hall, and the rest of the Bowery Boys gang appeared in dozens of low-budget films. Alice Cooper was inspired by one of them. "I heard the phrase 'School's out' in a Bowery Boys' movie." he says. "It was used the same way that someone would say 'Get smart, Satch.'"
Cooper then used it in the song that became his first Top 10 hit.

America's first nudist organization was founded in 1929, by 3 men.

W.C. FIELDS SEZ

The original movie curmudgeon had a lot to say.

"Never give a sucker an even break."

"Women are like elephants to me I like to look at 'em, but I wouldn't want to own one. "

"Anyone who hates children and dogs can't be all bad."

"Reminds me of my safari in Africa. Somebody forgot the corkscrew and for several days we had to live on nothing but food and water."

"Never try to impress a woman because if you do, you'll have to keep up that standard the rest of your life."

"Show me a great actor and I'll show you a lousy husband; show me a great actress, and you've seen the devil."

"I've been asked if I ever get the DTs. I don't know. It's hard to tell where Hollywood ends and the DTs begin."

"I am free of all prejudices. I hate everyone equally."

"I never vote *for* anyone. I always vote against."

"Start every day off with a smile, and get it over with."

"A thing worth having is a thing worth cheating for."

"'Twas a woman who drove me to drink....And I never had the courtesy to thank her for it."

"I always keep a supply of liquor handy in case I see a snake—which I also keep handy."

"All my available funds are completely tied up in ready cash."

"I have never struck a woman. Never! Not even my poor old mother."

"I like children. If they're properly cooked."

"If at first you don't succeed, try again. Then quit. No use being a damn fool about it."

A whopping 60% of all new cars sold in the '80s were recalled for some defect.

UNCLE JOHN'S LETTER OF THE YEAR

*Of all the mail we received—and there was plenty—one
stood out as our "Letter of the Year." Here it is.*

BACKGROUND: In our previous volume, we included a comment from Mary Tyler Moore about how far fans will go to get autographs. She said:

"I know a funny Carol Burnett story. Once a fan followed her into the bathroom. The fan poked her head under the stall and shoved a pen and a piece of paper at Carol for an autograph."

Okay, got it? Now here's our Letter of the Year.

June 4, 1989

Dear Uncle John,

I am a third grade teacher...I teach a literature selection during the year...and this year I selected *The Wizard of Oz*, one of my personal favorites. My son suggested that I read the excerpts and comments about this story in *Uncle John's Bathroom Reader*. I did, and was fascinated by the political implications of this child's tale.

However, this is not why I write. I am astounded to tell you that as I thumbed through your pages, I found an article on page 152— "Celebrity Mania"—that was about ME! I am referring to a quote of Mary Tyler Moore's regarding Carol Burnett.

Here is the real scoop. *I* was the fan referred to in the story. However, it does my heart good to know that not only the common people, but also the rich and famous like to embellish a good story now and then.

Many years ago, sometime in the early sixties, my husband and I had gone to Las Vegas. We tried to get tickets to see Carol Burnett's show. I think it must have been one of her very first forays away from the world of television and Garry Moore. [*Uncle John's note: She got her start on daytime TV, in "The Garry Moore Show".*]

Only one U.S. state is named after a president.

We were told that she was sold out. The disappointment of my life! (So far—I was young then.) Trudging away from the desk, I happened to see Carol going into the ladies' room. On impulse, I followed her in. Now my recollections are just a little different from Miss Burnett's. Ever the lady, I waited outside the stall, just as I would to use the facilities. I had no intention of "peeking under the stall." When Carol came out, I zipped inside, shut the door and sat down. Oh!, be still my heart—the seat was still warm. (Isn't this gross? Remember, I was very young.) That would have been enough for me. To live to tell the tale. Yet, when I came out to wash my hands, SHE was still there by the sink. Gathering up my courage I said to her . . .

"Oh MissBurnett,I'msosorrythatIcan'tgetticketsto seeyour-show whileweare-here.It'sabigdisappointment.CanIhaveyourautograph? Yourshowisallsoldout!!!!"

Whereupon she grabbed her head as only Carol Burnett can do and said in that great voice, "I had no idea that so many people would want to see me!" She added, "Why don't you and your husband come in to watch the dress rehearsal" . . . or whatever it was they were doing. "Just tell them at the door that I said it's O.K."

Well, I got my autograph—went to find my husband—walking on air! He said, "Sure, sure, sure. Who did you *really* get to sign that envelope?" He wouldn't go with me because he thought I was making it up, and I was too frightened to go alone. I never did get to see Carol Burnett do a show, but I still have the autograph. I'll never part with it.

Addendum: Just a couple of weeks ago I was installing a new toilet seat in my bathroom and I thought of Carol. (I'm sure she would be *thrilled* to know that I think of her every time I sit there!) Anyway, I was thinking that I should probably box up the old one and send it to her. Maybe she would like to sit on one of mine for a change.

Anyway, she has given me years of pleasure, not only in watching her, but in the telling and re-telling of my story. I know fans can be a pain...but I'd do it all over again.

Sincerely,

Cynthia L.

It takes 1/2 gallon of water to cook a pot of macaroni...and a gallon to wash the pot.

THE PATENTED CAR

*This is a bit of lost history. We take it for granted that anyone
who wants to can build a car. Few people realize that that
right actually had to be won in court at the beginning
of this century, by Henry Ford.*

CASHING IN
In the late 1870s George Selden, a lawyer/inventor special-
izing in patents, heard about the development of the automobile in Europe. He realized that it was a product of the future,
and "set his mind to working out the precise legal definition and
wording of a patent that would give him the sole right to license
and charge royalties on future automobile development in America." Some twenty years later, with the auto industry beginning to
show signs of life, he set up a partnership with a few wealthy Wall
Street sharks and began asserting his "rights" with automakers. To
his surprise, even the five biggest car manufacturers agreed to pay
him royalties rather than go to court.

THE CARMAKERS' CARTEL
By 1903, this royalty-paying alliance of carmakers had officially be-
come the Association of Licensed Automobile Manufacturers
(ALAM). Henry Ford, then a fledgling automaker, applied for
membership…and was refused. His reaction: "Let them try to put
me out of business!" He took out ads telling his dealers that "the
Selden patent does not cover any practicable machine," and dared
Selden's group to take him to court. They did.

BATTLING IN COURT
Ford and the ALAM battled it out for six years. Then in 1909, a
Federal judge determined that Selden's patent was valid; Selden
and his allies legally owned *all rights* to the car. Immediately, carmakers that had held off on joining the ALAM —including the
newly formed General Motors—fell in line to pay royalties.
    The ALAM magnanimously offered to settle cheaply with
Ford, but Henry fought on. "There will be no let up in this legal
fight," he announced angrily. Finally, on January 9, 1911, a Federal Court of Appeals ruled in Ford's favor. Selden and his cronies
were forced to give up; the ALAM was never heard from again.

Dirty snow melts quicker than clean snow.

YOU'RE PUTTING ME ON!

The history of some modern wearables.

WHAT A HEEL

In the 1600s, Louis XIV of France added a few inches to the heels of his boots because he was so short. To his annoyance, he started a fad in the Royal Court—soon everyone was wearing elevated heels. So he made his even higher. And so did everyone else. This went on until it got ridiculous. Eventually, men's heels got smaller—but women's stayed high. In the 1800s, American women copied the styles of Paris, and high heels—called "French heels" at first—became a part of American fashion.

TIES THAT BIND

The necktie fashion originated with a band of Croatian soldiers who showed up in France in the mid-1600s. Part of their uniforms were fancy scarves made of linen or muslin; and this looked so impressive to the French that they began wearing fancy linen scarves themselves. They called the scarves *cravats*. Meanwhile, King Charles II of England picked up on the fashion—and when cravats became part of *his* daily wear, the rest of England followed. Over the next century, the cravat evolved into the modern tie.

SNEAKING AROUND

The modern sneaker was introduced in 1917, when the National India Rubber Company came up with *Peds*. Or at least, that's what they wanted to call their new shoe. It turned out that the name *Peds* was already registered; so they quickly changed the name to *Keds* (with a K for "kids"). The original sneakers had black soles and brown tops, because those were the popular colors for traditional men's footwear.

TUX & ROLLS

Pierre Lorillard IV, scion of the tobacco company, lived in Tuxedo Park, N.Y. In 1886, he decided he was sick of the formalwear of the day, and had his tailor make suits without tails. In a daring move for Victorian high society gent, he planned to wear one of these

---

Americans use 18 billion disposable diapers every year.

scandalous suits to the annual Autumn Ball. But he chickened out at the last minute. Instead, his son and his son's friends wore the suits. No scandal here; since the Lorillards were rich, everyone copied them. The outrageous suit became a fashion. It was even named for its birthplace. And a century later, the tuxedo industry is grossing a half a billion dollars annually.

WRANGLING AROUND
The Blue Bell Overall company was the largest manufacturer of denim bib overalls in the world, but after World War II, they wanted to expand—and decided to add blue jeans to their line of clothing. The name they picked for their new product was Wrangler. At first, since Levi-Strauss had the better stores all sewn up, Blue Bell sold its Wranglers only to discount chains, like J. C. Penney's. But eventually they hired Hollywood stars to plug the jeans, and they became as fashionable as Levi's.

STRAIGHT-LACED
The shoelace was invented in England in 1790. Until then, shoes were always fastened with buckles.

MADE IN THE SHADES
According to Gene Sculatti, in *The Catalog of Cool*: "The first sunglasses were made in 1885 in Philadelphia. Seeking an alternative to costly amber and micalens glasses, a glazier simply put small circles of window glass out in the sun, exposing them to several summers' rays." Sunglasses were popular, but weren't faddish until the '20s, when a bankrupt French comb manufacturer began turning out an assortment of bizarre sunglass frames, trying to find something people would buy. They were shaped like "peacocks, butterflies, pistols, wings, masks, etc. These were gobbled up by the international pre-jet set of the '30s, and soon became true 'trinkets of the bourgeoisie.' " Since then, luminaries like Jackie O., Elton John, Marcello Mastroianni, Audrey Hepburn, and even Barry Goldwater have kept them stylish.

NEHRU WOULD BE PROUD
The Nehru jacket was popularized—briefly—by Johnny Carson, who wore it on TV in the '60s.

Just one part oil per million parts of water will make drinking water taste and smell funny.

MONSTER MOVIES

The inside dope on a few of the all-time great horror flicks.

FRANKENSTEIN (1931). The role that made Boris Karloff a star was originally offered to both Bela Lugosi and John Carradine; both turned it down. One of the factors: the monster costume weighed 62 pounds and the makeup took four hours to apply every day.

• Karloff had to wear 22-pound size 24 boots. He also donned two pairs of pants with steel struts shoved in them, and a double-thickness quilted suit.

• His facial makeup was one-sixteenth of an inch thick, and the bolts on the sides of his neck left long-term scars.

• The famous scene in which the monster carries Dr. Frankenstein was memorable for Karloff, too—he strained his back, and ultimately had to have an operation to fix it.

• Bette Davis wanted the part of Mrs. Frankenstein, but was turned down because she was "too aggressive."

DRACULA (1931). Bela Lugosi became the first great monster of the talkie era with his role in this film. He had been playing Count Dracula on Broadway since 1927, so he already knew the part. Unfortunately, he was only paid $500 for his classic film performance.

• Among the film's lighting tricks: "Twin pencil-spotlights" were shined in Lugosi's eyes to give Count Dracula his legendary hypnotic stare.

• The Castle Dracula and Carfax Abbey sets were so expensive to build that Universal Pictures kept and reused them. You can spot them in numerous Universal films of the '30s.

• The enormous spider web on Dracula's staircase was actually a string of rubber cement. And the mountains shown in the first scenes were really the Rockies—not the Alps or Carpathians.

THE MUMMY (1932) Boris Karloff's second big monster flick was inspired by the discovery of King Tut's tomb in 1922...and the widespread belief—because several men on the Tut expedition had died mysteriously—that there was a real-life curse connected to it.

• Karloff was wrapped every day in linen and gauze, and was covered with mud.

Survey results: 98% of American drivers think they drive better than anyone else.

• He had become so famous as Frankenstein's monster the previous year that he was billed simply as "Karloff." Only Greta Garbo could match that.

THE WOLF MAN (1941). Lon Chaney, Jr. starred; it was his favorite role. Based on a popular 1935 English film, *Werewolf of London*, it was a surprise hit. Universal released it two days after Pearl Harbor, and expected low box office receipts. But instead of being distracted *by* the news, Americans wanted to be distracted *from* it.
• Chaney's werewolf makeup took five hours to apply every day.
• The same makeup man who created the Mummy and Frankenstein's monster for Boris Karloff created Chaney's werewolf.
• The werewolf costume was actually made of yak hair.

THE THING (1951). Director Howard Hawks's flick about an alien discovered near an Arctic research station is notable for two reasons: First, it kicked off the whole "it came from outer space" genre in the '50s; and second, the actor playing the monster was James Arness—"Gunsmoke"'s Matt Dillon. Arness, who's 6 feet-5 inches tall, wore four-inch lifts. He was onscreen about 3 minutes.

THEM! (1954). Another B-film breakthough—the first of the "giant mutated insects" genre. In this one, huge killer ants were found in the desert. But again, it was one of the actors who made the film memorable—Fess Parker. In 1954 Walt Disney, planning a feature about Davy Crockett, couldn't find the right man to play the lead…until he saw *Them!* He immediately hired Parker, who became one of America's hottest actors as the King of the Wild Frontier—and later, as Dan'l Boone. Also featured in the film: Arness, who was a year away from TV stardom, and Leonard Nimoy.

THE CREATURE FROM THE BLACK LAGOON (1954). The star of this 3-D epic, the scaly creature who's become the symbol of all '50s cheapo monsters, was actually modeled after the Oscar statue given at the Academy Awards.
• Two different actors appeared inside the latex costume. On land, it was a big fellow named Ben Chapman. In water, it was champion swimmer Ricou Browning, whose main claim to fame was that a decade later, he created and trained TV's most famous aquatic hero—Flipper.

Michael Landon played the title role of *I Was a Teenage Werewolf* in 1957.

MYTH AMERICA

You've probably believed these stories since you were a kid. Most Americans have, because they were taught to us as sacred truths. Well, here's another look at them.

HILL OF BEANS
The Myth: The Battle of Bunker Hill—where the Americans first faced the Redcoats—was the colonists' initial triumph in the Revolutionary War.
The Truth: Not only did the British wallop the Americans in the encounter, the whole thing wasn't even fought on Bunker Hill. The American troops *had* actually been ordered to defend Bunker Hill, but there was an enormous foul-up and somehow, they wound up trying to protect nearby Breed's Hill, which was more vulnerable to attack. They paid for it—when the fighting was over, the Americans had been chased away by the British troops. Casualties were heavy for both sides; about 450 Americans were killed, and a staggering 1,000 (out of 2,100 soldiers) Redcoats bit the dust.

PILGRIMS' PROGRESS
The Myth: The Pilgrims were headed for Massachusetts.
The Truth: They were headed for "Hudson's River." Because of poor navigation and unexpected winds, the first land they sighted was Cape Cod. They tried to sail south, but "dangerous shoales and roaring breakers" prevented it. So they reluctantly turned back. By this time, the crew of the *Mayflower* (no, the ship wasn't manned by Pilgrims) was sick of them and hustled them off the boat as fast as they could.

The Myth: The Pilgrims landed at Plymouth Rock.
Background: This tale originated in 1741, more than 100 years after the Pilgrims arrived. It has been attributed to a then-95-year-old man named Thomas Fraunce, who claimed his father had told him the story when he was a boy. However, his father hadn't landed with the pilgrims—he reached America 3 years after they did.
The Truth: The Pilgrims first landed in Provincetown, Massachusetts.

In 1989, gamblers lost a record $4.43 billion in Nevada casinos.

AND SO FOURTH...

The Myth: American independence was declared on July 4th.

Background: Because the Declaration of Independence is dated July 4th, people associate that date with American independence. In fact, independence was declared first...and was confirmed with the document a few days later.

The Truth: The Continental Congress declared independence on July 2nd. One of the Founding Fathers, John Adams, is quoted as having written his wife on July 3rd: "The 2nd day of July, 1776, will be the most memorable...in the history of America. I am apt to believe it will be celebrated by succeeding generations, as the great anniversary Festival."

• **Note:** Actually, the first Independence Day celebration—by the Continental Congress—was on July 8th, 1776.

A SIGN OF THE TIMES

The Myth: In a hushed hall in Philadelphia on July 4, 1776, each signer of the Declaration of Independence proudly and publicly took his turn affixing his signature to the document.

Background: This tale was apparently concocted by Thomas Jefferson and Benjamin Franklin, who wrote about it in letters after the event.

The Truth: Only 2 people—John Hancock and Charles Thomson—signed the Declaration of Independence on July 4th. It wasn't until about a month later, on August 2, that the majority of the delegates signed it. And it wasn't until 5 years later, in 1781, that the last signature was finally added.

• How public was the signing? The Continental Congress would only admit that Hancock's and Thomson's names were on the document. Everyone else signed in secrecy. It wasn't until the following January that the signers' names were made public.

YANKEE DOODLE

The Myth: "Yankee Doodle" was originally a patriotic song.

The Truth: It was composed in England as an anti-American tune. The phrase "stuck a feather in his cap and called it macaroni" referred to a foppish English group called the Macaroni Club, whose members wore ludicrous "continental" fashions they mistakenly believed to be elegant. The British laughed at "Yankee Doodle dandies," bumpkins who didn't know how silly they really were.

BUSHSPEAK

President Bush has a unique way of presenting his ideas.
Newspapers have dubbed it "Bushspeak."

"America's freedom is the example to which the world expires."

To a gathering of Hispanic high school students:
"You don't have to go to college to achieve success. We need the people who do the hard, physical work."

On his years with Ronald Reagan:
"For seven and a half years I have worked alongside him, and I am proud to be his partner. We have had triumphs, we have made mistakes, we have had sex…"

On a tour of a Nazi death camp:
"Boy, they were big on crematoriums, weren't they?"

"If this country…ever loses its interest in fishing, we got real trouble."

Political analysis while on the campaign trail:
"It's no exaggeration to say the undecideds could go one way or another."

To the head of the Jordanian Army:
"Tell me, General, how dead is the Dead Sea?"

"I can announce that our dog is pregnant. This happened yesterday. A beautiful experience. We expect to have puppies in the White House."

"This isn't a signal. It's a direct statement. If it's a signal, fine."

On his gun control position:
"And you know, you look at the amount of people committing crimes with a gun—I looked up the gun registration, which I oppose. I went down —I told you or you heard me say this: But I had the guy doing up a file today."

"When I ran for office in Texas, they said, 'This guy's from New England.' I said, 'Wait a minute. I couldn't help that, I wanted to be near my mother at the time.'"

"He would have been in deep doo-doo."

Liberace's last custom-made piano was covered with 350 pounds of rhinestones.

ADVICE TO SINGLES

Before self-help books like How to Pick Up Girls *and* How to Marry
the Man of Your Choice *were available, people relied on aphrodisiacs
and rituals to score with the opposite sex. These honest-to-goodness
recipes were collected by love-starved historians.*

F OR THE MARRIAGE-MINDED:
"If you want to get married, stand on your head and chew a
piece of gristle out of a beef neck and swallow it, and you will
get anyone you want."

—American folklore

❤

"If you can walk around the block with your mouth full of water,
you will be married within a year."

—American folklore

❤

" To win your beloved's affection: Take a piece of clothing into
which you have freely perspired, and burn and powder it with some
of your hair. Mix with your spit and blood and introduce it into the
food and drink which your loved one will consume."

—English folklore

❤

APHRODISIACS:
"Take three pubic hairs and three from the left armpit. Burn them
on a hot shovel. Pulverize and insert into a piece of bread. Dip
bread in soup and feed to a lover."

*—Albertus Magnus,
Medieval philosopher*

❤

"Shed your clothes completely, and at the stroke of midnight beneath a cloudless moon, walk three times around a house. For each
step you take, throw a handful of salt behind you. If no one has
seen you by the time you have finished, the person you love will be
mad for you."

— Dutch folklore

❤

Annual event: The U.S. uses more steel making bottle caps than car bodies.

BASEBALL NAMES

If you're a baseball fan, you know these names by heart. But you probably don't know where they came from. Here are the stories behind some famous names.

Los Angeles Dodgers. Formed in Brooklyn, New York, in 1890. Brooklyn had hundreds of trolleys zig-zagging through its streets, and pedestrians were constantly scurrying out of their way. That's why their baseball team was called the Brooklyn Trolley Dodgers (later shortened to Dodgers). The team moved to L.A. in 1958.

Houston Astros. Formed in 1961, they were originally called the Colt .45s, after the famous gun. But by 1965, when their new stadium opened, Houston had become famous as the home of NASA's Mission Control. Both the stadium (Astrodome) and the team were named in honor of America's astronauts.

Pittsburgh Pirates. In 1876, they were known as the Alleghenies (after the neighboring Allegheny River). But in the 1890s, they earned a new nickname—the Pirates—when they stole a few players from a rival Philadelphia baseball club.

San Francisco Giants. The New York Gothams baseball club were fighting for a National League championship in 1886. After one particularly stunning victory, their manager proudly addressed them as "My big fellows, my giants." The name stuck. The New York Giants moved to San Francisco in 1958.

Cleveland Indians. From 1869 to 1912, the Cleveland baseball team had five different names—including the Forest Citys, the Naps, and the Spiders. Then in 1913 a popular player named Luis Francis Sockalexis died. He had been the first American Indian ever to play pro baseball and the team was renamed in his honor.

Chicago Cubs. Apparently they had no official nickname at the turn of the century (although they were informally called the Colts and the Orphans). Then, in 1902, a sportswriter dubbed them "the

Cubs" because it was short enough to fit into a newspaper headline. The name caught on, and 5 years later the team officially adopted it.

Cincinnati Reds. Formed in 1869, the team was originally called the Red Stockings. Later, they were known as the Reds—until the early '50s, when McCarthyism was rampant. No one wanted to be called a "Red" then—it sounded too much like "Commie." So the team actually made an official name change, to Redlegs. When the patriotic panic died down, they quietly switched back to Reds.

Detroit Tigers. Legend says that the Detroit Creams (the cream of the baseball crop) became the Tigers in 1896, when their manager decided their black and brown striped socks reminded him of tiger stripes.

Montreal Expos. The Canadian city was awarded a baseball franchise in 1968, partly because its 1967 World's Fair—called Expo '67—had been successful. The team was named in honor of the event.

New York Yankees. They were first called the Highlanders or Hilltoppers, because their ballfield was located at the highest point in the city. Again, sportswriters got fed up trying to fit the names into headlines. So in 1909, a newsman arbitrarily called them Yankees—patriotic slang for "Americans." After World War I, when jingoistic fervor was rampant ("The Yanks are coming"), the team officially became the Yankees.

Baltimore Orioles. Were named for the Maryland state bird in the early 1900s.

Kansas City Royals, San Diego Padres, Seattle Mariners, Texas Rangers, Toronto Blue Jays. All 5 are expansion teams. All 5 got their names in public "name-our-new-team" contests. The Padres, although formed in 1969, got their name in 1935. The original contest was held to name a *minor league* team. Thirty-four years later, San Diego was awarded a major league franchise, and the new ballclub adopted the old name.

The most-watched film in history is *The Wizard of Oz*. Over a billion people have seen it.

WHICH STOOGE ARE YOU?

*The B.R.I. is pleased to present this penetrating social
analysis by Ivan Stang, the brains behind the
Church of the Sub-Genius.*

There are three kinds of people in this world. I know, you've
heard that before. Everybody has their "three types of people," or their four types, or five types....
But there are three, and the models for these types come neither
from psychology nor ancient religion. They come from Columbia
Studios, and they are archetypally embodied in The Three Stooges.

The Stooges unwittingly—of course—left us a rich legacy of deft
interpretations of the most primal human behavior patterns. Their
short films, seen as a whole, form a tapestry in which the interac-
tions of people as individuals, corporations, and nations are dis-
tilled to a microcosm, a pure essence of existential folly.

There are but a small percentage of Moes in any given population: perhaps five percent. There are even fewer Curlys. The vast
bulk of humanity are Larrys. (Though represented by male characters, the three types also apply to women.)

THE MOE PERSONALITY

Moe is the active personality, and if not always dominant, always
striving to be. Moe is the one who spurs the others into action. He
devises plans to better their lot, but when his plans fail the other
two suffer the consequences. But is Moe any less the fool because
they follow his plans?

He is a natural manipulator, only partially because the others are
waiting to be manipulated. He would want to manipulate them
anyway, even if they weren't so willing.

THE LARRY PERSONALITY

Larry is a born follower, a blank slate that only reacts (and slowly
at that) to external stimuli. He never initiates action. He is Moe's
absolute tool, the truest "stooge." When Moe's abuse finally does
make him angry, he lashes out not at Moe, but at Curly. No matter
how he suffers under Moe's yoke, he never really rebels. He argues,
but gives up easily.

Were it not for the presence of his friends, Larry probably would

---

According to the U.S. Census, the average American eats 22 lbs. of lettuce a year.

live in peace—a dull, flat, mechanical peace. Though clumsy, he is still the most employable of the three—for the other two are incapable of following orders, although for different reasons.

THE CURLY PERSONALITY
Curly is the only likeable one, a truly rare human model. He is the holy man, the Divine Fool. He is as creative and active as Moe—but it is a spontaneous and joyous kind of creativity, no good for the kind of plotting and scheming required by a Moe-dominated society. He is a free spirit, but correspondingly unable to function well in a world of Moes and Larrys. He, like Larry, is perpetually abused, but he intuitively understands what is happening to him and reacts far more angrily—if equally ineffectually. He is everyone's favorite Stooge because he is the funniest; through his innate nobility and natural humility he constantly bests Moe, but it is in an unconscious way, and it is only apparent to the outside observer. Curly himself is hardly aware of his talents; his weakness is that he does not know his own strength, and cannot trust his own luck.

In real life, Curlys are usually branded by the Moes and Larrys around them as retarded, schizophrenic, maladjusted, or just plain stupid...whereas in reality, it is only Curly who understands the truth. Remaining cheerful through adversity, he wins battles not by fighting, but by "accidentally" unleashing "accidents" in which his enemies injure themselves.

STOOGE CO-EXISTENCE
Alien to feelings of avarice or ambition, Curly is the opposite of Moe. Yet the two are drawn together by some inexplicable balancing force of nature. The Larrys, though, are ever the in-betweeners, slug-like nonentities caught in the crossfire of cosmic dualities—yet remaining there by some herding instinct that makes being a casualty of the Moe-Curly battle preferable to life alone with other Larrys.

Only the existence of the blameless, bovine Larrys makes that of Moe or Curly possible. They are able to maintain their level of glandular brutality and senseless destruction only at the expense of the unquestioning, loyal worker drone whose income partially supports their excesses. Were he not there to diffuse Moe's anger by becoming another recipient of his blows, Curly would have been killed long ago, and Moe would have committed suicide out of loneliness.

The horror of it all is that the three types need each other to survive. Of all nature's cycles of parasitic symbiosis, the one involving the three human types is the most nightmarish. It rages around us all the time in real life, spreading death and madness, yet when we see it on the screen we call it "comedy."

NYUK NYUK NYUK:
THE STOOGES IN ACTION

A doctor doubts the Stooges' qualifications as surgeons.
Doctor: "Why, you don't even know how to deliver an anesthetic."
The Stooges pull out wooden mallets.
Moe: "Give him some anethesia."
Larry and Curly clobber him on the head with their mallets.

The Stooges are about to operate on a patient, planning out their strategy by playing tic-tac-toe on the sheet covering him.
Moe: "Give him another anesthetic, boys. I think it's wearing off.
Patient (sitting up): "No it isn't."
Larry (roughly pushing him down): "Lay down. Are you trying to make a fool out of us doctors?"
Wham!

Moe: "Whaddya up to now?"
Curly (bowling): "I just got a poifect score!"
Moe: "No ya haven't. Ya need another strike."
Wham!

Curly is holding an unwrapped cigar up to his ear.
Moe: "What're ya doin'?"
Curly: "Listenin' to the band. Nyuk, nyuk, nyuk."
Moe: "Would you like to hear some birdies?"
Curly: "I'd love it!"
Moe: "Take off yer hat!"
Wham!

Secretary: "Mattie Herring is here to see you."
Moe: "Mattie Herring? Sounds fishy. Send her in."
Secretary: "Now?"
Moe: "No, marinate her first."
Curly: "And don't forget the onions. Nuyuk, nyuk, nyuk."

The speed of a hard rain is about 20 mph.

WORD PLAY

In the first Bathroom Reader *we included some uncommon words, and their meanings, to help build anemic vocabularies. Here's another batch.*

Franch: To eat greedily

Rhotacism: Excessive use of the letter "R"

Manumission: The official act of freeing a slave

Netop: A friend

Gash-gabbit: Having a protruding chin

Girn: To bare your teeth in anger or in sadness

Wamfle: To walk around with flapping clothes

Charientism: An elegantly veiled insult

Juglandaceous: Pertaining to walnuts

Kakistocracy: Government of a state by its worst citizens

Ergophile: A person who loves to work

Lingible: Meant to be licked

Cicisbeo: A married woman's well-known lover

Moll-buzzer: A thief whose specialty is robbing women

Yerd: To beat with a stick

Mubblefubble: Mental depression

Nash-gob: An arrogant gossip

Zuber: The European breed of buffalo

Nazzard: A lowly or weak person

Alliaphage: A garlic eater

Nuddle: To push something with your nose

Glossolalia: Gibberish; babble

Ribazuba: Ivory from a walrus

Eristic: Argumentative

Roddikin: A cow or deer's fourth stomach

Mabble: To wrap your head

Scobberlotcher: An idle person

Irrefragable: Undeniable

Shench: To pour a drink for someone

Palilalia: Helplessly repeating a phrase faster and faster.

Shongable: A shoemaking tax

Slibbersauce: A disgusting substance

Walm: To bubble up

Cherubimical: Inebriated

Dendrofilous: Loving trees enough to live in them

Kinetosis: Travel sickness

Oligophrenia: Extreme mental retardation

Ranarium: A frog farm

American grow tomatoes at home more often than any other fruit or vegetable.

ONLY IN AMERICA

*It started out as a social protest song, and wound up a boring
patriotic anthem. Here is a fascinating true story
of how politics can influence popular music.*

BACKGROUND
The story of "Only in America," recorded by Jay and the
Americans in 1963 for United Artists Records, reveals a lot
about the racial consciousness of the music business—and about
how political censorship takes place behind the scenes in the U.S.

THE SONG:
The year was 1963. American blacks were demonstrating for civil
rights. One black leader, Medgar Evers, was shot and killed in Jackson, Mississippi and another, Martin Luther King, led a massive
March on Washington, delivering his immortal "I have a dream"
speech.

On the radio, a young white group called Jay and the Americans
was following up its 1962 hit, "She Cried," with a seemingly patriotic pop tune, "Only in America." Lead singer Jay Black sang about
the very American dream from which blacks were saying they were
excluded. In "the land of opportunity," he sang, a poor boy could
be parking cars one day and be a movie star the next, grow up to be
President, or win the ultimate rock 'n' roll prize, a "classy girl."

But the irony of "Only in America" was that it was originally
written for an all-black vocal quartet called the Drifters—one of
the most popular groups in America—who had consistently scored
with million-sellers like "Under the Boardwalk" and "On Broadway." And the original lyrics had a far different slant.

BEHIND THE SCENES
According to co-writer Barry Mann, the song was intended to deliver a strong message about black life in the United States. An
original verse was: "Only in America / Land of opportunity / Can
they save a seat in the back of the bus just for me./ Only in
America / Where they preach the Golden Rule / Will they start to
march when my kids want to go to school."

The bronze razor archeologists took out of King Tut's tomb was still sharp enough to use.

Arguing that the pop charts weren't ready for such strident social commentary, Atlantic Records asked for new lyrics.

"They said it would never get played," Mann recalls, "so we changed it to fit a WASP." But with the Drifters singing the re-vamped version, the song took on a different sort of irony. According to producer Mike Stoller, "They were afraid of it. They thought they'd get too much flak. It would be too controversial. We felt it would make a strong ironic statement—that it would be more ef-fective—four black guys singing about what was obviously not tak-ing place."

Stuck with an unreleasable song, the producers took their instru-mental track over to the other label they worked with, United Art-ists, where Jay and the Americans recorded. The group loved the song, UA bought the music tracks from Atlantic, and a white-washed "Only in America" wound up in the Top 25 in 1963.

Mike Stoller was disappointed. Because of the changes in the song and who sang it, people wouldn't have a clue about its original theme. "It was straight ahead. It didn't have any irony in it at all, as done by Jay and the Americans. The point behind the message in the lyrics was lost, as far as we were concerned. It had to have been done with a black group. With a white group, it was just a kind of patriotic song."

UNRELATED TRIVIA
According to *Celebrity Trivia*, by Edward Lucaire:
• "After his high school graduation, Johnny Carson hitchhiked to California, acquired a naval cadet's uniform, and managed to do three noteworthy things: He danced with Marlene Dietrich at the Stage Door Canteen; he was sawed in half by Orson Welles in a magic act (he volunteered from the audience); and he was arrested by the Military Police for impersonating a serviceman."
• Before she became an actress, Margaret Hamilton—who scared the daylights out of millions of children as the Wicked Witch of the West in the film version of *The Wizard of Oz*—taught nursery school and kindergarten.
• Once, while visiting Monte Carlo, Charlie Chaplin entered a "Charlie Chaplin look-alike contest." He not only didn't win...he came in *third*.
• Gary Cooper's real name was Frank. His agent renamed him "Gary" because her hometown was Gary, Indiana.

It takes 8 seconds to make a baseball bat in a bat factory.

THE FRISBEE STORY

Playing with a Frisbee is one of America's most popular outdoor activities. The story behind the product, from Charles Panati:

THE ORIGINAL FRISBIE

"In the 1870s, New England confectioner William Russell Frisbie opened a bakery that carried a line of homemade pies in circular tin pans embossed with the family surname. Bridgeport historians do not know if children in Frisbie's day tossed empty tins for amusement, but sailing the pans did become a popular diversion among students at Yale University in the mid-1940s. The school's New Haven campus was not far from the Bridgeport pie factory, which served stores throughout the region...."

THE INVENTOR

"The son of the inventor of the sealed-beam automobile headlight, [Walter Frederick] Morrison was intrigued with the possibility of alien visits from outer space, a topic that in the '50s captured the minds of Hollywood film makers and the American public. Hoping to capitalize on America's UFO mania, Morrison devised a lightweight metal toy disk (which he'd later construct of plastic) that in shape and airborne movements mimicked the flying saucers on movie screens across the country. He teamed up with the Wham-O Company of San Gabriel, California, and on January 13, 1957, the first toy 'Flyin' Saucers' debuted in selected West Coast stores."

THE FRISBEE IS BORN

"Within a year, UFOs in plastic were already something of a hazard on California beaches. But the items remained largely a Southern California phenomenon. To increase sales, Wham-O's president, Richard Knerr, undertook a promotional tour of Eastern college campuses, distributing free plastic UFOs. To his astonishment, he discovered students at two Ivy League schools, Yale and Harvard, playing a lawn game that involved tossing metal pie tins. They called the disks 'Frisbies' and the relaxation 'Frisbie-ing.' The name appealed to Knerr, and unaware of the existence of the Frisbie Pie Company, he trademarked the word "Frisbee" in 1959. And from the original pie tin in the sky, a national craze was launched."

You can make a glass of apple cider with three apples.

DUMB PREDICTIONS

Elsewhere in The Bathroom Reader, *we've included amazingly accurate predictions. These are amazingly dumb ones.*

The abolishment of pain in surgery is a chimera. It is absurd to go on seeking it today. Knife and pain are two words in surgery that must forever be associated in the consciousness of the patient. To this compulsory combination we shall have to adjust ourselves."

—**Dr. Alfred Velpeau, 1839**
Anesthesia was introduced 7 years later

"While theoretically and technically television may be feasible, commercially and financially I consider it an impossibility, a development of which we need waste little time dreaming."

—**Lee De Forest,
"Father of the Radio," 1926**

"At present, few scientists foresee any serious or practical use for atomic energy. They regard the atom-splitting experiments as useful steps in the attempt to describe the atom more accurately, not as the key to the unlocking of any new power."

—*Fortune* **magazine, 1938**

"What can be more palpably absurd than the prospect held out of locomotives traveling twice as fast as stagecoaches?"

—*The* **Quarterly Review,** **1825**

"The ordinary 'horseless carriage' is at present a luxury for the wealthy; and although its price will probably fall in the future, it will never, of course, come into as common use as the bicycle."

—*The* **Literary Digest,** **1889**

"The energy necessary to propel a ship would be many times greater than that required to drive a train of cars at the same speed; hence as a means of rapid transit, flying could not begin to compete with the railroad."

—*Popular Science* **magazine, 1897**

Sarah Bernhardt often slept in a coffin.

YOU ANIMAL!

*They're as famous as most human stars, but what do we
really know about them? Some gossip about
America's favorite animals:*

LASSIE
The most successful animal actor ever, starred in 7 feature
films and a TV series that ran for 19 years—2nd on the all-
time list behind "Gunsmoke." But there wasn't just 1 Lassie—there
were 6 of them. And they were all female impersonators. Lassie was
supposed to be a she-dog; in real life, "she" was always a he.

Lassie was created by writer Eric Knight in a 1938 *Saturday Evening Post* short story. But although the dog went on to make more
money than any animal actor in history, Knight got no royalties—
he'd already sold the rights to MGM in 1941 for a paltry $8,000.

SMOKEY THE BEAR
Smokey is the only celebrity in America with his own ZIP code—
20252. He's also the only bear in the world with his own secretarial
staff; the U.S. government employs 3 full-time secretaries to answer
his mail. Smokey was named after "Smokey Joe" Martin, Assistant
Fire Chief in New York City between 1919 and 1930.

CHEETAH
Tarzan's favorite chimp seemed angelic in the Tarzan movies, but
was dangerous to work with. During one scene in 1932's *Tarzan the
Ape Man*, a little of Jane's (Maureen O'Sullivan's) hair got in
Cheetah's eyes, blinding the chimp. Cheetah went crazy on the set
and bit O'Sullivan. Another time, Cheetah was supposed to kiss
O'Sullivan during a scene. As their faces met, the chimp sneezed
all over her.

One of the reasons Cheetah looked so convincing as a "thinking" animal was that many of the tricks the chimp already knew
were written into the Tarzan scripts. For example, Cheetah was
adept at crawling on his stomach. So in *Tarzan and His Mate*
(1934), a scene was included in which the chimp escaped from an
attacking rhinoceros by crawling through the tall grass.

RIN TIN TIN

Rinty was film's first bona fide animal superstar. He made his film debut in 1922, and his box office success over the next few years literally saved Warner Brothers' Studio from bankruptcy. During the '20s, when he made some 22 movies and was voted the #1 movie star in America (no kidding), Rinty was insured for $250,000. In the early '30s, he lived in a Hollywood mansion across the street from Jean Harlow. His sons and grandsons were among the dogs used in later films, and in the 1954-59 TV series.

ELSIE THE COW

The Borden milk symbol started as a cartoon in Borden's ads in 1938. But at the 1939 New York World's Fair, visitors to the Borden exhibit kept asking, "Where's Elsie?" Borden needed an answer, so they picked the most attractive cow in their milking exhibit—a 975 lb. Jersey named "You'll Do, Lobelia"—and renamed her Elsie. They built her a special display—a "bovine boudoir"—that was so successful she got a screen contract, playing Buttercup in the 1940 version of *Little Men*. Elsie became a national celebrity: She went on tour and raised $10 million in U.S. War Bonds; she gave birth to a calf in the window of Macy's department store (behind a modest curtain, of course); she was even awarded a "Doctorate of Bovinity" at Ohio State in 1948.

MORRIS THE CAT

America's best-known catfood salesman was originally named "Lucky" by his owner—because he was discovered at an animal shelter in Hinsdale, Illinois about 20 minutes before he was going to be "put to sleep." As Morris, he was the the first animal star ever featured on "Lifestyles of the Rich and Famous."

TOTO

Almost didn't make it into MGM's 1939 film *The Wizard of Oz*; the MGM prop department was using W. W. Denslow's original illustrations as a casting guide, but they couldn't identify the breed of dog in the pictures. Sketches were sent all over the world, but no one responded—until Hollywood trainer Carl Spitz happened to see the illustrations. He knew right away that they were looking for his Cairn Terrier, Terry. When Spitz took Terry to the studio, someone grabbed him and shouted "That's the dog we want!"

Cosmic coincidence? Both Elvis and his mom died when they were 42.

COOKING WITH POWER TOOLS

Here's a handy cooking idea from Jack Mingo, author of the
Official Couch Potato Handbook.

Many of you have power tools sitting around your homes that you never use. Almost all of them, with a little imagination, can be adapted for food preparation. For example: Take a household power drill, poke the bit through the plastic lid of a 15 oz. styrofoam cup, and voilà! You've got a blender that's ideal for highspeed whipping. A jigsaw is great for slicing and dicing. A good belt sander will peel potatoes in a jiffy. And a butane torch is perfect for Pop Tarts flambé.

Caution: Power tool cooking should be attempted only if tools are properly shielded and grounded. Wear safety lenses. Some power tools will interfere with TV reception, so confine preparation to commercials. Power tool cookery is NOT recommended while bathing.

Here are three of our favorite power tool recipes:

THE CHEESE CHOC-DOG
Ingredients
- 1 Package hot dogs
- 1 Loaf generic white bread
- 1 Can aerosol cheese product
- Electric Drill with 1/4" bit
- 1 Squeeze-bottle of Hershey's Chocolate syrup
- Safety Lenses

Instructions
1. Put on safety lenses.
2. Hold unopened package of hot dogs with ends pointing toward you.
3. Using slow speed, carefully drill each hot dog lengthwise.
4. Open package and remove hot dogs. Each should now have a hole down the center.
5. Fill cavities with aerosol cheese product.
6. Place hot dog on slice of white bread. Pinch bread into a trough around the hot dog and squirt liberally with chocolate syrup. Pop

in toaster oven for 10-12 minutes, or until cheese is runny.

TUBE-STEAK PATÉ

This is the award-winning recipe in the 1982 Chef Aldo International Couch Potato Bake Off. I highly recommend it for its near-European sensibility.

Ingredients
- 1 Oscar Mayer all-meat hot dog
- 1 Tsp. sweet pickle relish
- 2 Green olives, pimentos left in
- 8 Saltine crackers
- Mayonnaise
- Pepper
- Power tool blender (or real blender)

Instructions
1. Rev blender up to full speed and drop in hot dog.
2. Add relish and olives. Let blend at high speed for 90 seconds.
3. Spread the saltine crackers generously with mayonnaise.
4. Spread paté on crackers; add pepper to taste. Makes 8 servings.

EXTRA SHARP CARROT CAKE

This extra-easy version of the old favorite is almost indistinguishable from traditional recipes (the cola and spices even turn the Bisquick a rich, golden brown color). You can double the recipe and use a regular size aluminum pie tin.

Ingredients
- 2-3 Skinny carrots
- 1/2 Handful brown sugar
- 1 Can generic cola
- 1 Pot pie tin
- 1 Handful Bisquick
- 1/2 Handful pumpkin pie spices
- Electric pencil sharpener

Instructions
1. Shred carrots in clean pencil sharpener.
2. Line bottom of pot pie tin with carrot shavings.
3. Add Bisquick, sugar, and spices.
4. Knead slowly with hands, adding a small amount of the cola. Continue to knead and add cola until batter is the consistency of fresh Play-Doh.
5. Adjust sugar and spices to taste.
6. Bake in toaster oven at 400° for 15-22 minutes.
7. Remove from oven. When cool, carrot cake can be frosted with canned or aerosol frosting. A real health treat.

Swedes drink more coffee than anyone else.

INVENTION IN THE NEWS:

While many B.R.I. members enjoy reading current news-
papers on the seat of learning, the B.R.I.'s staff historian
is particularly fond of old ones. "It's like reliving history,"
he says. For some time now, he's been searching through
old issues of The New York Times, *looking for an account*
of the Wright Brothers' flight in 1903. He hasn't found it,
and here's why: Only one newspaper, the Norfolk Virginia
Pilot, *published an account of the first airplane flight.*
Luckily, B.R.I. member Gene Brissie had a copy.
Here's part of it.

FLYING MACHINE SOARS 3 MILES IN TEETH OF HIGH WIND OVER SAND HILLS AND WAVES AT KITTY HAWK ON CAROLINA COAST
No Balloon Attached to Hold It!!

December 17, 1903

The problem of aerial navigation without the use of a balloon has been solved at last!

Over the sand hills of the
North Carolina coast yesterday, near Kittyhawk, two Ohio
men proved that they could
soar through the air in a flying
machine of their own con-
struction, with the power to
steer and speed it at will.

This, too, in the face of a
wind blowing at the registered
velocity of twenty-one miles
an hour!

Like a monster bird, the invention hovered above the
breakers and circled over the
rolling sand hills at the com-
mand of its navigator and, after soaring for three miles, it
gracefully descended to earth
again, and rested lightly upon
the spot selected by the man
in the car as a suitable landing
place.

While the United States
government has been spending
thousands of dollars in an effort to make practicable the
ideas of Professor Langley, of
the Smithsonian Institute,
Wilbur and Orville Wright,
two brothers, natives of Day-
ton, Ohio, have, quietly, even
secretly, perfected their invention and put it to a successful
test.

They are not yet ready that
the world should know the
methods they have adopted in

According to *Billboard* magazine, Connie Francis is the #1 female singer of the last 35 years.

conquering the air, but the *Virginian Pilot* is able to state authentically the nature of their invention, its principles and its chief dimensions. . . . [Ed. note: the flight began with the plane rolling down a track.]

Wilbur Wright, the chief inventor of the machine, sat in the operator's car, and when all was ready his brother unfastened the catch which held the invention at the top of the slope. The big box began to move slowly at first, acquiring velocity as it went, and when halfway down the hundred feet the engine was started. . . . When the end of the incline was reached the machine shot out into space without a perceptible fall.

Keeping its altitude, the machine slowly began to go higher and higher until it finally soared sixty feet above the ground.

Maintaining this height, the forward speed of the huge affair increased until a velocity of eight miles was attained.

All this time the machine headed into a twenty-one-mile wind.

The little crowd of fisherfolk and coast guards, who have been watching the construction of the machine with unconcealed curiosity since September, were amazed.

They endeavored to race over the sand and keep up with the thing in the air, but it soon distanced them and continued its flight alone.

Steadily it pursued its way, first tacking to port, then to starboard, and then driving straight ahead.

"It is a success," declared Orville Wright to the crowd on the beach after the first mile had been covered.

But the inventor waited. Not until he had accomplished three miles, putting the machine through all sorts of maneuvers en route, was he satisfied.

Then he selected a suitable place to land and, gracefully circling, drew his invention slowly to the earth, where it settled, like some big bird, in the chosen spot.

"Eureka!" he cried.

The success of the Wright brothers in their invention is the result of three years of hard work.

The spot selected for the building and perfecting of the machine is one of the most desolate upon the Atlantic seaboard; no better place could scarcely have been selected to maintain secrecy.

It is said the Wright brothers intend constructing a much larger machine, but before this they will go back to their homes for the holidays.

The real James Bond was an ornithologist, not a spy.

WORD PLAY

What do these familiar phrases really mean? Etymologists have researched them and come up with these explanations.

FEATHER IN YOUR CAP
Meaning: An achievement.
   Background: Dates back to 1346, when, according to scholars, "the English Black Prince was awarded the crest of John, King of Bohemia—3 ostrich feathers—after distinguishing himself at the Battle of Crecy." It started a tradition; thereafter, any knight who fought well was allowed to wear a feather in his helmet.

PRIVATE EYE
Meaning: A private detective.
Background: The Pinkerton Detective Agency, founded in 1850, used the motto "We Never Sleep," and accompanied it with a picture of an open eye. It was commonly referred to as "The Eye," and Pinkerton agents, hired by private concerns, were called "Private Eyes."

LOCK, STOCK, AND BARREL
Meaning; The whole thing.
Background: Guns. The lock (firing mechanism), stock (wooden mount), and barrel constituted the main parts of an old rifle.

DOG DAYS
Meaning: The hottest days of summer.
Background: The Ancient Romans believed that there was a period during the summer when "the brightest star in the heavens, the dog star 'Sirius,' added its heat to the sun's, making these days a veritable inferno."

GREAT SCOTT!
Meaning: An exclamation of surprise or amazement.
Background: One of America's most admired soldiers during the 19th century was General Winfield Scott, hero of the Mexican War in 1847. He inspired the phrase in the mid-1800s.

When he's feeling amorous, the male sea otter grabs the female's nose with his teeth.

FAMOUS CHEATERS

You've heard the old adage, "Cheaters never win."
But when they do win, we never find out about
them. We only know about the ones who
get caught. Like these folks:

THE CULPRIT: Rosie Ruiz, a 26-year-old New Yorker.

SCENARIO: Ms. Ruiz appeared to be the fastest woman runner in the 26-mile Boston Marathon in 1980, stumbling across the finish line with an impressive time of 2 hours, 31 minutes, and 56 seconds. The only thing was, no one remembered seeing her run the course. And she couldn't recall anything about the route she was supposed to have taken. Very suspicious. Then a friend revealed that Ruiz's impressive showing in the New York Marathon a few months earlier was a fraud. Rosie, claimed the friend, had skipped most of the race and taken the subway to the finish line. Was Boston a fraud, too? Ruiz denied it.

VERDICT: After an embarrassing public controversy, race officials determined that Rosie had only run the last two miles of the marathon, and stripped her of her title.

AFTERMATH: In 1984, Ruiz was arrested in Miami for trying to sell two kilos of cocaine to a cop. Police said she was a member of an all-woman cocaine ring.

THE CULPRIT: Dave Bresnahan, a catcher for the Williamsport (Pennsylvania) Bills.

SCENARIO: It was September, 1987, a minor league baseball game—Williamsport vs. Reading.

Reading was at bat, with two outs and a man on third. After a pitch, the catcher (Bresnahan) leaped to his feet and threw to the third baseman, apparently trying to catch the runner off base. He missed by a mile—the "ball" sailed into the outfield and the runner headed home...only to find the catcher waiting there with the ball in his hand, ready to tag him out. How did Bresnahan get the ball so fast? Answer: he never actually threw the ball—instead, he threw a potato he'd hidden in his uniform.

At any one time, there are 1800 thunderstorms taking place somewhere in the world.

VERDICT: Unfortunately, the authorities didn't appreciate this prank. Not only was the runner called safe and Bresnahan ejected from the game, but the following day the parent Cleveland Indians released Bresnahan from the team.

AFTERMATH: Bresnahan moved to Arizona and got a job selling real estate. But his stunt became so famous that a year later, the Williamsport Bills invited him back to recreate it…and to honor him by retiring his number!

THE CULPRIT: Janet Cooke, a reporter for the *Washington Post.*

SCENARIO: Cooke arrived at the Post with impressive credentials—she said she'd graduated from Vassar with honors and had gotten a master's degree at the University of Toledo. She was assigned to do local stories, and in 1980 told her editor that she'd heard of an 8-year-old who was addicted to heroin. "Find that kid," the editor reportedly told her, "and it's a front-page story." Cooke came back with a detailed account of how a ghetto woman had allowed her lover to inject—and addict—her young son. The tale was titled "Jimmy's World," and it caused an immediate furor in Washington. Cooke refused to reveal her sources, so the mayor put the full resources of the police behind an effort to find the child. The board of education was bombarded with questions and complaints. But the newspaper stood by Cooke. In fact, they nominated her for a Pulitzer Prize, journalism's most prestigious award. And she won. But as reporters gathered biographical information for their story about her, they discovered she had lied about her background. And the Post's executives discovered, to their horror, that Cooke had fabricated the entire story of "Jimmy's World."

VERDICT: Cooke, in tears, offered her resignation. The *Post* accepted it. The Pulitzer went to Teresa Carpenter of the *Village Voice,* instead.

AFTERMATH: The *Post* published a front-page story criticizing itself. On the legal front, several members of the Washington Board of Education sued Cooke and the *Post* to recover the money the city has spent trying to find "Jimmy," and for damages for being falsely accused of concealing "Jimmy" 's identity.

FABULOUS FLOPS

Next time you read about some amazing
overnight success, remember these
equally fabulous stinkers.

THE GTO SHOE

In the '60s, Thom McAn Shoes cashed in on every fad. They marketed Beatle Boots, Monkee Boots, Chubby Checker Twister boots, and even Ravi Shankar "Bombay Buckles." But they lost their magic touch when they tried to ride the hot car fad of the mid-'60s with GTO shoes, "the world's first high-performance shoe." Promoted in conjunction with Pontiac's celebrated GTO, the footwear came equipped with "pointed toes, beveled accelerator heels, and double-beam eyelets."

The Pontiac GTO was a huge success, but most of Thom McAn's GTO shoes wound up being donated to charity.

INSTANT FISH.

In the early '60s, one of the owners of the Wham-O Mfg. Co.—makers of Hula Hoops and Frisbees—was on vacation in Africa. One evening, he camped beside a dry lake bed; during the night it rained, and the lake filled up. The next day he noticed there were fish in the lake. "How could that be?" he thought. "Fish don't grow overnight."

When he got back to California, he asked a biologist friend what had happened, and was told that there was indeed a fish in that part of the world whose eggs lay dormant until they were exposed to water. Then the eggs hatched and the fish emerged.

It sounded like an incredible idea for a product—"Instant Fish." At his urging, Wham-O hurriedly built huge fish tanks in their factory and imported thousands of fish so they could start collecting their eggs.

Meanwhile, the annual New York Toy Fair, where toy store owners from all over the U.S. buy merchandise, was taking place....And "Instant Fish" was the smash of the show. In one week, Wham-O took orders for $10 million worth of fish (an incredible amount in the mid-'60s). Even when the company refused to take any more orders, people sneaked to Wham-O's hotel rooms and slipped orders under the door. "Instant Fish" was a gold mine. Except that nobody told the fish. They just couldn't lay eggs fast enough to supply all the excited toy store owners. Desperate, Wham-O owners tried everything they could think of: They tried covering the windows to darken the inside of their plant; they tried warmer room temperatures...and they tried cooler ones; they even tried piping romantic music into the tanks. But nothing worked. Wham-O finally had to admit that "Instant Fish" had laid its own enormous egg. And after shipping only a few of the fish, they canceled all the orders.

"TURN ON"

In 1968 and 1969, "Laugh-In" was TV's #1 show. Hoping to buy themselves a copycat hit, ABC hired "Laugh-In" executive producer George Schlatter to create an identical series. And by mid-1969, he'd put together "Turn-On," which ABC promoted as "the second coming of 'Laugh-In'," a "visual, comedic, sensory assault." "Turn-On" premiered on Feb. 5, 1969. It was so bad that the next day, phone calls poured in from ABC affiliates all over the U.S., saying that they refused ever to carry the show again. Embarrassed, the network cancelled it immediately, making it the shortest-lived primetime series in TV history.

THE ANIMAL OF THE MONTH CLUB

In the '50s and '60s, mail order "thing-of-the-month" clubs were big business—worth close to a billion dollars a year. Americans were buying a Fruit-of-the Month, a Candy-of-the-Month, a House-of-the-Month (architectural plans), a Cheese-of-the-Month, Flowers-of-the-Month, and so on. How far could the fad go? Creative Playthings took it to the limit when it introduced an "Animal of the Month Club" in the late '60s. Every month, the company promised, an exotic "pet," such as an Argentine toad snail, a musk turtle, a newt, a Mongolian gerbil, or others, would arrive in the mail at subscribers' houses.

But shipping exotic pets turned out to be a crazy—and cruel—idea. In 1968, for example, Creative Playthings had orders for 4,000 Argentine toads and couldn't find enough of them in the Argentine swamps to supply the demand. But that wasn't the worst of their problems. Ever try bulk-mailing animals? The creatures-of-the-month often arrived squashed, or dehydrated. Mercifully, Creative Playthings took its losses and gave up.

In 1681, the last dodo bird died.

UNCLE WALT'S SECRETS

Everyone knows about Walt Disney—or do they?
Check it out for yourself.

TRANGE LOVE AFFAIR
Walt once confessed, "I love Mickey Mouse more than any woman I've ever known."

HIS PASSION FOR TRAIN WRECKS

Like Gomez Addams, Walt relaxed with model trains—but Walt's were big enough to ride on: The Disney "ride 'em" scale model railroad was half a mile long; it circled his estate, and even wound through a tunnel under his wife's flower beds.

The Disneys spent a great deal of time riding the little train. If you were a really good friend, Uncle Walt made you an official "vice president" of his railroad.

But Disney was more like Gomez than met the eye. According to *Everybody's Business*: "Disney especially enjoyed planning wrecks because he had so much fun repairing the damage. Once, after buying two new engines, he told George Murphy (then an actor and one of the road's 'vice-presidents'; later a U.S. senator): 'Boy, we're sure going to have some wrecks now!' "

PEN-ULTIMATE SECRETS

• Most people believe that Walt was a cartooning genius. But according to author Richard Schickel in *The Disney Version*, he couldn't draw Donald Duck or any of his other famous characters! According to *Everybody's Business*:

•"Disney was known to ask his animators to show him how to turn out a quick sketch of Mickey Mouse to accompany autographs."

• "Walt grew up on a small farm in Missouri, where he picked up a feeling for what middle America wanted in their movies. He also picked up a bit of anti-Semitism, which he showed in a rather nasty caricature of a Jewish peddler in his first big cartoon success, *The Three Little Pigs*."

• "Disney's real signature bore no resemblance to the famous logo that appeared on all his products. Ironically, a number of people have thrown away authentically signed books and records under the impression that the autographs were fake."

More films are made in India each year than in any other country.

THE BIRTH OF A FLAKE

You probably think that corn flakes have always been with us.
Not so. The cereal flake was accidentally born
less than a century ago. Here's the tale.

BACKGROUND
It all started with a devoutly religious woman named Sister Ellen Harmon White, a Seventh Day Adventist who in 1844 decided it was time for her to ascend to heaven in a laundry basket. Along with others in her congregation, she stood for hours on a Maine hilltop, waiting to be carried away…but nothing happened. Sister Ellen wasn't disappointed, however. She took it as a sign that God still had important things for her to do in this world—and she set out to accomplish them.

In 1863, she and her husband traveled to Otsego, Michigan, where she had a vision: The Lord told her that people could only achieve "purity of mind and spirit" by eating properly—water, fruits, and vegetables, with a little bit of bread made from Graham flour. Another vision told her to open a sanitarium in nearby Battle Creek, where people could heal themselves with this diet.

THE BATTLE CREEK SANITARIUM

1866, the Western Health Reform Institute at Battle Creek was opened. It had no doctor on its staff for ten years. But in 1876, a 25-year-old Adventist who had just graduated from Bellevue Medical College—Dr. John Harvey Kellogg—was hired to run it. Kellogg's first official act was to hire his younger brother, William Keith (W. K.) as chief clerk.

Kellogg set out to turn the institution into an influential one. He changed the name to Battle Creek Sanitarium, and screened potential patients so that no one who was seriously ill was ever admitted. What he wanted were "tired businessmen, sufferers from dyspepsia…and neurotics." So people were invariably cured, and the San (as it was called) began attracting the wealthy and famous from all over the country. John D. Rockefeller, Henry Ford, Harvey Firestone, and others were among the guests. At the same time, Kellogg wrote voluminously, making his somewhat looney medical views influential with common Americans who would never make it to Battle Creek.

KELLOGG GETS FLAKEY

The diet in this now world-famous institution was strictly vegetarian. But to make the food more palatable to non-vegetarians, the Kelloggs and their staff set up a special kitchen in which they experimented with new dishes. Among their creations: hamburger substitutes, a coffee substitute called Caramel Coffee, and cereal flakes.

The flakes were an accident. Kellogg originally required his patients to begin each meal by chewing a piece of hard zwieback bread. But when a patient broke a tooth on it, he started experimenting with substitutes. One experiment entailed running boiled wheat dough through rollers, turning it into thin sheets before it was toasted and ground into flour.

On one occasion in 1895, Kellogg left some pans full of dough sitting while he was called away on an emergency. When he returned (it's not clear exactly how much later), he ran the dough through the rollers—but instead of thin sheets, he got a bunch of flakes. He toasted them and served them to his patients… who loved them. The flake was born.

NOT A CORNY JOKE

Kellogg and his staff came up with two flake variations—rice and corn. The corn was a flop (too tough and tasteless) until someone got the idea to use only the heart of the corn, and to flavor it with malt. Then it instantly became the most requested variety.

Realizing that he was sitting on a commercial bonanza, Dr. Kellogg set up the Sanitarium Health Food Company with his brother (keeping it separate from the San and the Adventist Church) and began selling his flakes. In the first year, he sold over 100,000 pounds of them. Business kept growing, and Kellogg kept getting wealthier.

"CEREAL SODOM"

But then things suddenly got out of hand. Dozens of cereal entrepreneurs moved in on Kellogg's territory and cut his profits. Subtly capitalizing on the reputation of the San, 42 Battle Creek-based cereal companies sprang up, each making ludicrous health claims for its products…and each making a fortune. Sister Ellen Hanson White was furious; she felt Dr. Kellogg had desecrated the Divine vision that inspired the San, and Battle Creek had now become a

---

A minnow's teeth are in its throat.

"cereal Sodom." On the other side, Will Kellogg was pressuring his brother to cash in like all the other cereal companies—which Dr. Kellogg adamantly opposed. His practices were already attracting some unfavorable attention from the medical profession, and he didn't want to focus any more attention on himself.

DR. KELLOGG LOSES CONTROL
Here's what happened: Dr. Kellogg, a tight man with a dollar, had been giving out stock in his cereal company to employees in lieu of pay raises. But it backfired, because his brother Will quietly bought the stock up until, in 1906, he had control of the entire enterprise—which he renamed the Kellogg Toasted Corn Flakes Company. He immediately placed an advertisement in the *Ladies' Home Journal*, which brought in a flood of orders. Sales leapt from 33 cases a day to 2,900 cases a day. But Dr. Kellogg wasn't happy about it. He called William a traitor...and the two never spoke to each other again.

Meanwhile, the Kellogg's Corn Flake Company prospered. As *Everybody's Business* puts it: "By 1909 the company was selling more than 1 million cases a year. Two years later, the advertising budget had reached $1 million, part of which was used to erect the world's largest electric sign on the Mecca Building at Times Square in New York, with K in *Kellogg* 66 feet tall."

THE KELLOGGS' FATE
Both of the Kellogg brothers were expelled from the Seventh Day Adventist church. The San, even without religious affiliation, flourished under Dr. Kellogg's direction until 1933. Then the Depression deprived it of many wealthy clients, and its source of revenue. Deeply in debt, it was forced to close in 1938. John Harvey Kellogg lived until 1942 when, at the age of 91, he succumbed to pneumonia.

William (W. K.) Kellogg, whose signature is on every box of Kellogg's cereal, lived to be 92 years of age. He died in 1951. His legacy: a $5 billion dried breakfast cereal business.

BY THE WAY...
Remember these cereals? Rice Krinkles; King Vitaman; Frosty-Os; Crispy Critters; Apple Jacks; Puffa Puffa Rice; Wheat Honeys....

THE ADDAMS FAMILY

"They're creepy and they're kooky, mysterious and spooky...."
You know the rest. But here are a few things you didn't
know about TV's weirdest sitcom family.

HOW IT STARTED

Charles Addams' ghoulish cartoon characters first appeared in *The New Yorker* magazine and developed a cult following strong enough to warrant several volumes of cartoons. It was one of these collections that inspired the TV show. Early in 1963, TV executive David Levy noticed an Addams book in a N.Y. store window. "Eureka!" he thought. "There's an idea for a great TV show." Unaware that Addams had already rejected other TV offers, Levy called *The New Yorker* and made an appointment to meet him. They met at the Plaza Hotel.

"Addams was tall and young-looking for his age, with a twinkle in his eye," recalls Levy. "He spoke laconically, with a very dry wit. I remembered a famous quote of his: Emerging from a big screening of Liz Taylor's Cleopatra with actress Joan Fontaine on his arm, he was asked if he enjoyed the movie. He said 'Yes.' What part? 'I liked the asp.'

"I had all this in mind when I met him, but for two hours over drinks we talked of *nothing* but novelist John O'Hara!"

It was a strange way to discuss a TV series.

Addams and O'Hara, it turned out, had been drinking buddies since Prohibition. And Levy had worked with O'Hara on TV adaptations of his short stories. The O'Hara connection made all the difference. After two hours, Addams suggested that they meet the next day to finalize an agreement...and "The Addams Family" TV series was born.

INSIDE FACTS
Go, Gomez

After John Astin's first sitcom, "I'm Dickens, He's Fenster," was cancelled, he auditioned for "The Addams Family," and was turned down...for the part of *Lurch*. He didn't even try out for Gomez. But the producer spied John leaving the room, grabbed him, and offered him the lead role on the spot. The only condition: Astin had to grow a mustache. He grabbed the role.

Hair Today...
It took Carolyn Jones two hours every day to put on Morticia's makeup. The final touch: she wore a wig made of—what else?—human hair.

• Believe it or not, Jones was only the producer's 3rd choice to play Morticia! ABC insisted that they needed a "name" actress, and Jones was the only well-known performer in the running (she had been nominated for an Oscar in 1956)—so she got the part.

Itt's Alive!
Cousin Itt's (you remember, the ball of fur with a hat on) voice was supplied by "Addams" producer Nat Perrin, who recited gibberish into a tape recorder and played it back at a higher speed.

Name Game
Addams, who'd never given his characters first names, had to come up with some for the TV show. (It was one of the few contributions he actually made to the sitcom; other than that, he did nothing except give his approval.) Within a week he'd decided on all of them—except for Mr. Addams, who almost wound up being called "Repelli" (for repellent) instead of Gomez.

True Fans
• When Ringo Starr met John Astin in 1965, he greeted Astin by grabbing his hand and kissing his way up his arm. And Astin hadn't said a word of French!
• In the early '80s, punk-rocker Siouxsie Sioux, of Siouxsie and the Banshees, wrote in a "portrait-of-the-artist" column, "My role model, inspiration, and heroine is Morticia Addams."
• Lurch got fan mail from teenage girls who thought he was cuter than the Beatles.

Home Sweet Home
The unique interior of the Addams house was inspired by the real-life Manhattan apartment of Charles Addams, which contained suits of armor, an antique cross-bow collection, and other odds-and-ends (with the emphasis on "odds").

ROAD KILL

*One of the stranger studies in human behavior we've ever heard of
was a recent experiment to find out how people react to animals
on the highway. Here's what they found out.*

THE TEST

David Shepherd, a biology professor at Southeastern Louisiana University, put rubber reptiles "on or near roads" and watched how 22,000 motorists reacted to them. His conclusion: "There are apparently very few animals hit accidentally on the highway."

WHAT THEY DID

To find out how drivers would respond to reptiles on the road, Shepherd and his crew put fake snakes and turtles in places where drivers would hit them if they kept driving straight; they also put the rubber reptiles where drivers had to go way out of their way to hit them. Shepherd's comment: "We found that while eighty-seven percent of drivers tried to avoid the animals, six percent went out of their way to hit them—with snakes getting squashed twice as often as turtles."

WEIRD REACTIONS

Apparently, there's something about a reptile on the road that makes some drivers bloodthirsty. A few examples Shepherd witnessed:
• "A truck driver crossed the center line, went into the opposite lane of traffic, and drove onto the shoulder of the road to run over a 'turtle.' "
• A normal housewife who saw what she thought was a snake in the road swerved to kill it, "then turned around to run over it five more times."
• "A policeman crushed a 'snake' with his tires, then stopped and pulled his gun. I quickly jumped from some bushes and explained it was a fake."

His conclusion: "Some people just have a mean streak toward animals."

The patent for the ball-point pen was awarded to John J. Loud of Weymouth, Mass. in 1888.

MANIAC

Believe it or not, the gruesome horror flick, The Texas Chainsaw Massacre, *inspired one of the best-selling dance tunes of the '80s.*

GOOFING AROUND
One night, musician/songwriter Michael Sembello and his writing partner rented a copy of *The Texas Chainsaw Massacre*, a particularly gruesome horror film. After watching it on Sembello's VCR, they decided—just for kicks, because they were sick of love songs—to write a tune about a mass-murderer. They did a rough version of the song, put it on cassette, then went back to working on other projects.

RUSHIN' ROULETTE
A few weeks later, record producer Phil Ramone asked Sembello to supply some music for an upcoming Paramount film—a dance movie called *Flashdance*. Michael came up with 2 or 3 songs he thought might work; then he asked his wife to copy them onto a tape and send them off to Paramount. She went into the studio and picked up a cassette, did the copying, and rushed it into the mail.

The next day his wife took a call from someone at Paramount. The guys at the studio had listened to all the songs, and there was one they were crazy about—they'd tested it with a specific dance scene, and it worked perfectly. They definitely wanted to use it in the film. "Which song?" she asked. The reply: "I don't know. It's the song at the very end of the tape that keeps repeating something about a maniac." Sembello's wife was horrified—it was the song about the mass murderer! She'd sent the tape without realizing it was at the very end of the cassette. "No, no, that's not supposed to be on the cassette!" she pleaded. But Paramount was adamant—they loved it and wanted it.

NEW CHARACTER
When Michael found out, he was so shocked that he didn't even believe his wife. But Ramone confirmed it, adding that Paramount wanted the lyrics changed to fit the dance scene. In this new version, the maniac was dance-crazy, not bloodthirsty.

"Maniac"—the song no one was ever supposed to hear—became Sembello's first hit—a million-seller, #1 song, and Oscar nominee.

Ford Motor Co. manufactured a plastic auto—the first ever—in 1941.

WARHOLISMS

Andy Warhol understood modern America. Some comments:

"Try the Andy Warhol New York City Diet: When I order in a restaurant, I order everything I don't want, so I have a lot to play around with while everyone else eats."

"An artist is a person who produces things that people don't need to have but that he—for some reason—thinks it would be a good idea to give them."

"It's not what you are that counts, it's what they *think* you are."

"Employees make the best dates. You don't have to pick them up and they're always tax deductible."

"Sex is the biggest nothing of all time."

"Being born is like being kidnapped. And then sold into slavery."

"It's the movies that have really been running things in America ever since they were invented. They show you what to do, how to do it, when to do it, how to feel about it, and how to *look* when you feel about it."

"The most exciting attractions are between opposites that never meet."

"The nicer I am, the more people think I'm lying.'"

"I always run into strong women who are looking for weak men to dominate them."

"I never think that people die. They just go to department stores."

"After being alive, the next hardest work is having sex."

"Dying's the most embarrassing thing that can ever happen to you."

"I am a deeply superficial person."

"The more information you get, the less fantasy you have."

"Muscles are great. Everybody should have at least one that they can show off."

A Saudi Arabian woman can get a divorce if her husband doesn't give her coffee.

THE CONDENSED MAN

One of the most famous names in American food is Borden's.
This tale of Gail Borden, an inventor and classic American
eccentric, comes from Everybody's Business.

SMALL IS BEAUTIFUL

"Gail Borden was obsessed by the idea that food could be preserved by condensing, but his early experiments were unsuccessful....A condensed meat 'biscuit' he invented for Texans headed for California during the 1850s Gold Rush proved to be nutritious, but tasted awful....Undeterred, Borden continued his experiments with dehydrating and concentrating foods. 'I mean to put a potato into a pillbox, a pumpkin into a tablespoon, the biggest sort of watermelon into a saucer,' he declared."

THE PERFECT HOST

"He once subjected friends to a dinner party consisting entirely of the products of his experiments: condensed and concentrated soups, main course, fruits, and extracts. While Borden ate heartily and discoursed enthusiastically on the fine flavors of his concoctions, his guests toyed unhappily with their food. All firmly refused second helpings.

"Afterward, the unfortunate diners were lured onto another of Borden's inventions, the 'land schooner,' a contraption that used wind power to move on land. Its sails raised, the schooner moved down the beach, gaining speed at an alarming rate. Borden's passengers yelled for him to stop—at which point it was discovered that the braking mechanism was ineffective. As panic broke out, Borden swung the rudder the wrong way, and the schooner splashed into the waves, capsizing and dumping all hands into the sea. Unhurt, the group scrambled ashore. 'Where's Gail?' inquired one of Borden's dripping guests....'Drowned, I...hope!' "

CONDENSED FOR ETERNITY

"Neither drowned nor discouraged, Borden went on...to found what...became a giant corporation, built on his 1863 discovery of a process for making condensed milk. As he rode the train to work in New York City each day, he passed a cemetery where he had built his own tombstone—in the shape of a can of condensed milk."

The Neanderthal Man's brain was bigger than yours is.

THE FABULOUS '60s

Odds and ends about America's favorite decade, from the fabulous book 60s!, by John and Gordon Javna.

SOUP'S ON

Not everyone appreciated Pop Art. When Andy Warhol's first Campbell's Soup Can paintings went on display in an L.A. art gallery in 1961—for $100 apiece—another gallery down the street contemptuously stacked soup cans in its windows with the sign: "The real thing, 29¢."

WARHOL AGAIN

For a show at a gallery in Toronto in 1965, Warhol moved 80 of his Pop Art sculptures of Brillo boxes, cornflakes boxes, and the like across the Canadian border—only to discover that they were classified as "merchandise" instead of "art" by the Canadian government. That meant that the gallery owner had to pay an import duty, which he refused to do. He told newsmen that Canada had embarrassed itself and was now the "laughingstock of the art world." Government spokesmen countered that the boxes looked too much like their commercial counterparts, and "the only thing the artist adds is his signature."

"But," said Warhol, "I don't sign them."

MR. SPACEMAN

On April 12, 1961, one of man's impossible dreams was realized when Yuri Gagarin, a 27-year-old Russian test pilot, orbited the earth. He thus became the first man in history to actually see our planet. His 108-minute flight for the Soviet Union made him a worldwide hero. After the experience, he returned to testing new aircraft. Tragically, he was killed in a plane crash in 1968 and did not live to see man walk on the moon.

GIMME A BURGER, BABY

McDonald's menu in 1964:
- Hamburgers 15¢
- French fries 12¢
- Shakes 20¢.

Have you forgotten? The first "Rocky" film won an Oscar for Best Picture.

FIVE REACTIONS TO THE MOON LANDING

In 1969, the whole world watched as Neil Armstrong and crew walked on the moon. Some unusual reactions.

1. In Ghana: Nagai Kassa VII, a tribal chief, listened to the Apollo 11 saga on his shortwave radio through the Voice of America. Reportedly, he was worried that the astronauts would fall off the moon, and was amazed that they were able to fit on it at all. "The moon is so small as I see it that I didn't think there would be enough room," he said.

2. In India: Astrologers wondered if the moon was "too tainted for use in soothsaying, now that a man has walked on it."

3. In Alaska: Unimpressed by the scientific aspects of the lunar escapade, an Eskimo interpreted the moon landing for a reporter as a way to predict the weather. He said it was a sure sign of a "hard winter next year."

4. Somewhere in the Arab World: Al Fatah, the terrorist organization, objected that Arab newspapers were giving more attention to the moon landing than to "terrorist missions against Israel."

5. In New York City: The lunar landing was celebrated with a "moon bash" in Central Park. The Department of Parks invited the millions of New Yorkers to enjoy huge screens with live TV coverage, searchlights, a film collage, synthetic Northern Lights, dancing to "moon music," inflatable sculpture, and a blue-cheese picnic.

MISS AVERAGE AMERICA

Our all-time favorite beauty contest is the National College Queen Pageant, a little-known pageant that awarded some lucky college girl a title and prizes for excelling in the most mundane activities imaginable. "We are idealizing the well-rounded average," explained the show's promoter in 1962. Some of the events in which contestants had to compete:

• Blouse-ironing
• Cooking hamburgers
• "Doodling designs with colored inks on electric blankets"
• Carrying coffee cups and pots across a room to the judges' table and pouring (to evaluate "skill and poise as a hostess")
• Sandal decoration
• A fierce debate on "right and wrong hairstyles."

An Indian woman can legally wed a goat.

TV's RULES TO LIVE BY

More words of wisdom from Prime Time Proverbs.

"Remember—the Eagle may soar but the weasel never gets sucked up into a jet engine."
—**Rick Simon,**
Simon and Simon

"The first thing to do when you're being stalked by an angry mob with raspberries, is to release a tiger."
—**John Cleese,**
Monty Python's Flying Circus

"Always enter a strange hotel room with extreme caution, especially one with a samurai warrior in it."
—**Thomas Magnum,**
Magnum P.I.

"If you can't fight 'em, and they won't let you join 'em, best get out of the county."
—**Pappy Maverick,**
Maverick

"Just keep laughin'."
—**Bozo the Clown,**
Bozo's Circus

"The older you get, the better you get—unless you're a banana."
— **Rose,**
The Golden Girls

"Like my old skleenball coach used to say, 'Find out what you don't do well, then don't do it.' "
— **Alf,**
ALF

"As we say in the sewer, if you're not prepared to go all the way, don't put your boots on in the first place."
—**Ed Norton,**
The Honeymooners

"An ounce of prevention is worth a pound of bandages and adhesive tape."
—**Groucho Marx,**
You Bet Your Life

"It's been the lesson of my life that nothing that sounds that good ever really happens."
—**Alex Reiger,**
Taxi

"Never wear polyester underwear if you're going to be hit by lightning."
—**Roz,**
Night Court

"A watched cauldron never bubbles."
Morticia Addams,
The Addams Family

Donald Duck comics were banned from libraries in Finland because he doesn't wear pants.

GIMME SOME SKIN

When you meet someone socially, what do you do? Shake hands?
Tip your hat? Here's the background story on
some traditional greetings.

THE HANDSHAKE

From *Extraordinary Origins of Everyday Things*:

"In its oldest recorded use, a handshake signified the conferring of power from a god to an earthly ruler....

"In Babylonia, around 1800 B.C., it was required that the king grasp the hands of a statue of Marduk, the civilization's chief deity. The act, which took place annually during the New Year's festival, served to transfer authority to the potentate for an additional year. So persuasive was the ceremony that when the Assyrians defeated and occupied Babylonia, subsequent Assyrian kings felt compelled to adopt the ritual, lest they offend a major heavenly being....

"Folklore offers an earlier, more speculative origin of the handshake: An ancient villager who chanced to meet a man he didn't recognize reacted automatically by reaching for his dagger. The stranger did likewise, and the two spent time cautiously circling each other. If both became satisfied that the situation called for a parley instead of a fight to the death, daggers were reinserted into their sheaths, and right hands—the weapon hands—were extended as a token of goodwill. This is also offered as the reason why women, who throughout history were never the bearers of weapons, never developed the custom of the handshake."

TIPPING YOUR HAT, BOWING, CURTSYING, ETC.

From *Extraordinary Origins of Everyday Things*:

"The gentlemanly practice of tipping one's hat goes back in principle to ancient Assyrian times, when captives were required to strip naked to demonstrate subjugation to their conquerors. The Greeks required new servants to strip from the waist up. Removing an article of clothing became a standard act of respect. Romans approached a holy shrine only after taking their sandals off. And a person of low rank removed his shoes before entering a superior's home—a custom the Japanese have brought, somewhat modified,

---

Each $1,000 raise in a wife's salary increases the chances for divorce or separation by 1%.

into modern times. In England, women took off their gloves when presented to royalty. In fact, two other gestures, one male, one female, are remnants of acts of subjugation or respect: the bow and the curtsy; the latter was at one time a full genuflection.

"By the Middle Ages in Europe, the symbol of serfdom to a feudal lord was restricted to baring the head. The implicit message was the same as in earlier days: 'I am your obedient servant.' So persuasive was the gesture that the Christian Church adopted it, requiring that men remove their hats on entering a church.

"Eventually, it became standard etiquette for a man to show respect for an equal by merely tipping his hat."

GIVING A MILITARY SALUTE.

The formal military salute seems to have started in medieval England, when soldiers were commonly clad in armor. Two possible explanations for its origin:

• At jousting tournaments, knights paraded past the queen with hands held over their eyes, a symbolic gesture suggesting they were protecting themselves from her "blinding beauty."
• When two knights in armor met on the road, they raised their visors to show respect...and to demonstrate that they had no violent intentions. This position—one hand held at the forehead—became a formal military greeting. It outlasted the practice of wearing armor.

BUSINESS CARDS

Today, business cards are a means of establishing credibility as a professional. But until the early part of this century, they were "calling cards," and they were used exclusively for social purposes. They were "upper class"; presenting a calling card when you met or visited someone indicated that you didn't have to work for a living. And there was an elaborate etiquette surrounding their use (e.g., should a single woman leave a calling card for a gentleman?). But as the middle classes got into the act, the calling card became another means of making a business contact. Today, that's all it is.

GOOD-BYE

Good-bye is probably a shortened version of the old term, "God be with you."

FAMOUS FOR 15 MINUTES

We included this feature—based on Andy Warhol's comment that "in the future, everyone will be famous for 15 minutes"— in the first Bathroom Reader. Here it is again, with new stars.

THE STAR: Robert Opel, a 33-year-old unemployed actor.

THE HEADLINE: "Streaker Steals Oscar Show."

WHAT HAPPENED: Near the end of the 1974 Academy Awards ceremony, host David Niven was introducing the woman who would present the Best Picture award—Elizabeth Taylor. "She is," he was saying fondly, "a very important contributor to world entertainment, and someone quite likely—"

Suddenly his speech was interrupted by screams and laughter as a naked man streaked across the stage in back of him. Niven stuttered for a second, then recovered and commented, "Ladies and gentlemen, that was bound to happen. Just think, the only laugh that man will probably ever get is for stripping and showing off his shortcomings." Then he gave the floor to Taylor, who quipped, "That's a pretty tough act to follow."

Meanwhile, the streaker had been caught backstage and was produced by security, fully clothed, for the press. "I have no official connection with the Academy," Robert Opel told reporters. But observers speculated that Oscar show producer Jack Haley, Jr. had created the whole incident as a publicity stunt. He denied it, declaring: "I would have used a pretty girl instead."

THE AFTERMATH: Opel made an appearance on "The Mike Douglas Show," debuted as a stand-up comedian in Hollywood, and was hired to streak at other Hollywood affairs (e.g., one honoring Rudolf Nureyev). Then he disappeared from public view. Five years later, he made the news again when was brutally murdered at a sex paraphernalia shop he owned in San Francisco.

THE STAR: Jimmy Nicol, a little-known English drummer.

THE HEADLINE: "Ringo Heads to Hospital as Beatles Tour with New Drummer."

WHAT HAPPENED: In June, 1964 the Fab Four were getting

publicity shots taken at a photographer's, when drummer Ringo Starr suddenly collapsed. He was rushed to a hospital, and was diagnosed as having tonsillitis. This was a huge problem—the Beatles were about to leave for a world tour. Their solution: They hired a local session drummer named Jimmy Nicol to play with them while Ringo recovered. Overnight, the bewildered Nicol became a member of the world's most popular band.

Nicol played with the Beatles for two weeks—in Holland, Hong Kong, and Australia. Ringo finally felt well enough to join the band Down Under, and after one last performance—with Ringo watching—Jimmy reluctantly returned to England.

THE AFTERMATH: Inspired, Nicol started his own band, called the Shubdubs. Unfortunately, they went nowhere.

THE STAR: Jackie Mitchell, 17-year-old lefthanded pitcher for the Chattanooga Lookouts, a minor league baseball team.

THE HEADLINE: "Female Hurler Fans Ruth and Gehrig."

WHAT HAPPENED: It was April 2, 1931. The mighty New York Yankees were "working their way north at the end of spring training," playing minor league teams along the way. Today, they were in Chattanooga, Tennessee. When the first two Yankee batters got hits, the manager decided to make a pitching change. He brought in his latest acquisition, a local player who had never pitched in a pro game before—Jackie Mitchell. She was, in fact, the first woman *ever* to play in a pro game. And the first batter she had to face was Babe Ruth. A tough situation; but she was tough. Jackie struck the Babe out in 5 pitches…and then proceeded to strike out "Larrupin' Lou" Gehrig in 3.

It was an impressive debut for a rookie, but it was a little suspect —Joe Engel, owner of the Lookouts, was known for publicity stunts, and this game had been planned for April 1 (the April Fools' Day game was rained out). Still, Jackie insisted to her dying day that it was on the level, and you can't argue with record books.

AFTERMATH: *The New York Times* praised Jackie in an editorial, hailing her feat as a blow for women's rights.

Mitchell never made it as a pro—she played ball around Chattanooga for 6 years, then quit to marry and to take over the family business (optometry). She died in 1987.

THE STAR: Harold Russell, a disabled World War II veteran.

THE HEADLINE: "Non-actor Wins Oscar for First Film Role."

WHAT HAPPENED: In 1946, director William Wyler made a film called *The Best Years of Our Lives*, depicting the personal struggles of several returning World War II vets. It was a hot topic, and the movie attracted a first-class cast: Frederic March, Myrna Loy, Virginia Mayo, Dana Andrews…and Harold Russell.

Russell had lost both his hands in an explosion at a Georgia training camp during the war. The Army asked him to appear in a short film about disabled veterans, and Wyler spotted him in it.

The director essentially cast Russell as himself—a severely disabled man trying to readjust to everyday life. Wyler wouldn't let him take acting lessons; and his performance was so powerful that it carried the film. *The Best Years of Our Lives* captured 7 Oscars—including best picture, best actor (Frederic March), best director, best screenplay, and best supporting actor—Russell.

AFTERMATH: Russell didn't appear in another film for 34 years. He can be seen in the 1980 feature, *Inside Moves*.

THE STAR: Valerie Solanas, founder of SCUM—the Society for Cutting Up Men.

THE HEADLINE: "Warhol Felled By SCUM."

WHAT HAPPENED: Valerie Solanas had hung around Andy Warhol's studio in the '60s. She'd even appeared in his movie, *I, a Man*. So the artist whom friends called "the ultimate voyeur" was shocked when Valerie pulled out a gun one day in June, 1968 and shot him. Solanas, it turned out, was irked that Warhol hadn't bothered commenting on the script of a play she'd left with him.

Andy was seriously wounded; doctors only gave him a 50-50 chance to survive. Meanwhile Valerie turned herself in, telling the patrolman to whom she surrendered, "He had too much control over my life." She was immediately sent for psychiatric observation, while she and her organization were splashed across the tabloid front pages.

AFTERMATH: Warhol lived, Solanas was imprisoned, and the whole incident stands as an ironic reminder that no one—not even the man who first articulated the idea—is immune when someone's 15 minutes arrive.

Painting accounts for almost half the cost of automobile assembly.

NEAR MISSES

A surprising amount of movie parts that turn lesser lights into stars are cast simply because bigger stars have turned the roles down. Take these, for example:

CASABLANCA (1942). The lead role was originally offered not to Humphrey Bogart, but to movie tough guy George Raft—who turned it down because he didn't like the script. Earlier, Raft also turned down the part of Sam Spade in *The Maltese Falcon* (1941) because he didn't trust the young director (John Huston), and the lead in *High Sierra* (1941) because he thought it was bad luck to die onscreen. Bogart took both of those roles, too, and built a career on them.

DRACULA (1931). The choice for the film was Universal's master of horror, Lon Chaney, Sr. But Chaney died in August, 1930, a few months before filming began. Second choice: Bela Lugosi, who'd played the vampire on Broadway. Lugosi was rushed to Hollywood, became a surprise star, and was typecast as a movie ghoul for the rest of his career.

THE WIZARD OF OZ (1939). This was supposed to star "Americas's Sweetheart," Shirley Temple. MGM was willing to trade the services of its two biggest stars—Clark Gable and Jean Harlow—to 20th Century Fox to get the little actress. But Darryl Zanuck, Fox's chief, refused—so the part of Dorothy went to little-known Judy Garland. Ironically, Miss Temple was cast in a similar movie the following year, called *The Blue Bird*. It bombed and ruined her film career.

More Shuffling:
•W. C. Fields was supposed to be the Wizard, but he was dropped when he held out for more money. His replacement was Frank Morgan.
• Ray Bolger was supposed to be the Tin Woodsman, and Buddy Ebsen was supposed to be the Scarecrow. But they traded parts. Then Ebsen's lungs got infected when he inhaled the metallic dust sprayed on his costume, and he spent the next six weeks in an iron lung. He was replaced by Jack Haley.

The experts say: if you shop for food while hungry, you'll spend 3 times as much.

MIDNIGHT COWBOY (1969): Dustin Hoffman's intended co-star was Michael Sarazin. But Sarazin turned it down...and Jon Voight became an overnight star.

GONE WITH THE WIND (1939): The original Scarlett and Rhett were Bette Davis and Errol Flynn. That was Jack Warner's idea, anyway, when Warner Brothers still planned to finance the film. But Davis absolutely refused to have anything to do with Flynn, so Warner pulled out. When MGM got involved, producer David O. Selznick asked them for Gary Cooper to play Rhett—but he was refused. Finally he wound up with Clark Gable, who took the part simply because he wanted some quick money to finance an impending divorce.
• Despite the hoopla about finding *the* actress to play Scarlett at the last minute, Selznick apparently knew who he wanted quite early. When he saw Vivien Leigh in the British film *A Yank at Oxford*, his mind was made up. The rest was just p.r.

FRANKENSTEIN (1931): After the success of *Dracula*, Bela Lugosi was in line for all the good monster parts—including this one. But he turned *Frankenstein* down when he found out the monster wouldn't have any dialogue. Instead, an English actor named William Henry Pratt (Boris Karloff) got the role and became an international star.

ON THE WATERFRONT (1954): Marlon Brando won an Academy Award for his performance, but the producers originally wanted Montgomery Clift to star instead.

SOMEBODY UP THERE LIKES ME (1956): Young, little-known actor Paul Newman lost several choice parts to James Dean—including the role of Cal in *Giant*, and the lead in this biography of boxer Rocky Graziano. Then suddenly, before shooting on *Somebody Up There* started, Dean was dead. Newman was picked to step in, and the movie was his springboard to stardom.

TARZAN THE APE MAN (1932): Swimming star Johnny Weissmuller made a living with Tarzan pictures for decades, but only because Clark Gable turned the first one down.

You use up as many calories sitting in a sauna for 15 minutes as you do jogging for a mile.

THEIR REAL NAMES

We know them as Doris Day, Woody Allen, etc. But that's not what their parents called them. Here are some celebs' real names.

Muddy Waters: McKinley Morganfield
Liberace: Wladziu Valentino Liberace
Wolfman Jack: Bob Smith
Stan Laurel: Arthur Stanley Jefferson
Dean Martin: Dino Crocetti
Twiggy: Leslie Hornby
Peter Lorre: Laszlo Lowenstein
Jerry Lewis: Joseph Levitch
Lauren Bacall: Betty Perski
James Stewart: Stewart Granger
Yves Montand: Ivo Livi
Shelley Winters: Shirley Schrift
Van Morrison: George Ivan
W. C. Fields: W. C. Dunkenfield
Roy Rogers: Leonard Slye
Charles Bronson: Charles Buchinsky
Irving Berlin: Israel Baline
Stevie Wonder: Steveland Judkins Morris
Doris Day: Doris Kappelhoff
Boris Karloff: William Henry Pratt
Natalie Wood: Natasha Gurdin
Tammy Wynette: Wynette Pugh

Kirk Douglas: Issur Danielovitch
Rock Hudson: Roy Fitzgerald
Sophia Loren: Sophia Scicolone
Tony Curtis: Bernie Schwartz
John Wayne: Marion Michael Morrison
David Bowie: David Jones
Greta Garbo: Greta Gustafsson
Woody Allen: Allen Konigsberg
Fred Astaire: Fred Austerlitz
Lucille Ball: Dianne Belmont
Anne Bancroft: Anne Italiano
Jack Benny: Joseph Kubelsky
Yul Brynner: Taidje Kahn, Jr.
George Burns: Nat Birnbaum
Michael Caine: Maurice Mickelwhite
Joan Crawford: Lucille Le Sueur
Rodney Dangerfield: John Cohen
John Denver: Henry John Deutschendorf, Jr.
Werner Erhard: Jack Rosenberg
Douglas Fairbanks: Julius Ullman
Redd Foxx: John Sanford
Mel Brooks: Mel Kaminsky

How big is a standard grave? 7' 8" long x 3' 2" wide x 6' deep.

MYTH AMERICA

Here are a few more patriotic stories we all learned when we were young…and which are all 100% baloney.

The Myth: Nathan Hale, an American soldier during the Revolutionary War, was captured by the British and sentenced to hang. When the Redcoats asked if he had any last words, he replied defiantly: "I regret that I have but one life to lose for my country."
The Truth: He never said that—or anything close to it. According to the diary of a British soldier who was there, Captain Frederick MacKenzie, Hale's last words were brave, but not very inspiring. They were: "It is the duty of every good officer to obey the orders given him by his commander-in-chief."

The Myth: Abraham Lincoln hurriedly composed his most famous speech—the Gettysburg Address—on the back of an envelope while riding on a train from Washington, D.C. to the site of the speech in Gettysburg.
Background: The story apparently originated with Lincoln's son, Robert, who first created it in a letter he wrote after his father was assassinated.
The Truth: Lincoln actually started writing the speech two weeks before the event, and wrote at least five drafts before even leaving Washington for Gettysburg. He wasn't particularly keen on speaking spontaneously—in fact, he even refused to say anything to the crowd that met him at the Gettysburg train station because he was afraid he might say something foolish.

The Myth: The Liberty Bell got its name when it was rung on July 4, 1776 to commemorate declaring independence.
Background: This tale was invented by writer George Lippard in his 1847 book, *Legends of the American Revolution.*
The Truth: The Liberty Bell was installed in Philadelphia in 1753—23 years before the colonists rebelled—and it has nothing whatsoever to do with the Revolution. Its nickname, "Liberty Bell," was coined by abolitionists in 1839. They were referring to the end of slavery in America, not freedom from England.

That's great: The Russian Czar, Peter the Great, was nearly 7 feet tall.

MUSTANG: CAR OF THE '60s

*The original Ford Mustang, a sporty car for "everyman," intro-
duced in 1964, is now a symbol of the entire decade.
Its early history is fascinating.*

The Mustang was the most successful car ever introduced by
the American auto industry. But in terms of the '60s, it was
more than a car. Its popularity was an expression of the simple truth of the decade—that everyone wanted to look, feel, and
act young.

ORIGIN OF THE CAR

• The Mustang was the pet project of Ford General Manager Lee
Iacocca, who kept notes on new car ideas in a little black book. Because Ford kept getting letters from car buffs who wanted a car like
the 1955 T-Bird, Iacocca felt there was a market for a new "personal sports car" waiting to be developed. Research also showed that
the population was getting younger, and that young people bought
more cars per capita than any other segment of the population.

• Based on these findings—and Iacocca's instinct—Ford decided
to create a car that was sporty yet low-priced, so young people and
middle-income groups could afford it. But it also had to be capable
of taking enough options to make it a luxury car.

• The new project was dubbed "T-5." Ford engineers and designers
worked under maximum security in a windowless room, known as
"The Tomb"; even the wastepaper was burned under supervision.

• Over a three-year period they came up with many two-seat proto-
types—XT-Bird, Allegro, Aventura, and Mustang I (loved by car
enthusiasts, but considered too sporty by Iacocca)—but all were
scrapped in favor of a four-seat model with a large trunk. It was
completed in spring 1963.

• The Mustang was designed to be versatile. The buyer had options: two different engines, whitewalls, power disc brakes, racing
hubcaps, sports console, and so on. As Dr. Seymour Marshak,
Ford's market research manager, said admiringly, "This flexibility
makes this car the greatest thing since the Erector Set."

•Since Ford figured the T-5's market was the young sports car

The most popular color for cars is white. 10% of all cars sold in the U.S. are white.

buyer, the name "Torino" was chosen because it sounded like an Italian sports car. The projected ad campaign called it "the new import . . . from Detroit."

• But last-minute market research showed that this car could appeal to all buyers, and a new name had to be chosen. Colt, Bronco, and Maverick (all used for later cars) were considered. But "Mustang" seemed best for T-5, bringing to mind cowboys, adventure, and the Wild West. As one Ford man put it, "It had the excitement of the wide-open spaces, and it was American as all hell."

• The Mustang was introduced on April 17, 1964. On that day, over 4 million people visited the 6,500 Ford dealers across the country to get a look at it...and they bought 22,542 of them.

• In the first three months of production, a record 100,000 Mustangs were sold. It was an instant status symbol, with people vying for the limited supply as though it was a contraband item.

MUSTANG FEVER
The introduction of the Mustang on April 17, 1964 was a big event. Here are 5 of the bizarre things that happened that day.

1. A Mustang was the pace car for a stock car race in Huntsville, Alabama. When it drove onto the track, thousands of people scaled the retaining wall to get a better look at it. The race was delayed for over an hour.

2. A cement truck crashed through the plate-glass window of a Seattle Ford dealer when the driver lost control of his vehicle. The reason: He was staring at the new Mustangs on display there. They looked "like some of them expensive Italian racers," he explained.

3. A Chicago Ford dealer was forced to lock the doors of his showroom models because too many people were trying to get into them at the same time.

4. A Texas dealer put a new Mustang on a lift to show a prospective customer the underside of the vehicle. By the time his demonstration was over, the showroom was filled with people, and he had to leave the Mustang up in the air for the rest of the day.

5. A New Jersey Ford dealer had only one Mustang and 15 eager buyers, so he auctioned it off. The winner of the auction insisted on sleeping in the car to be sure the dealer didn't sell it to someone else before his check cleared.

STRANGE LAWSUITS

*These days, it seems like people will sue each other over
practically anything. Here are a few real-life
examples of unusual legal battles.*

THE PLAINTIFF: An unidentified 40-year-old woman from Poughkeepsie, New York.

THE DEFENDANT: Her plastic surgeon.

THE LAWSUIT: The woman had an operation to tighten her stomach in 1979. When it was over, she discovered that her belly-button was now 2-1/2 inches off center. She claimed "the operation had left a large deformed hole in her stomach and had disrupted her business and her life." She sued the doctor for malpractice.

VERDICT: She was awarded $854,000 by the New York State Supreme Court, and ultimately settled with the doctor for $200,000. A year later, she had her bellybutton surgically corrected.

THE PLAINTIFF: An unidentified woman from San Francisco.

THE DEFENDANT: Her priest.

THE LAWSUIT: The woman embezzled around $30,000 from the Catholic Church, and was overcome by guilt. "I couldn't take the pressure anymore," she said. "I needed to talk with someone, and the only person I could talk with was my priest." So she went into the confessional and admitted what she'd done. She expected absolution and forgiveness; instead, the priest turned her in to the police. She spent 7 months in jail, and when she got out, she sued the priest for $5 million for "violation of confidentiality."

VERDICT: Settled out of court.

THE PLAINTIFFS: Bruce and Susan S., from Manitoba, Canada.

THE DEFENDANT: Winnipeg International Airport.

THE LAWSUIT: One day in 1988, the couple and their baby daughter, Anna, showed up at the Winnipeg Airport to catch a flight. At the gate, the airport security guard X-rayed their carry-on luggage—and then picked up Anna and sent her through the X-ray

---

machine, too. The couple immediately took their daughter to a hospital to see if the X-rays had harmed her. She was okay, but they still sued the airport—"for the time lost while waiting for test results as well as the fare of the missed flight."
VERDICT: Settled out of court.

THE PLAINTIFF: Robert K., "a 36-year-old Philadelphia real estate manager."
THE DEFENDANT: The Transcendental Meditation Society and the guru Maharishi Mahesh Yogi.
THE LAWSUIT: Mr. K. worked with TM groups for 11 years, but he finally sued them because "he was never able to achieve the 'perfect state of life' they promised, and he suffered psychological disorders as a result. One broken agreement: he had been told he would be taught to 'fly' through self-levitation, but he learned only to 'hop with the legs folded in the lotus position.' "
VERDICT: "A U.S. district court jury in Washington, D.C. awarded him nearly $138,000 in damages."

THE PLAINTIFF: A 19-year-old man from New York City.
THE DEFENDANT: The City Transit Authority.
THE LAWSUIT: The 19-year-old decided to commit suicide by throwing himself off a subway platform into the path of an oncoming train. The train didn't stop in time to avoid hitting him, but it didn't kill him, either—he lost a leg, an arm, and part of the other arm. So he sued the Transit Authority, claiming "the motorman was negligent in not stopping the train quickly enough."
THE VERDICT: They settled out of court for $650,000—despite the fact that while they were negotiating the settlement, the man threw himself off a subway platform—and failed to kill himself—a second time.

AND LET'S NOT FORGET...
Two 1974 cases involving CBS-TV. The first one, a claim by studio technician Hamilton Morgan that "The Beverly Hillbillies" was originally his idea, was settled out of court (reportedly with a big cash settlement to Morgan). The second charged that CBS's Paladin character in "Have Gun, Will Travel" was pirated from a retired rodeo performer. The case went to court, and CBS lost.

The book most often read by high school English classes: Shakespeare's *Romeo and Juliet*.

"COME UP AND SEE ME..."

Comments from film actress Mae West.

"Marriage is a great institution, but I'm not ready for an institution yet."

"It's hard to be funny when you have to be clean."

"She's the kind of girl who climbed the ladder of success, wrong by wrong."

"Between two evils, I always pick the one I haven't tried before."

"I generally avoid temptation—unless I can't resist it."

"It's not the men in my life that counts—it's the life in my men."

"He who hesitates is last."

"When women go wrong, men go right after them."

"Too much of a good thing can be wonderful."

"I used to be Snow White...but I drifted."

"I only like two kinds of men—domestic and foreign."

"Is that a gun in your pocket, or are you glad to see me?"

"Give a man a free hand and he'll run it all over you."

"I've been in more laps than a napkin."

"A man in the house is worth two in the street."

"He's the kind of man a woman would have to marry to get rid of."

"Brains are an asset...if you hide them."

"I don't look down on men, but I certainly don't look up to them either. I never found a man I could love—or trust—the way I loved myself."

"When I'm good, I'm very good. But when I'm bad, I'm better."

"I always say, keep a diary and one day it will keep you."

"I've always had a weakness for foreign affairs."

The average bank teller loses about $250 every year.

WE'VE ONLY JUST BEGUN

*Ads are so pervasive in society that we often don't even
know one when we hear it. Like this one.*

Some people think "We've Only Just Begun" is a great love
song. Actually, it's a bank commercial.

BACKGROUND: In 1968, officials of the Crocker Bank in California approached a San Francisco ad agency about trying to attract young people to their institution. There was a strong anti-establishment feeling among college graduates at the time, and the bank felt it had to make an extra effort to reach them.

The ad executive in charge of the project came up with a basic approach. "The one thing that all young people have in common," he explained later, "is that they're starting out on new things—beginning careers, setting up a household for the first time, and so on. So the ad campaign was developed around that theme." The slogan: "We've only just begun."

THE BUCK STARTS HERE: The ad exec got an inspiration—he decided to pay a songwriter to create a *real* song called "We've Only Just Begun," instead of just a coming up with a jingle. That way, if the song made the charts, there would be extra benefits to his client whenever it was played on the radio. So he commissioned tunesmith Paul Williams to write a song with the phrase "We've Only Just Begun" in it.

As part of the deal, the bank used it on their commercials—but Williams was also free to do whatever he wanted with it.

What did he do with it? He sold it to the Carpenters, who recorded a saccharine version that sold millions of records, and became a wedding and elevator standard.

Meanwhile, the bank made its money back by licensing commercial right for the song to other banks around the country.

THE ULTIMATE IRONY: The bank realized it didn't *want* young people's business. Young adults flocked to the Crocker Bank to borrow money, but they didn't have any collateral. They turned out to be bad risks, and the ad campaign was stopped.

U.S. airports are busier on Thursdays than any other day.

NOTHING TO SNEEZE AT

*Why do we say "God Bless You" when we sneeze? Charles
Panati checked it out, and came up with the answer in
his* Extraordinary Origins of Everyday Things.

Gesundheit,' say Germans; 'Felicita,' say Italians; Arabs clasp
hands and reverently bow. Every culture believes in a bene-
diction following a sneeze. The custom goes back to a time
when a sneeze was regarded as a sign of great personal danger."

SNEEZING SUPERSTITIONS
"For centuries, man believed that life's essence, the soul, resided in
the head and that a sneeze could accidentally expel the vital force.
This suspicion was reinforced by the deathbed sneezing of the sick.
Every effort was made to hold back a sneeze, and an inadvertent or
unsuppressed sneeze was greeted with immediate good luck chants."

THE GREEK SNEEZE
"Enlightenment arrived in the fourth century B.C. with the teach-
ings of Aristotle and Hippocrates, the 'father of medicine.' Both
Greek scholars explained sneezing as the head's reaction to a foreign or offensive substance that crept into the nostrils. They observed that sneezing, when associated with existing illness, often
foretold death. For these ill-boding sneezes, they recommended
such benedictions as 'Long may you live!' 'May you enjoy good
health!' and 'Jupiter preserve you!' "

THE ROMAN SNEEZE
"About a hundred years later, Roman physicians extrapolated the
lore and superstition surrounding a sneeze.

"The Romans preached the view that sneezing, by an otherwise
healthy individual, was the body's attempt to expel the sinister spir-
its of later illnesses. Thus, to withhold a sneeze was to incubate disease, to invite debility and death. Consequently, a vogue of sneezing swept the Roman Empire and engendered a host of new post-
sneeze benedictions: 'Congratulations' to a person having robustly
executed a sneeze; and to a person quavering on the verge of an exhalation, the encouraging 'Good luck to you.' "

THE CHRISTIAN SNEEZE

"The Christian expression 'God bless you' has a still different origin. It began by papal fiat in the sixth century, during the reign of Pope Gregory the Great. A virulent pestilence raged throughout Italy, one foreboding symptom being severe, chronic sneezing. So deadly was the plague that people died shortly after manifesting its symptoms; thus, sneezing became synonymous with imminent death.

"Pope Gregory beseeched the healthy to pray for the sick. He also ordered that such well-intended though leisurely phrases as 'May you enjoy good health' be replaced with his own more urgent and pointed invocation, 'God bless you!' And if no well-wisher was around to invoke the blessing, the sneezer was advised to exclaim aloud, 'God help me!'

"Pope Gregory's post-sneeze supplications spread throughout Europe, hand in hand with the plague, and the seriousness with which a sneeze was regarded was captured in a new expression, which survives to this day: 'Not to be sneezed at.' "

WORLD-CLASS SNEEZING

• According to the *Guinness Book of World Records*, "The most chronic sneezing fit ever recorded is that of Donna Griffiths." On January 13, 1981, the 12-year-old from Pershore, England began sneezing and kept sneezing every day for 978 days. The previous record was 194 days.

• In the first year, she sneezed an estimated one million times.

•Her first "sneeze-free day" in almost three years was September 16, 1983.

The *Guinness Book* has somehow also come up with an account of the most powerful sneeze ever recorded:
"The highest speed at which expelled particles have been measured to travel," it says, is "103.6 miles per hour."

MISC. LAST THING ON THE PAGE

The phrase "Bring home the bacon" comes from the 1700s, when the term *bacon* was criminal slang for "booty" or "loot." If you brought home the *bacon*, you fulfilled your mission and returned with "the goods," which is how we use it today.

The first gold record ever awarded went to Glenn Miller for "Chattanooga Choo-choo."

SO LONG, ROUTE 66

You may not know it, but America's most famous highway is slowly disappearing, a victim of progress.

Although many American highways have been celebrated, few can match the romance and lore of Route 66—the 2,200-mile-long highway that was once the primary route between Chicago and Los Angeles. Route 66 has been immortalized in song ("Get Your Kicks on Route 66") and on the screen (the hit 1960s TV series).

Although it has now been bypassed by superhighways, it's still cherished by an enthusiastic cult of motorists who venture off the new interstates in search of a piece of America's history—which they seem to find on the old Route 66 backroads that still exist.

ROUTE 66 FACTS

• Route 66 began as a series of cattle and wagon train trails. By the early 1900s, the route was known as the "National Old Trails Highway."

• It was first designated Route 66 in 1926, while it was still mostly dirt and gravel. At the time, East-West routes were given even numbers, North-South got odd numbers. Route 66's Midwest path landed it between Route 2 (the northernmost route running from Maine to Idaho) and Route 96 (on the southern Texas border).

• In 1937, paving was completed. The finished highway went through eight states (Illinois, Missouri, Mississippi, Oklahoma, Texas, New Mexico, Arizona, and California) and three time zones.

• Route 66 was the road of choice for "Dust Bowl" Okies fleeing to California during the Depression of the early 1930's. John Steinbeck included Route 66 in his classic *The Grapes Of Wrath*, calling it "the mother road" on which the Joad family travelled West.

• Route 66 nicknames: The Will Rogers Highway, the Postal Highway, and the Ozark Trail.

• The TV show "Route 66" was actually filmed in Oregon and Florida. The series ran from October 7, 1960 until September 18, 1964. It starred Martin Milner and George Maharis as Tod Stiles and Buz Murdock. They drove a '62 Corvette.

• **The beginning of the end:** President Eisenhower ordered the construction of 42,500 miles of interstate highways in 1956. New superhighways like Interstate 40—which runs parallel to Route 66 from Oklahoma City to L.A.—eventually replaced the country backroads. As a result, small businesses which once thrived by the highway began to disappear in favor of fast-food franchises and hotel chains. Three interstates—40, 44, and 55—eventually replaced Route 66, whose last original stretch of highway (Williams, AZ) closed in the mid-1980s.

THE SONG

• In 1946, Bobby Troupe was driving from his home in Pennsylvania to try and make it as a songwriter in Los Angeles. At one point in the trip, his wife, Cynthia, suggested that he try and write a song about Highway 40. Troupe didn't think much of the suggestion. "Then later, out of Chicago, when we realized that we'd be following the same highway all the way to California," Troup recalls. "She whispered, kind of hesitantly because of the put-down on the first suggestion, 'Get your kicks on Route 66.' " By the time Troupe and his wife hit L.A. the song was nearly complete. Nat King Cole was the first to record it—everyone from Nelson Riddle and the Rolling Stones to Depeche Mode have done their version of "Route 66."

ROUTE 66 LANDMARKS

• Route 66 officially began on Jackson Boulevard and Michigan Avenue in Chicago. It ended at Ocean Avenue and Santa Monica Boulevard in Santa Monica, California, where a plaque can still be found dedicated to the Will Rogers Highway. It reads: "This Main Street of America Highway 66 was the first road he travelled in a career that led him straight to the hearts of his countrymen."

• The state of Arizona has preserved 105 miles of Route 66 as a historic state highway—it contains the longest drivable stretch of the road that still exits, running from Seligman to Topock, Arizona.

• Clark Gable and Carole Lombard spent their first honeymoon night on Rte. 66, in the Beale Hotel in Kingman, Arizona in 1939.

• Route 66 crosses the Texas panhandle and goes through Amarillo, home of the Cadillac Ranch (immortalized by Bruce Springsteen).

• Major cities you can still see on Route 66: Chicago, St. Louis, Oklahoma City, Amarillo, Albuquerque, and L.A.

The leaders in per capita consumption of chocolate: #1, Switzerland; #2, Norway. #3, Britain.

HELLO, I'M MR. ED

*A horse is a horse, of course, of course. Unless he's on TV.
Then anything can happen. Mr. Ed is probably TV's first
legitimate animal folk hero.*

HOW IT STARTED.
Arthur Lubin couldn't understand it. His films about
Francis the Talking Mule had made a small fortune, but he
still couldn't interest the TV networks in a similar concept he'd
created for the small screen. He envisioned a show about a talking
horse named Mr. Ed. (The idea was inspired by a series of magazine
stories about a horse that not only talked, but frequently got
drunk.) But no one—not even his projected star, comedian Alan
Young—would consider the series when Lubin proposed it in 1954.

Lubin kept trying, and three years later, in 1957, he finally found
a backer who agreed to bankroll a pilot film—comedian George
Burns, who along with his pal, Jack Benny, thought the concept of
a talking horse was hilarious.

Now that Lubin had some money, he approached Young again
with a concrete offer. But again Young turned him down. "It's not
the kind of thing I want to do," said Alan, who'd had his own CBS
variety show in the early '50s (but was now working in England).
Lubin went ahead and made a pilot anyway, using a different actor;
in fact, all the stars in the original pilot were different from the TV
show—even Mr. Ed. But he still couldn't sell the show.

Lubin was nothing if not persistent. He offered the part to Young
again a few years later. And this time Young decided it was his only
chance to get back into American TV. So he accepted. Lubin
wanted to call it "The Alan Young Show," but Young refused that.
"Why should I take the rap if it bombs?" he asked. So it became
"Mr. Ed."

When the networks didn't pick up the show, the Studebaker
Company (a now-defunct auto maker) purchased it and put it into
syndication in 1960. To everyone except Lubin's (and Burns's)
surprise, it was an instant hit. A year later, CBS bought it, making
it the first syndicated show ever to be picked up by a network. It
aired until 1965 on Sunday nights.

INSIDE FACTS

Les Is More

• Mr. Ed, an 1100-lb. golden palomino, wouldn't respond to any of his co-stars. He only took orders from his trainer, Les Hilton—which meant that Hilton had to be on the set all the time, barking out commands or giving them with hand signals.

• Hilton was often hidden in the scene or lying on the floor just out of camera range. If you're watching Mr. Ed and you want to know where Hilton is, just watch Ed's eyes. Ed is always looking at him (even if it seems that he's involved in the action).

Vital Stats

Ed's real name was Bamboo Harvester. He was born in 1954, and supposedly died in 1979 at the age of 25. His daily diet was 20 lbs. of hay, washed down with a gallon of sweet tea.

Take Five

Like any star, Ed could be moody and difficult to work with. When he was tired of working, he'd just walk off the set. And when he was hungry, shooting stopped while he strolled over to his bale of hay and ate. When he was bored, he'd cross his hind legs and yawn.

Historic Preservation

The classic Mr. Ed theme was first recorded in Italy—by an opera singer! It was so bad that Arthur Lubin started looking for a new song to use. But Jay Livingstone, Oscar-winning ("Que Sera, Sera") co-writer of the tune, recorded his own version which Lubin liked enough to use on the show. Livingstone sings it on the air.

Stunt Horse

There was no stand-in while Ed performed his stunts. He could really open the barn door (left or right side) and answer the telephone. He couldn't really talk, though. His lips were moved by a nylon bit.

The Voice

The voice of Mr. Ed was kept a secret. It was actually Allen "Rocky" Lane, a former cowboy star. For obvious reasons, Lane billed himself as "an actor who prefers to remain anonymous."

In 1900 only 41% of all Americans lived to be 65. In 1989, 79% do.

FREUDIAN SLIPS

From the mind of Sigmund Freud...

"America is a mistake, a giant mistake!"

"When a man is freed of religion, he has a better chance to live a normal and wholesome life."

"Anatomy is destiny."

"What progress we are making. In the Middle Ages they would have burnt me; nowadays they are content with burning my books."

"Thought is action in rehearsal."

"The great question...which I have not been able to answer, despite my thirty years in research into the feminine soul, is 'What do women want?' "

"Sometimes a cigar is just a cigar."

"The more the fruits of knowledge become accessible to men, the more widespread is the decline of religious belief."

"Neurosis seems to be a human privilege."

"The goal of all life is death."

"The first human being who hurled an insult instead of a stone was the founder of civilization."

"When one of my family complains that he or she has bitten his tongue, bruised her finger, and so on, instead of the expected sympathy, I put the question, 'Why did you do that?' "

"We hate the criminal, and deal with him severely, because we view in his deed, as in a distorting mirror, our own criminal instincts."

"When making a decision of minor importance, I have always found it advantageous to consider all the pros and cons. In vital matters, however, such as the choice of a mate or profession, decisions should come from the unconscious, from somewhere within ourselves. In the important decisions of our personal lives we should be governed by the deep inner needs of our nature."

41% of all Americans say they want their child to be President of the United States.

PRESIDENTIAL CURIOSITIES

*Nowadays, former presidents—even disgraced ones—are treated
with respect and deference. So it's enlightening to find out that the
presidential office wasn't always a royal one.*

F ACT: The government of the United States completely
ignored the death of one former president because he was
considered a traitor.

THE PRESIDENT: John Tyler (10th president, 1841-45).

BACKGROUND: A Virginia aristocrat, Tyler was William
Henry Harrison's running mate in 1840. When Harrison died in
1841, he became president. But 20 years later, the 71-year-old
joined the Confederacy. He died in 1861 while serving as a
Virginia representative in the Confederate Congress, and was
buried with full honors by the rebels. In Washington, however, his
death was never publicly acknowledged.

FACT: One president had to borrow money to get to his own
inauguration.

THE PRESIDENT: George Washington (1st president,
1789-97).

BACKGROUND: Washington wasn't poor—he was among
America's largest landowners. But when it came time to travel to
New York City for his inauguration in 1789, he didn't have any
money. So "The Father of Our Country" had to borrow about $600
to get there. One consolation: his presidential salary was $25,000.

FACT: One ex-president was so destitute in his final years that
circus impresario P. T. ("There's a sucker born every minute")
Barnum actually offered him $100,000 to take a nationwide tour
with his personal memorabilia.

THE PRESIDENT: Ulysses S. Grant (18th president, 1869-77).

BACKGROUND: In the early 1880s, Grant invested his life
savings—about $100,000—in a banking firm in which one of his
sons was a partner. The head of the company turned out to be a
swindler, and the firm went broke in 1884. Grant was not only
penniless, but had terminal cancer when Barnum wrote that year

---

You have more sweat glands in your hands and feet than anywehere else on your body.

and suggested a quick money-making tour. Grant refused. Instead, in an effort to leave his wife something after his death, he wrote his memoirs. Mark Twain published them posthumously, and they earned over $500,000 for the Grant estate.

FACT: Another ex-president was so broke that friends created a lottery in his name and began selling raffle tickets in Washington.

PRESIDENT: Thomas Jefferson (3rd president, 1801-1809).

BACKGROUND: Brilliant in other fields, Jefferson apparently had no head for business. When he came close to bankruptcy in his final years, friends and political allies put together the "Thomas Jefferson Lottery" to benefit the ex-president. Fortunately, Jefferson was spared this embarrassment when enough money was raised privately to keep him financially afloat.

FACT: One president never voted in a presidential election until *he* was the one running for office.

THE PRESIDENT: Zachary Taylor (12th president, 1849-50).

BACKGROUND: "Old Rough and Ready," a national military hero in the Mexican War, was completely apolitical until he was bitten by the presidential bug. When an aide first suggested that he run for the office, he reputedly answered "Stop your nonsense and drink your whiskey!"

When he actually was nominated by the Whigs, he didn't find out about it until weeks after the convention. The Whig party's letter informing him of the news arrived collect, and Taylor refused to pay the postage due—so he never read it. The nominators had to send another letter—prepaid—to tell him. When Taylor voted in the national elections of 1848, it was the first time he'd ever voted for a president—and he probably wouldn't have bothered then either, if he hadn't been on the ballot.

FACT: One president was a licensed bartender.

THE PRESIDENT: Abraham Lincoln (16th president, 1861-65).

BACKGROUND: In 1833, Honest Abe was co-owner of a saloon in Springfield, Illinois, called *Berry and Lincoln*. He needed his license to sell booze.

Letters galore: Chinese script has more than 40,000 characters.

MONEY TALK

What do you really know about your money?

THE GREENBACK DOLLAR

The Federal government didn't start printing paper money until 1861.

• When the Civil War broke out, people began hoarding coins—and soon there was virtually no U.S. money in circulation. So Congress was forced to authorize the Treasury Department to create paper currency.

• These bills were nicknamed "Greenbacks" after the color ink used on one side. Lincoln, then president, was pictured on them.

• Congress stipulated that paper money had to be signed either by the Treasurer of the United States or people designated by him. Today the signature is printed on the bills, but in 1862 money had to be signed by hand. So 6 people—2 men and 4 women—worked in the attic of the Treasury building every day, signing, sorting, and sealing our first $1 and $2 bills.

THE BUCKS START HERE

Today, paper money worth over $12 billion is printed every year—an average of more than $10 million a day.

• About 2/3 of the paper money printed is $1 bills.

• A $1 bill lasts for about 1-1/2 years in circulation.

• The average bill is exchanged 400 times in its lifetime.

• It costs the government about 2.5¢ to print a $1 bill. It costs the same amount to print a $100 bill.

• Modern U.S. currency is printed on special paper, a blend of rag bond, cotton, and linen, supplied by a single manufacturer, Crane and Company of Massachusetts.

• U.S. paper money is printed three separate times—once each for front and back, and then it's reprinted with an overlay of green ink.

• The current U.S. dollar is 1/3 smaller than it was in 1929.

VITAL STATS

Size of a bill: 2.61 inches x 6.14 inches.
Thickness: .0043 inches. (233 of them make a stack an inch high.)
Weight: 490 bills equals a pound. A million $1 bills weigh approximately a ton.

Laid end-to-end around the equator, it would take 257,588,120 dollar bills to circle the earth.

THE BIG BUCKS

• There are officially 12 different denominations of U.S. paper money, ranging from $1 to $100,000.

• The highest denomination printed in the last 45 years is a $100. In fact, everything over $100 has been officially "retired" from circulation for 30 years.

• The $100,000 bill has never been available to the public. It's only for transactions between the Treasury Department and the Federal Reserve.

• The $2 bill was resurrected in 1976—the only piece of new engraved currency in 60 years. It was a flop; the mint recently got rid of the last remaining bills in storage by burning them.

• Who's on what? $50—Ulysses S. Grant ; $100—Ben Franklin; $500—William McKinley; $1,000—Grover Cleveland; $5,000—James Madison; $10,000—Salmon P. Chase; $100,000—Woodrow Wilson.

COIN OF THE REALM

• The first U.S. coin to bear the words, "United States of America," was a penny piece made in 1727. It was also inscribed with the plain-spoken motto: "Mind your own business."

• All American coins struck since 1792, when the first United States mint was established in Philadelphia, have been stamped with the word, "Liberty."

• The average coin circulates for a minimum of 15-20 years.

• Originally, the dime, quarter, and half dollar were 90% silver, 10% copper. But in the early '60s, the price of silver began to climb, and government officials worried that people would melt coins down for the precious metals.

• The result: Congress passed the 1965 Coinage Act, eliminating all silver from the three coins. Instead, the composition was changed to "clad" metal—a combination of three strips of metal. The faces are made of 75% copper and 25% nickel; the core is pure copper, which you can see on the side.

• In 1965, anticipating the disappearance of old quarters due to the value of the silver, the government issued almost 2 billion new ones (compared to an average annual production of 225 million). That's why you find so many 1965 quarters in circulation.

• Nickels are now made of 75% copper, 25% nickel.

• Pennies are now bronze. They contain 95% copper, 5% zinc.

AROUND THE HOUSE

The origins of a few common items.

BAND-AIDS (1921).
In 1921 Earle Dickson, an employee of Johnson & Johnson, married a woman who kept injuring herself in the kitchen.
• As he carefully bandaged her cuts and burns with gauze and adhesive tape numerous times, he became frustrated; the clumsy bandages kept falling off. So he decided to create something "that would stay in place, be easily applied, and still retain its sterility." He stuck some gauze in the center of a piece of adhesive tape, and covered the whole thing with crinoline to keep it sterile. It worked.
• He made up a bunch for his wife, and took a few in to show his co-workers. The company's owner, James Johnson, heard about it and asked for a demonstration—which convinced him to begin manufacturing the product
• By the '80s, over 100 billion Band-Aids had been sold. Dickson, who became an exec at J & J, was amply rewarded for his efforts.

IVORY SOAP (1879).
Harley Procter and his cousin, chemist James Gamble, came up with a special new soap in 1878. It was smooth and fragrant, and produced a consistent lather...but it wasn't Ivory—it was called White Soap—and it didn't float.
• One day in 1879, the man operating P & G's soap-mixing machine forgot to turn it off when he went to lunch. On returning, he discovered that so much air had been whipped into the soap that it actually floated.
• For some reason, the batch wasn't discarded—it was made into bars and shipped out with the other White Soap. Soon, to their surprise, P&G was getting letters demanding more of "that soap that floats." So they started putting extra air in every bar
• Now that they had a unique product, they nedded a unique name. And they found it in the Bible. Procter was reading the 45th Psalm—which says: "All thy garments smell of myrrh, and aloes, and cassia, out of the ivory palaces..." —when it hit him that *Ivory* was just word he was looking for.
• In October, 1879 the first bar of Ivory Soap was sold.

That's huge: In the 4th century, the Romans had a stadium that held 380,000 spectators.

VELCRO (1957).

A young Swiss inventor named George De Mestral went for a hike one day in 1948. When he returned, he was annoyed to find burrs stuck to his clothes. But his annoyance turned to fascination. Why, he wondered, wouldn't it be possible to create synthetic burrs that could be used as fasteners?

• Most people scoffed at the idea; but a French weaver took him seriously. Using a small loom, the weaver hand-wove two cotton strips that stuck together when they touched. The secret: one strip had hooks, the other had loops.

• But De Mestral had to figure out how to mass-produce it...and he needed tougher material than cotton, which quickly wore out.

• Years passed; De Mestral experimented constantly. Finally he found a suitable material—nylon, which, it turned out, became very hard when treated with infrared light.

• Now he knew how to make the *loops* by machine—but he still couldn't figure out how to mass-produce the *hooks*.

• Finally a solution hit him. He bought a pair of barber's clippers and took them to a weaver. With the clippers, he demonstrated his idea—a loom that snipped loops as it wove them, creating little nylon hooks. He worked on the project for a year—and when it was finally completed, Velcro ("Vel" for velvet, "cro" for crochet) was born. The product had taken a decade to perfect.

THE ELECTRIC TOASTER (1919).

The first electric toasters, which appeared around 1900, were primitively constructed heating coils that were terrible fire hazards.

• However, they were a luxury—it was the first time in history that people didn't need to fire up a stove just to make a piece of toast.

• There was a built-in problem, though—the bread had to be constantly watched or it would burn to a crisp.

• In 1919, Charles Strite, a Minnesota factory worker, got sick of the burnt toast in the company cafeteria. So in his spare time, he designed and patented the first pop-up toaster. Then he went into business manufacturing them. It took years to work out the bugs, but by 1926, Strite's "Toastmasters" were relatively foolproof.

• A few years later, a New York businessman purchased Strite's company, and invested heavily in advertising—which proved to be the key ingredient in making the toaster a common household. appliance. Every home "had to have one"...and now they do.

That's a lotta nerve: You have 45 miles of nerves in your body.

ACCORDING TO JEFFERSON

Wisdom from Thomas Jefferson, one of our Founding Fathers.

"A little rebellion now and then is a good thing."

"The man who reads nothing at all is better educated than the man who reads nothing but newspapers."

"The tree of liberty must be refreshed for time to time with the blood of patriots and tyrants. It is its natural manure."

"I tremble for my country when I reflect that God is just."

"Never buy what you do not want, because it is cheap; it will be dear to you."

"Question with boldness even the very existence of a God; because, if there be one, he must more approve of the homage of reason than that of a blindfolded fear."

"Never spend money before you have it."

"The art of life is the avoiding of pain."

"The Earth belongs...to the living. The dead have neither rights nor powers over it."

"The tax which will be paid for education is not more than the thousandth part of what will be paid to kings, priests, and nobles who will rise up among us if we leave the people to ignorance."

"Resistance to tyrants is obedience to God."

"To the press alone, chequered as it is with abuses, the world is indebted for all the triumphs which have been gained by reason and humanity over error and oppresion."

"Do not bite at the bait of pleasure till you know there is no hook beneath it."

"The legitimate powers of government extend to such acts as are injurious to others. But it does me no injury for my neighbor to say there are twenty gods, or no God. It neither picks my pocket nor breaks my leg."

If you're average, you've got a vocabulary of about 10,000 words.

LIMERICKS

Limericks have been around since the 1700s. The authors of these silly ditties (except for the one by Edward Lear) are unknown.

There was a young fellow
  named Clyde,
Who once at a funeral was
  spied.
When asked who was dead,
He smilingly said,
  "I don't know—I just came
for the ride."

There was a young man of
  Calcutta
Who had a most terrible
  stutta,
He said: "Pass the h. . .ham,
And the j . . .j . . .j . . .jam,
And the b....b...b...b...b...
  b...butta."

There was a young man from
  Darjeeling,
Who got on a bus bound for
  Ealing;
It said at the door:
"Don't spit on the floor,"
So he carefully spat on the
  ceiling.

There was an old fellow named
  Cager
Who, as the result of a wager,
Offered to fart
The whole oboe part
Of Mozart's *Quartet in F
  Major.*

There was a young fellow of
  Lyme
Who lived with three wives at
  one time.
When asked: "Why the third?"
He replied: "One's absurd,
And bigamy, sir, is a crime."

There was a brave fellow
  named Gere,
Who hadn't an atom of fear.
He indulged a desire
To touch a live wire,
And any last line will do
  here.

An epicure, dining in Crewe,
Once found a large mouse in
  his stew.
Said the waiter: "Don't shout,
Or wave it about,
Or the rest will be wanting
  one, too."

A mouse in her room woke
  Miss Dowd,
Who was frightened and
  screamed very loud.
Then a happy thought hit
  her—
To scare off the critter,
She sat up in bed and
  meowed.
            —Edward Lear

INSIDE MOTHER GOOSE

We've sung and recited these rhymes since we were kids. Little did we know that they weren't just nonsense. Here's the inside scoop about what they really meant.

Humpty Dumpty *sat on a wall, Humpty Dumpty had a great fall. All the King's horses and all the king's men, couldn't put Humpty together again.*

Background: According to Katherine Thomas in *The Real Personages of Mother Goose*, this rhyme is 500 years old and refers to King Richard III of England. In 1483 his reign ended when he fell from his mount during battle; he was slain as he stood shouting "My kingdom for a horse!"

• Richard's fall made him Humpty Dumpty. Originally the last line was "Could not set Humpty up again"—which can be interpreted as either putting him back on his horse, or back on the throne.

Old King Cole *was a merry old soul, a merry old soul was he. He called for his pipe and he called for his bowl, and he called for his fiddlers three."*

Background: There was actually a King Cole in Britain during the third century. No one knows much about him, but historians agree that he's the subject of the poem. Of interest: There's a Roman amphitheater in Colchester, England which has been known as "King Cole's Kitchen" for centuries.

Little Jack Horner *sat in a corner, eating his Christmas pie. He stuck in his thumb and he pulled out a plum, and said "What a good boy am I."*

Background: In the mid-1500s, when King Henry VIII was confiscating lands belonging to the Catholic church, the Abbot of Glastonbury—the richest abbey in the British kingdom—tried to bribe the monarch by sending him a special Christmas pie. Inside the pie, the abbot had enclosed the deeds to 12 manor houses.

The courier who delivered the pie to the king was the abbot's aide, Thomas Horner.(The name "Jack" was contemporary slang for any male, particularly a "knave"). On his way, Horner stopped, stuck in his hand, and pulled out one of the deeds from the pie—a plum called Mells Manor. Shortly after, Horner moved into Mells, and his family still lives there today (although they deny the story).

Ironically, the abbot was later put on trial for his life—and Horner was one of the judges who condemned him to death.

Jack be nimble, Jack be quick, Jack jump over the candlestick.
Background: for centuries, jumping over a candlestick was a method of fortune-telling in England. According to *The Oxford Dictionary of Nursery Rhymes*: "A candlestick with a lighted candle was placed on the floor and if, when jumping over it, the light was nmot extinguished, good luck was supposed to follow during the coming year."

Ring around the rosy, a pocket full of posies.
Ashes, ashes, we all fall down
Background: According to James Leasor in *The Plague and the Fire*, this "had its origin in the [London Plague of 1664]. Rosy refers to the rosy rash of plague....The posies were herbs and spices carried to ward off the disease; sneezing was a common symptom of those close to death. In the *Annotated Mother Goose*, the authors note that the third line is often given as a sneezing noise ("At-choo, at-choo"), and that " 'We all fall down' was, in a way, exactly what happened."

WHO WAS MOTHER GOOSE?
No one's quite sure. There are at least two possibilities, according to *The Annotated Mother Goose*:
• Charles Perrault, a French writer, "published a collection of fairy tales called *Tales of My Mother Goose* in 1697. The book contains eight stories: 'Little Red Riding Hood,' 'Bluebeard,' 'Puss In Boots,' " etc.
• But many scholars maintain that Mother Goose was actually one Elizabeth Foster Goose, of Boston, Mass. In 1692, when she was 27, Elizabeth married a widower named Isaac Goose and immediately inherited a family of 10 children. One of her step-daughters married a printer several years later and the printer enjoyed listening to "Mother Goose" recite old rhymes to the younger children. In 1719, he published a collection called *Songs for the Nursery, or Mother Goose's Melodies*.

In 1980, there was only one country in the world with no telephones—Bhutan.

BUT THEY'D NEVER BEEN THERE

*Songs about places can be so convincing that it's hard to believe
the people who wrote them haven't been there themselves.
But that's often the case. Three prime examples:*

TAKE ME HOME, COUNTRY ROADS; JOHN DENVER

John Denver sounds so sincere singing this song that it's
hard to believe he wasn't born and raised in West Virginia. But he
wasn't. Denver didn't even write it; two musicians named Bill
Danoff and Taffy Nivert did.

And they didn't grow up in West Virginia either. In fact, they'd
never even been there when the song was composed.

It was actually written while they were on their way to a Nivert
family reunion in *Maryland*. As they drove through the
countryside, along the winding, tree-lined roads, Bill passed the
time by writing a little tune about their rural surroundings.
Gradually, it became "Take Me Home, Country Roads."

How did West Virginia get into the song? A friend of Bill's kept
sending him picture postcards from the Mountain State with notes
like, "West Virginia's almost heaven." Bill was so impressed by the
postcards that he incorporated them into the lyrics of the song.

John Denver discovered the tune in 1970, while he was
performing at a Washington, D.C. folk club. Bill and Taffy were
also performing there, and one evening they played Denver their
half-finished "Country Roads." The three of them stayed up all
night finishing it. Denver put it on his next RCA album; it made
him a star, and made Bill and Taffy some hefty royalties.
Presumably, they've been to West Virginia by now.

WOODSTOCK; CROSBY, STILLS, NASH, AND YOUNG

The most famous tribute to the most famous musical event in rock
history was written by Joni Mitchell. Millions of young Americans
have listened to the hit versions by Crosby, Stills, Nash, and Young
and by Matthews' Southern Comfort (as well as an album cut

featuring Joni herself) and imagined enviously what it was like to be at Woodstock.

But what they don't know is that Joni *wasn't at the festival.* She was watching it on TV, like most of America.

She'd been traveling with Crosby, Stills and Nash (who played one of their first gigs ever at the mammoth rock concert), and they were all staying in New York City before heading up to the festival. But Mitchell's managers, David Geffen and Elliot Roberts, decided she wouldn't be able to make her scheduled appearance on "The Dick Cavett Show" if she went to Woodstock—so they cancelled her appearance there; Joni was left behind in New York.

Mitchell says: "The deprivation of not being able to go provided me with an intense angle on Woodstock. I was one of the fans."

But in the song, she sounds like one of the eyewitnesses.

PROUD MARY;
CREEDENCE CLEARWATER REVIVAL

This million-selling single about an old Mississippi paddlewheeler established Creedence Clearwater Revival as America's chief exponent of "swamp rock."

They were quickly recognized as the most promising artists to emerge from New Orleans since Fats Domino.

There was only one catch: Creedence Clearwater Revival wasn't from New Orleans. They were from El Cerrito, California. And they had never even been to New Orleans. In fact, the farthest east that songwriter John Fogarty had ever gotten was to Montana. And the closest thing to a bayou that he'd ever seen was the swampland around Winters, California.

Actually, Proud Mary wasn't originally going to be a Mississippi riverboat at all. Fogarty initially envisioned her as a "washer woman." But the first few chords he played with reminded him of a paddle-wheel going around. That brought him to thoughts of the Mississippi River, and Mary became a boat.

How did Fogarty manage to pull it off so well? The best explanation he could come up with for his "authentic" sound was that he'd listened to a lot of New Orleans music (like Fats Domino) when he was young.

IRRELEVANT NOTE: Not even one of the 13 actors who played Charlie Chan in movies, radio, Broadway, or TV were Chinese or of Chinese ancestry.

The most extras ever used in a movie was 300,000, for the film *Gandhi* in 1981.

PRIME TIME PROVERBS

TV's comments about everyday life in America
From Prime Time Proverbs, *by Jack Mingo and John Javna.*

ON AGING
Dorothy: "Age is just a state of mind."
Blanche: "Tell that to my thighs."

—*The Golden Girls*

Fred Sanford: "I still want to sow some wild oats!"
Lamont Sanford: "At your age, you don't have no wild oats—you got shredded wheat!"

—*Sanford and Son*

ON RELATIONSHIPS
"You can make a man eat shredded cardboard. . . . If you know the right tricks."

—**Jeannie's sister,**
I Dream of Jeannie

Sam Malone: "You've made my life a living hell."
Diane Chambers: "I didn't want you to think I was easy."

—*Cheers*

ON HUMAN NATURE
"I'm only human, Meathead... and to be human is to be violent."

—**Archie Bunker,**
All in the Family

"Everyone's a character—some of us just haven't met the right writer yet."

—**Dash Goff,**
Designing Women

"I think man is the most interesting insect, don't you?"

—**Marvin Martian,**
The Bugs Bunny Show

ON ANATOMY
Cosmetic Clerk: "You know what the fastest way to a man's heart is?"
Roseanne: "Yeah. Through his chest!"

—*Roseanne*

ON MARRIAGE
"Just because we're married to men doesn't mean we've got anything in common with them."

—**Ethel Mertz,**
I Love Lucy

"Why can't they invent something for us to marry instead of women?"

—**Fred Flintstone,**
The Flintstones

All wet: The average 150-lb. man should consume 2.9 quarts of water (in any form) each day.

MARK TWAIN & POLITICS

In 1912, Mark Twain declared he was running for the presidency. Here's what he told the press:

On His Reasons for Running: "A patriotic American must do something around election time, and…I see nothing else to do but become a candidate for President. Even the best among us will do the most repulsive things when smitten with a Presidential madness."

On His Position: "I am in favor of anything and everything anybody is in favor of."

On His Character: "The rumor that I buried a dead aunt under my grapevine was correct. The vine needed fertilizing; my aunt had to be buried, and I dedicated her to this high purpose. Does that unfit me for the Presidency? The Constitution of this country does not say so. No other citizen was ever considered unworthy of this office because he enriched his grapevine with his dead relatives. Why should I be selected as the first victim of an absurd prejudice?"

On Corruption: "We have humble God-fearing Christian men among us who will stoop to do things for a million dollars that they ought not to be willing to do for less than two million."

On the Arms Race: "The idea is that these formidable new war-inventions will make war impossible by and by—but I doubt it."

On Women's Rights: "Their wonderful campaign lasted a great many years, and is the most wonderful in history, for it achieved a revolution—the only one achieved in history for the emancipation of half a nation that cost not a drop of blood."

On Civil Rights: "It is a worthy thing to fight for one's freedom; it is another sight finer to fight for another man's."

On Liberty: "I believe we ought to retain all our liberties. We can't afford to throw them away. They didn't come to us in a night. The trouble with us in America is that we haven't learned to speak the truth. We have thrown away the most valuable asset we have—the individual right to oppose both flag and country when by one's self we believe them to be in the wrong."

Every person has a unique tongue-print.

GET SMART

*The most popular satire in the history of TV was this spy
takeoff starring Don Adams and Barbara Feldon.*

HOW IT STARTED.
The spy craze began quietly in 1963 with the release of the
first James Bond film, *Dr. No*. By the end of 1964, there
were 2 more Bond epics and a hit TV spinoff ("The Man from
UNCLE"). Spies were everywhere, and Dan Melnick, a packager at
Talent Associates, decided to parody them on TV. He picked
comedy writers Mel Brooks (still years away from his first film) and
Buck Henry to create the satire. "No one had ever done a show
about an idiot before," Brooks said in 1965. "I decided to be the
first."

The appropriate name for a sitcom idiot, they figured, was Smart.
And since every secret agent needed a number, they gave theirs
86—the code bartenders use to cut off service to a drunk ("86 that
guy"). Smart also needed a beautiful companion, so they created a
slightly daffy Mata Hari named "99" (instead of "69") to costar.

"We had no special comedian in mind for Smart," Henry said at
the time. "We wrote dialogue suitable for any standup comedian.
But we had our eyes on a definite Mata Hari—Barbara Feldon."

ABC loved the idea and commissioned a pilot script. But when
they read what Brooks and Henry had written, they backed out of
the deal. The story had the evil KAOS threatening to blow up the
Statue of Liberty, which ABC called "dirty and un-American."
Instead, the show was sold to NBC.

"Get Smart" became the highest-rated new show of the 1965–
66 season, and the episode ABC rejected was nominated for an
Emmy.

SIC 'EM
Barbara Feldon was the first of many models who became famous
by starring in TV ads. Her big break: A commercial for a men's hair
product called Top Brass. She stretched out on a rug and purred,
"Sic 'em, tiger." That got her so much attention that she was
offered TV guest roles as an actress. A spot as an industrial spy on a
show called "East Side, West Side" earned her the role of 99.

No wonder they're confused: There are 68,000 miles of telephone lines in the Pentagon.

WOULD YOU BELIEVE...

Don Adams and comedian Bill "Jose Jimenez" Dana were old friends. So when Dana got his own sitcom in 1963 ("The Bill Dana Show"), he included Adams in the cast, playing a dumb house detective named Byron Glick—essentially the same role he played as Maxwell Smart. Dana's show was cancelled in 1965, leaving Adams free to take the starring role in "Get Smart" the same year.

THE VOICE

In the '50s, Adams' stand-up comedy routine included impersonations of famous personalities, including actor William Powell. For Max's voice, he just did his Powell imitation in a higher pitch.

THE OLD ONE-LINER TRICK

Max was famous for one-liners like "Sorry about that, Chief," and "Would you believe..." They became fads, with kids adopting them as hip slang. But it wasn't an accident. From the outset, Don Adams anticipated it and insisted the show's writers build them into the stories. Most of them were already part of Adams' comedy routine. He brought "Would you believe..." from "The Bill Dana Show" and borrowed "Sorry about that" from Ernie Kovacs' protege, Joe Mikalos. As the old lines got stale, writers began adding new ones, like "The old _____ trick."

THE BURGER KING

Here's a whopper. Which cast member had the most successful post-"Get Smart" acting career? King Moody, who played the semi-regular villain, Starker. He became Ronald McDonald on McDonald's TV commercials.

TRUE CONFESSIONS

Don Adams on the quality of the show: "At first, I wanted every show to be a classic. [But] I then came to the realization that when you do a show every week, you can't be a classic. If you can do 3 out of 5 which are good, you should be happy with that."

NAME GAME

According to Buck Henry, Agent 99's real name was never revealed. In one episode, she was introduced as "Susan Hilton." But in the end, she explained to Max that it was just a cover name.

Room to breathe: In 1610, the population of the American colonies was 350 people.

MORE EPITAPHS

*More unusual epitaphs and tombstone rhymes from our
wandering B.R.I. tombstone-ologists.*

Seen in Enosburg, Vermont:
In memory of Anna
Here lies the body of our
  Anna,
Done to death by a banana.
It wasn't the fruit that laid her
  low,
But the skin of the thing that
  made her go.

Seen in Burlington, Mass.:
Anthony Drake
Sacred to the memory of
  Anthonly Drake,
Who died for peace and
  quietness sake.
His wife was constantly
  scoldin' and scoffin',
So he sought for repose in a
  $12 coffin.

Seen in Winslow, Maine:
Beza Wood, 1792-1837
Here lies one Wood
  enclosed in wood,
One within the other.
The outer wood is very good.
We cannot praise the other.

*Seen in Boot Hill Cemetery,
Dodge City, Kansas:*
He played five Aces.
Now he's playing the harp.

*Seen in the English
countryside:*
Mary Ford, 1790
Here lieth Mary—the wife of
  John Ford.
We hope her soul is gone to
  the Lord.
But if for Hell she has changed
  this life,
She would rather be there
  than be John Ford's wife.

Seen in Canaan, N.H.:
Sarah Shute, 1803-1840
Here lies, cut down like unripe
  fruit,
The wife of Deacon Amos
  Shute.
She died of drinking too much
  coffee,
Anno Domini eighteen forty.

Seen in Burlington, N.J:
Mary Ann Lowder, 1798
Here lies the body of Mary
  Ann Lowder,
Who burst while drinking a
  Seidlitz powder.
Called from this world to her
  Heavenly Rest
She should have waited till it
  effervesced.

If a Turkish person is wearing violet, he or she might be in mourning.

THE ORIGIN OF LEVI'S

Blue jeans are as American as apple pie and bathroom reading. In fact, you might have a pair around your ankles right now.

CANVASING THE CUSTOMERS

In 1850—during the California gold rush—a 17-year-old named Levi Strauss moved from New York City to San Francisco to sell dry goods to the miners. • He tried to sell canvas to them for their tents, but found little interest in it. So he made pants out of the material instead.

• The miners loved them. Although the pants weren't particularly comfortable, they were the first pants durable enough to withstand the miners' rugged living conditions.

• People nicknamed the pants Levi's, after their creator.

A RIVETING EXPERIENCE

Some years later, Levi Strauss began using denim in his pants. It was still tough, but it was softer and more comfortable than canvas.

• He also found that when the denim pants were dyed blue, they wouldn't show soil and stains as much. Miners appreciated this, and Levi's became even more popular.

• Meanwhile, miners found that after heavy use, the pockets often ripped the pants at the seams.

• A Nevada tailor named Jacob Davis solved that problem for his customers by securing each pocket seam with a rivet. It worked so well, in fact, that Davis wrote to Levi Strauss offering to sell him the idea. Strauss took him up on it; copper rivets first appeared on Levis in 1873. They became a hallmark of the company's product.

LEVI'S' MIDDLE-AGE SPREAD

Levi's were working people's pants for their first 75 years. Then, in the '30s, an advertisement for jeans ran in *Vogue* magazine. The reaction was so great that jeans became the rage. Jitterbugging teenagers started wearing them with the cuffs rolled up, and they've been fashionable ever since.

• Meanwhile, the Levi Strauss Company branched out into manufacturing other items as well as blue jeans...and by 1970 it had become the largest clothing manufacturer in the world.

Breathe deep: Your right lung takes in more air than your left one does.

MYTH AMERICA

*Here's a myth in reverse—a tale most people believe
is fictional, but is actually true.*

THE MYTH: Uncle Sam is a fictional character, created by cartoonists as a symbol of America's government and our "national character."

BACKGROUND: Ironically, while Americans routinely believe historical tales which are completely false, we're skeptical of some that are actually true. This is a case in point. For years, it was assumed there was no real Uncle Sam. Then, in 1961, a historian stumbled on proof that "Uncle Sam" had actually existed.

THE TRUTH: There's a detailed account of the Uncle Sam story in Charles Panati's book *Extraordinary Origins of Everyday Things*: Here are some excerpts:.

BACKGROUND

• "Uncle Sam was Samuel Wilson. He was born in Arlington, Massachusetts, on September 13, 1766....At age 14, [he] joined the army and fought in the American Revolution."

• "With independence from Britain won, Sam moved in 1789 to Troy, New York, and opened a meat-packing company. Because of his jovial manner and fair business practices, he was affectionately known to townsfolk as Uncle Sam."

OUR "UNCLE SAM" IS BORN

• "During the War of 1812, government troops were quartered near Troy. Sam Wilson's fair-dealing reputation won him a military contract to provide beef and pork to soldiers. To indicate that certain crates of meat produced at his warehouse were destined for military use, Sam stamped them with a large 'U.S.'—for 'United States,' though the abbreviation was not yet in the vernacular."

•"On October 1, 1812, government inspectors made a routine tour of the plant. They asked a meat packer what the ubiquitously stamped 'U.S.' stood for. The worker, himself uncertain, joked that the letters must represent the initials of his employer, Uncle Sam."

• "The error was perpetuated. Soon soldiers began referring to all military rations as bounty from Uncle Sam. Before long, they were calling all government-issued supplies property of Uncle Sam. They even saw themselves as Uncle Sam's men."

UNCLES SAM'S WARDROBE

"The...familiar and colorful image of Uncle Sam we know today arose piecemeal, almost one item at a time, each the contribution of an illustrator."
- "The first Uncle Sam illustrations appeared in New England newspapers in 1820."
- "Solid red pants were introduced during...Jackson's presidency."
- "The...beard first appeared during Abraham Lincoln's term, inspired by the President's own beard, which set a trend at the time."
- "By the late nineteenth century, Uncle Sam was such a popular national figure that cartoonists decided he should appear more patriotically attired. They adorned his red pants with white stripes and his top hat with both stars and stripes. His costume became an embodiment of the country's flag."
- "It was Thomas Nast, the famous...cartoonist of the Civil War and Reconstruction period, who made Uncle Sam tall, thin, and hollowcheeked. Coincidentally, Nast's Uncle Sam strongly resembles drawings of the real-life Sam Wilson. But Nast's model was actually Abraham Lincoln."
- "The most famous portrayal of Uncle Sam—the one most frequently reproduced and widely recognized—was painted in this century by American artist James Montgomery Flagg. The stern-faced, stiff-armed, finger-pointing figure appeared on World War I posters captioned: 'I Want You for U.S. Army.'...Flagg's Uncle Sam, though, is not an Abe Lincoln likeness, but a self-portrait."

A MYTH UNCOVERED

- "During these years ...the character of Uncle Sam was still only a myth. The identity of his prototype first came to light in early 1961. A historian, Thomas Gerson, discovered a May 12, 1830, issue of the New York Gazette newspaper in the archives of the New York Historical Society. In it, a detailed firsthand account explained how Pheodorus Bailey, postmaster of New York City, had witnessed the Uncle Sam legend take root in Troy, New York."
- Sam was officially acknowledged during JFK's administration, "by an act of the 87th Congress, which states that 'the Congress salutes 'Uncle Sam' Wilson of Troy, New York, as the progenitor of America's National symbol.' "

The Earth spins faster on its axis in September than it does in March.

THE FACTS ABOUT G.I. JOE

G.I. Joe, the first successful doll for boys, seems to be going as strong today as he was the year he was introduced.

HIS BIRTH. By 1963 Mattel's Barbie doll was so popular that Don Levine, creative director of the Hasbro Toy Co., suggested manufacturing a boys' version. "But instead of fashion," he explained, "we'll make it a soldier, and we'll sell extra uniforms and weapons."

• But would boys buy dolls? Hedging its bets, Hasbro decided never to call it a "doll"—only an "action soldier." And they decided to give it a scarred face to make it seem more masculine.

HIS NAME. Hasbro planned to make different sets of uniforms for each branch of the service (Army, Navy, Air Force, Marines) and give each a different name—Salty the Sailor, Rocky the Marine, etc. But the marketing department insisted on one name. One night, Levine happened to see the 1945 film *The Story of G.I. Joe* on television, and realized that "G.I. Joe" was perfect.

HIS BODY. Unlike Barbie, the boy's doll had to be fully movable. But Hasbro wasn't sure if it could be done. One day Levine was walking past an art-supply store when he noticed a display of small wooden, jointed models that artists use to draw different body positions. He bought a dozen, and they copied the construction.

HIS LIFE.

1964: Joe is introduced to the toy industry; toy store owners avoid him, sure that American parents won't buy their sons dolls. But Hasbro sticks with it, and in the first year over $30 million worth of G.I. Joe and accessories are sold—including 2 million dolls.

1968: With the increasing unpopularity of the war in Vietnam, parents begin to reject war toys. Joe's sales plummet to less than a third of their previous level. He's almost wiped out, but Hasbro saves the day by changing him from a soldier to an adventurer.

1978: *Star Wars* action figures are hot, and no one wants a G.I. Joe anymore. He's dead meat. Hasbro drops him from their line.

1982: Joe returns. Raised from the dead with his "G.I. Joe Team," he storms the toy market and becomes the #1 seller again. From 1982-88, he racks up over $600 million in sales. Go Joe!

It must be love: women's hearts beat faster than men's.

POLITICAL DOUBLE-TALK

*Every year, the Committee on Public Doublespeak of the
National Council of Teachers of English "honors" public figures
(or organizations) who "use language that is grossly deceptive,
evasive, confusing, and self-contradictory." Here are some
examples, taken from their annual news releases.*

In 1980:
* President Jimmy Carter declared that the failed effort to rescue American hostages in Iran was an "incomplete success."

In 1981:
* The Department of Agriculture decided that ketchup was a vegetable and could "be counted as one of the two vegetables required as part of the school lunch program."

In 1982:
* The Environmental Protection Agency prohibited its employees from using the term "acid rain." Instead, they were told to use the term "poorly buffered precipitation."
* Lewis Thurston, chief of staff for New Jersey's governor, Thomas Kean, insisted that "staff members do not have chauffeurs." Rather, they have "aides who drive."
* When it was pointed out that a commercial sponsored by the Republican National Committee misrepresented the facts, a Republican official declared: "Since when is a commercial supposed to be accurate?"

In 1984:
* When American troops in Lebanon were evacuated to ships offshore, Secretary of Defense Caspar Weinberger claimed this did not constitute a withdrawal. "We are not leaving Lebanon," he said. "The Marines are merely being deployed two or three miles to the west."
* Investigating an accident, the National Transportation Safety Board called an airplane crash "controlled flight into terrain."
* The Pentagon called peace "permanent pre-hostility."
* The CIA called mercenary soldiers hired to fight in Nicaragua "unilaterally controlled Latino assets."

Hard to Believe: Chemically speaking, your blood is very close to sea water.

In 1986:
•NASA referred to the *Challenger* astronauts' bodies as "recovered components," and their coffins as "crew transfer containers."
• Disregarding Due Process of Law, Attorney General Edwin Meese suggested that if a person is arrested, he's almost certainly guilty. "If a person is innocent of a crime," he explained, "he is not a suspect." Then he insisted to a reporter that "I...consider myself in the forefront of the civil rights movement in the country today."
• The Defense Department defined a hammer as a "manually powered fastener-driving impact device," a flashlight as an "Emergency Exit Light," and a tent as a "frame-supported tension structure."
• When a missile flew out of control and crashed, the Defense Dept. said it had merely "impacted with the ground prematurely."

In 1987
• Oliver North said he wasn't lying about his actions in Iran-Contra—he was "cleaning up the historical record," and creating "a different version from the facts." In discussing a false chronology of events which he helped to construct, North said he "was provided with additional input that was radically different from the truth," adding: "I assisted in furthering that version."
• The U.S. Army called killing "servicing the target."
• The U.S. Navy called a limited armed conflict "violent peace."
• South Africa's Deputy Minister for Information set the record straight, commenting that "We do not have censorship. What we have is a limitation of what newspapers can report."

In 1988:
• Senator Orrin Hatch of Utah explained that "Capital punishment is our society's recognition of the sanctity of human life."
• The Chrysler Corporation, on laying off 5,000 workers, said it had simply "initiated a career alternative enhancement program."
• In a report, the U.S. Department of Agriculture called cows, pigs, and chickens "grain-consuming animal units."
• General Motors announced, as it closed an entire plant, that it was making a "volume-related production schedule adjustment."
• The Massachusetts Department of Public Works called road signs "ground-mounted confirmatory route markers."

Dieter's secret: If you eat 11 pounds of potatoes, you only gain one pound of weight.

BATHROOM ECOLOGY

We all know and love the bathroom—but we still have a lot to learn about it. Believe it or not, the way we use it can affect the world around us in significant ways. Here's some valuable information from the great new book, 50 Simple Things You Can Do to Save the Earth, *by the Earthworks Group.*

THE TOILET

• Each time your toilet is flushed, it uses 5 to 7 gallons of water—in fact, 40% of the pure water you use in your house is flushed down the toilet.

Bathroom Ecology: You can save 1-2 gallons with each flush if you put something in the tank that reduces the amount of water the tank will hold. This is called a "displacement device."

• Don't use a brick. Small pieces can break off and damage your plumbing system.

• Small juice bottles, dishwashing soap bottles, or laundry soap bottles work well. Soak off the label, fill the bottle with water, put on the cap, and put it in the tank.

• Be careful that the bottle doesn't interfere with the flushing mechanism.

• You may need to experiment with bottle sizes—different toilets need different amounts of water to flush effectively. Option: put a few stones in the bottom of the bottle to weight it down.

Savings: 1-2 gallons per flush.

Results: If the average toilet is flushed about 8 times a day, that means a savings of 8-16 gallons every day, 56-112 gallons a week, 2900-5800 gallons a year. If only 10,000 people were to put a bottle in the tank, that would equal a savings of 29 to 58 million gallons a year! And if 100,000 people did it…well, use your own imagination.

THE SINK

• A running faucet puts 3-5 gallons of water down the drain every minute.

• You use 10-15 gallons of water if you leave the tap running while you brush your teeth.

• If you shave with the water on, you use 10-20 gallons each time.

You knew this, of course: A peanut isn't a nut.

Bathroom Ecology: If you just wet and rinse your brush when you brush your teeth, you use only 1/2 gallon of water. *Savings:* Up to 9 gallons each time you brush.

• If you fill the basin when you shave, you use only 1 gallon of water. *Savings:* Up to 14 gallons each time you shave.

• Install a Low-Flow Faucet Aerator. It's a simple device that screws onto the end of your faucet and cuts the flow *in half.* But don't worry—since it mixes air in with the water, the water comes out just as fast as before.

• Low-flow faucet aerators sell for less than $4 at hardware and plumbing stores everywhere.

THE SHOWER & BATH

• Showers account for a whopping 32% of home water use.

• A standard shower head has a flow rate of 5 to 10 gallons of water per minute. So a 5-minute shower uses around 25 gallons.

Bathroom Ecology: First of all, take showers instead of baths. Depending on the size of the tub, a bath will generally use around 50 gallons of water…or more—which is about double the water use of a shower.

• Try installing a "low-flow shower head." It can reduce your overall water use by 50% or more.

• With a low-flow shower head, a family of four accustomed to 5-minute showers will save nearly 22,000 gallons of water per year.

• For a family of four, the $ savings from a low-flow shower head can amount to $100 a year in water saved, plus $150 a year in energy costs-—for all that hot water you don't have to heat.

• So the cost of a low-flow shower head—generally, less than $15 at any plumbing supply or hardware store—can be recouped in a month.

AEROSOL CANS

• At one time, aerosol cans routinely used gases called CFCs as propellants. But it was discovered that CFCs were harmful to the Earth's ozone layer, and CFCs were banned. End of problem? No. Their replacements—gases like butane and propane—are also harmful to the environment. They mix with sunlight to create smog…which contributes to the acid rain problem.

Bathroom Ecology: Use non-aerosols whenever possible.

Around the world, more people eat herring than any other fish.

MODERN MYTHOLOGY

These characters are as famous in our culture as Pegasus or Hercules were in Greek myths. Where did they come from?

THE PLAYBOY BUNNY. When Hugh Hefner was a little boy, one of his prized possessions was "a blanket with bunnies all over it." Apparently, he never outgrew it—when he started *Playboy* magazine, he used the same bunny as his symbol.

THE JOLLY GREEN GIANT. In the early 1920s, the Minnesota Valley Canning Company introduced a new, large variety of peas to the American market. They called the peas "green giants," and because the law required it to protect their trademark, they put a picture of a Green Giant on the label. Where did they get the original art? They lifted it from *Grimm's Fairy Tales*. Oddly enough, the original giant was white, not green; he looked like a dwarf, not a giant; and he wasn't jolly—he was scowling. His image eventually softened, and he became such a powerful symbol that the company changed its name to the Green Giant Co.

BETTY CROCKER. The Washburn Crosby Company, a Minneapolis flour maker, got so many letters asking for baking advice that in 1921, they made up a character to write back to consumers. They picked the name "Betty" because it sounded "warm and friendly," and "Crocker" was picked to honor a former company director. To come up with a signature for Betty (so she could sign "her" letters), the company held a contest for its women employees. The winner—which is still used today—was submitted by a secretary.

THE QUAKER OATS MAN. In 1891, seven oatmeal millers combined to form the American Cereal Company. One of the seven was Quaker Mill of Ravenna, Ohio, which had trademarked the Quaker man 14 years earlier. So when the American Cereal Company changed its name to Quaker Oats in 1901, the Quaker man was revived as its symbol. The real Quakers weren't too happy about this, by the way. They tried to get Congress to prohibit manufacturers from using religions' names on their products.

The average American eats 10 lbs. of chocolate a year.

FAST FOOD FACTS

Fascinating factoids about fast food.

There are more than 55,000 fast food restaurants in the U.S.

When Colonel Sanders started selling chicken in the late '50s, he was 65 years old. His only goal was to make $1,000 a month.

Two-thirds of the eateries in the U.S. serve fast food. And two-thirds of the people who go out to eat get their meals at fast food restaurants.

Fast food fries are usually sprayed with sugar, which gives them their brown coloring when cooked.

Domino's offers 10 different toppings for its pizza. That means you can get 3.9 million different combinations of pizzas there.

Pepsico, Pepsi's parent company, is one of the world's largest fast food restaurateurs. Among its holdings: Kentucky Fried Chicken, Taco Bell, and Pizza Hut. All serve Pepsi, of course. Pepsico also owns Frito-Lay.

Every day, approximately 46 million Americans eat at fast food restaurants.

Colonel Sanders wasn't particularly fond of Kentucky Fried Chicken after he sold it. He called the "extra-crispy" chicken "a damn fried doughball stuck on some chicken," and he said the KFC gravy was "pure wallpaper paste."

Wendy's was named after the daughter of the company's founder, Dave Thomas.

Thomas claims his square burgers are designed for grill efficiency. Others say it's "a marketing ploy." The four corners hang out over the edge of the bun, making the burger look bigger.

Regional fast food numbers:
#1. The Midwest; 30.5% of the population eats fast food at least once a week.
#2. The South; 30.4%.
#3. The West Coast; 23%.
#4. The East Coast; 16.5%.

There are 525 McDonald's eateries in Japan.

There is a city called Rome on every continent in the world.

THOREAU'S THOUGHTS

Thoughts from Henry Thoreau, the outspoken American iconoclast of the 19th century.

"Distrust any enterprise that requires new clothes."

"It is a characteristic of wisdom not to do desperate things."

"If Christ should appear on Earth, he would be denounced as a mistaken, misguided man, insane and crazed."

"It takes two to speak the truth—one to speak, and one to listen."

"Simplify, simplify."

"The mass of men lead lives of quiet desperation."

"What men call social virtues, good fellowship, is commonly but the virtue of pigs in a litter, which lie close together to keep each other warm."

"Blessed are they who never read a newspaper, for they shall see Nature, and through her, God."

"It is only when we forget all our learning that we begin to know."

"Do not be too moral. You may cheat yourself out of much life."

"Aim above morality. Be not simply good, be good for something."

"You cannot kill time without injuring eternity."

"The highest condition of art is artlessness."

"What man believes, God believes."

"A man is rich in proportion of the number of things he can afford to let alone."

"Business! I think there is nothing—not even crime—more opposed to poetry, to philosophy, to life itself, than this incessant business."

"There are a thousand hacking at the branches of evil to one who is striking at the root."

"Not until we are lost—in other words, not until we have lost the world—do we begin to find ourselves."

Dairy delight: The average American eats 26 lbs. of cheese every year.

THE TRUTH ABOUT SPIRO T. AGNEW

You'd think that if a Vice President of the U. S. was accused of taking bribes—and had to resign because of it—we'd all remember the incident in detail. That's not the case with Spiro Agnew; his resignation in 1973 was quickly overshadowed by Watergate. But hey—let's not forget the guy. He's part of American history.

AGNEW'S CAREER

• In 1962, he ran for Baltimore County Executive. He was elected, and served until 1966.

• In 1966, he ran for governor of Maryland as a Republican. As it happened, the Democrats nominated a reactionary who stood no chance of being elected. Agnew won.

• In 1968, ghetto riots hit Baltimore. "Agnew met with the leaders of the state's black moderates," reported *Time* magazine, "and before the TV cameras, dressed them down for not controlling the rioters. The incident established Agnew as a hard-liner on race and caught the eye of Richard Nixon."
The result: Nixon picked him as his running mate.

• In 1969, Agnew emerged, said *U.S. News & World Report*, as "one of the most controversial Vice Presidents the United States has seen in many a day." He was a strident moralist and a "law and order" man whose trademark was violent verbal attacks. His speeches were peppered with phrases like "parasites of passion," and "nattering nabobs of negativism."

• He was reelected with Nixon in 1972, and looked like the heir apparent to the Presidency. Then it all collapsed. In 1973, the *Wall Street Journal* learned that Agnew was under investigation in Maryland for having taken kickbacks from building contractors while he was both county executive and governor.

• On Oct. 10, 1973, after months of negotiating, Agnew resigned. He appeared in court and pled "No Contest" to income tax evasion—which the judge pointed out was equivalent to a guilty plea. It was part of an extensive plea-bargaining process that enabled him to avoid jail. The Government insisted, however, that they be allowed to make their case aginst him public.

In 1976, the theme song from the TV show "Happy Days" hit #5 on the *Billboard* charts.

THE GOVERNMENT'S EVIDENCE

One of several contractors who admitted paying bribes to Agnew was named Lester Matz. Here's a part of the government's report on one of the incidents he recaled. It took place in 1969, a few months after Agnew had become V.P.:

"Matz called the Vice President's office in Washington and set up an appointment to meet with Mr. Agnew. On a piece of yellow legal-sized paper, Matz calculated the sum then 'owed' to Mr. Agnew for work received by Matz's company from the State of Maryland. He met with Mr. Agnew, showed him the calculations, and briefly reviewed them for him. He then handed him an enveloped containing approximately $10,000 in cash....Mr. Agnew placed this envelope in his desk drawer.

"Matz also told the Vice President that the company might 'owe' him more money in the future....They agreed that Matz was to call Mr. Agnew's secretary when he was ready to make the next payment and to tell her that he had more 'information' for Mr. Agnew. This was to be a signal to Mr. Agnew that Mr. Matz had more money for him.

"After this meeting, Matz returned to Baltimore and told [an associate] of the payment. He also told [him] that he was shaken by his own actions, because he had just made a payoff to the Vice President of the United States."

AGNEW'S STATEMENT IN COURT

In a cleverly worded statement, Agnew made it seem as though he was denying the charges against him.

For example: The government said he took kickbacks. As Agnew explained it: "I admit that I did receive payments during the year 1967 which were not expended for political purposes, and...that contracts were awarded by State agencies in 1967 and other years to those who made such payments, and that I was aware of such awards....I stress, however, that no contracts were awarded to contractors who were not competent to perform the work, and in most instances State contracts were awarded without...payment of money by the contractor."

Careful reading of the text, however, shows that he was really saying something like: "Sure I took money, but not all the time, and only from good contractors."

ELEMENTARY, MY DEAR STEVE

Can you match wits with the world-famous sleuth, Leslie Boies?
Here are more mysteries for you to solve. Answers are on p. 223.

It was a dark, rainy night. Leslie Boies, the celebrated solver-of-mysteries, was driving north from Thomasville on a narrow country road in her 1957 DeSoto coupe. Her faithful companion, Steve, was at the wheel. It was a critical situation—they had to reach the little town of Montez before sunrise if they were going to save Raymond Redel, the famous chair designer, from his nefarious son-in-law.

Suddenly they came to a crossroads…and they discovered that the signpost had been knocked down. Steve hopped out to take a look. One of the arrows on the sign said "Montez, 23 miles"…But there was no way to tell which road it had been pointing to.

"We're lost, Leslie," Steve exclaimed forlornly.

"I declare, Steve, sometimes you are so dense," Leslie sighed. Then she informed Steve how to tell which road was the right one.

How did Leslie know which way to go?

2. Steve was lounging around the apartment, reading the paper. "Hey, Les," he called, "There's a town I was reading about where nobody ever shaves himself—they all let the barber do it."

Leslie walked in, practicing yo-yo tricks she planned to perform in the upcoming Detective's Follies. "Well, Steve, if that's true, then who shaves the barber?"

Steve looked puzzled. "Maybe there are two barbers in town."

Leslie shook her head. "No, my uncle lives there and I know there's only one."

Steve shrugged. "I give up."

Who does shave the barber?

3. Steve came home one day and found Leslie hard at work on a new murder case.

"Sorry to bother you, Honey, but I'm a little perplexed about

---

The Ancient Egyptians had bowling alleys similar to ours.

something. I could use your help to get it resolved."

Leslie looked up, and focused affectionately on Steve

"How can I help my faithful companion?" she offered.

"Well, on the way home today, I ran into two women."

Leslie's expression darkened. "Ye-e-s?"

"Well, they looked exactly alike, so I asked if they were twins. They said no, but they had the same mother and father, and they were born on the same day in the same year. When I asked how that was possible, they just laughed and walked away. Were they putting me on?"

Leslie smiled. "Nope. They were telling the truth."

How was that possible?

4. It was late in the evening. Renowned detective Leslie Boies was studying fingerprint technology when Inspector Gordon Van Gelder of the St. Martin's Police arrived. Steve, a lanky 6-footer she called her "pet guy," let the Inspector in.

Inspector Van Gelder knew Leslie too well to beat around the bush. "Here's the scoop," he said. "A guy named Mingo's been murdered, and I can't figure out how it was done. He and his pal, Arnie, went into Noona's Bar down on 9th St. together and each ordered a Scotch on the rocks. Arnie had to get home, so he drank his fast. But Mingo stayed and nursed his awhile, drinking it slowly. And then he just keeled over and died.

"I know the drinks and the glasses were exactly the same. No one slipped anything into Mingo's drink, and Arnie—who's fine, by the way—definitely didn't doctor Mingo's drink at all. So I can't understand how one of them could have died and the other walked away healthy. The lab report will probably tell me what happened, but I'd sure like to figure it out before then. Can you help?"

Leslie smiled indulgently, reached for a pad and a pencil, and jotted down a few words. "Arrest the bartender, Inspector," she said, handing him the paper. "This will tell you how he did it."

After Van Gelder left, Steve turned to his companion. "Well, are you going to to tell me how it happened?"

"Why, it was elementary, my dear Steve," she replied, winking at him.

How was the murder committed?

YOGI SEZ

Gems from Yogi Berra, Hall of Fame
catcher for the New York Yankees.

"It's deja vu all over again."

[Explaining a loss]
"We made too many wrong mistakes."

"The game's not over 'til it's over."

"You give 100% in the first half of the game, and if that isn't enough, in the second half you give what's left."

[On quotes like these]
"I really didn't say everything I said."

[Asked why he hadn't been to a favorite restauarant lately]
"It's so crowded, nobody goes there anymore."

"If people don't want to come out to the ballpark, nobody's going to stop them."

[On being honored with a "Yogi Berra Night"]
"I want to thank all you people for making this night necessary."

[Asked, during spring training, what his hat size was]
"I don't know. I'm not in shape yet."

"You've got to be careful if you don't know where you're going, because you might not get there."

"We have deep depth."

[On seeing a Steve McQueen movie]
"He must have made that before he died."

"I never blame myself when I'm not hitting. I just blame the bat and if it keeps up, I change bats...After all, if I know it isn't my fault that I'm not hitting, how can I get mad at myself?"

[On meeting King George IV]
"Nice to meet you, King."

"Baseball is ninety percent mental. The other half is physical."

"It gets late early out there."

Pollsters say that 40% of dog and cat owners carry pictures of the pets in their wallets.

NICKNAMES

What would you call celebrities if you knew them personally? According to Carl Sifakis in The Dictionary of Historic Nicknames, *you might know them by names like these:*

Johann Sebastian Bach. In his lifetime, the great composer's music was considered so boring and out of date that even his own family called him "The Old Wig."

Humphrey Bogart. If you were a Hollywood acquaintance, you night have known him as "Whiskey Straight."

Claudette Colbert. The Oscar-winning actress worried so much about the way she looked during filming that her cameramen dubbed her "The Fretting Frog."

Christopher Columbus. Historians call him a great explorer, but his own crew wasn't so kind. When his quest for riches led them to insect-infested tropical islands instead of gold and silver, they christened him "The Admiral of the Mosquitoes."

Davy Crockett. No one who knew Davy believed a word of his outrageous stories about his exploits in the wild. Acquaintances called him "The Munchausen of the West"—a name inspired by Baron von Munchausen, the popular fictional character of the late 1700s, whose trademark was absurdly exaggerated claims about his own life.

Wyatt Earp and Bat Masterson. The heroes of Western legends and prime-time TV shows were apparently as interested in other pursuits as they were in law and order. On various occasions they owned saloons, gambling establishments, and even a brothel or two. In their home, Dodge City, Kansas, they were known as "The Fighting Pimps."

Dwight David Eisenhower. In his hometown of Abilene, Kansas, the other kids knew him as "Ugly Ike."

Billy Graham. In his early days, the famous crusading evangelist was known as "The Preaching Windmill" because of "his exuberant arm flailing."

Sam Houston. The most celebrated hero in Texas' fight for independence from Mexico during the 1830s is known today as "The Father of Texas." But Indians who knew him called him "Big Drunk."

Robert F. Kennedy. America remembers him as RFK, or Bobby. Lyndon Johnson always called him "The Little Shit."

Spiro T. Agnew. Nixon's vice president was known by adversaries as "Spiro T. Eggplant."

Abraham Lincoln. "Honest Abe's" nickname didn't come from politics—it came from his youthful efforts as "a judge and referee at cockfights."

Richard Nixon. Nicknames haven't been kind to the ex-prez. When he was in college, he was so humorless that classmates called him "Gloomy Gus." And he spent so much time studying that he was dubbed "Iron Butt." When he ran for Congress in 1950, he earned the title "Tricky Dick."

Leo Tolstoy. The author of *War and Peace* is considered one of the greatest novelists in history. But people who knew him as a child—even his own family and close friends—called the troubled youth "Crybaby Leo."

Henri de Toulouse-Lautrec. The famous French painter suffered through childhood accidents that gave him the appearance of a dwarf—but not in every way. When he lived in a brothel, the prostitutes, amused by the contrast in size between "his large male member" and the rest of his body, dubbed him "the Teapot."

Warren G. Harding. Probably should have been called "The Rodney Dangerfield of Politics," but in 1920 when he was elected president, Rodney wasn't around yet. Instead, he was called "Everybody's Second Choice," because he was nominated as a compromise candidate in a "smoke-filled room."

MT. RUSHMORE

Here's Charles Panati's version of how the four big faces got there, from Extraordinary Origins of Everyday Things.

HOW IT GOT ITS NAME.

"The full story of the origin of Mount Rushmore begins 60 million years ago, when pressures deep within the earth pushed up layers of rock. The forces created an elongated granite-and-limestone dome towering several thousand feet above the Dakota prairie lands. The first sculpting of the mountain was done by nature. The erosive forces of wind and water fashioned one particularly protuberant peak, which was unnamed until 1885.

"That year, a New York attorney, Charles E. Rushmore, was surveying the mountain range on horseback with a guide. Rushmore inquired about the impressive peak's name, and the guide, ribbing the city lawyer, answered, 'Hell, it never had a name. But from now on we'll call the damn thing Rushmore.' The label stuck. And later, with a gift of five thousand dollars, Charles Rushmore became one of the earliest contributors to the presidential memorial."

THE MEMORIAL

"The idea to transform a gigantic mountaintop into a colossus of human figures sprang from the mind of a South Dakota historian, Doane Robinson. In 1923, Robinson presented to the state his plan to simultaneously increase South Dakota's tourism, strengthen its economy, and immortalize three 'romantic western heroes.' [Ed. note: The original plan was to sculpt the heads of Kit Carson, Jim Bridger, and John Colter.] A commission then sought the skills of renowned sculptor John Gutzon de la Mothe Borglum, an authority on colossi.

"Idaho born, Borglum started as a painter, then switched to sculpture, and his fame grew in proportion to the size of his works. The year Doane Robinson conceived the idea for a Mount Rushmore memorial, Borglum accepted a commission from the United Daughters of the Confederacy to carve a head of General Robert E. Lee on Stone Mountain in Georgia.

"Mount Rushmore, though, beckoned with the greater challenge. Borglum opposed sculpting Western heroes. The notion was provincial, he argued. A colossus should capture prominent figures. In a letter dated August 14, 1925, Borglum proposed the faces of four influential American presidents."

THE SCULPTURE.

"Construction on the 6,200-foot-high wilderness peak was fraught with dangers. And the mountain itself was inaccessible except by foot or horseback, which necessitated countless climbs to lug up drills and scaffolding. But for Borglum, two features made the remote Rushmore peak ideal. The rocks faced southeast, ensuring maximum sunlight for construction, and later for viewing. And the peak's inaccessibility would protect the monument from vandals.

"Bitter winters, compounded by a chronic shortage of funds, continually threatened to terminate construction. Weathered surface rock had to be blasted away to expose suitably firm stone for sculpting. The chin of George Washington, for instance, was begun thirty feet back from the original mountain surface, and Theodore Roosevelt's forehead was undertaken only after 120 feet of surface rock were peeled away.

"Borglum worked from a scale model. Critical 'points' were measured on the model, then transferred to the mountain to indicate the depth of rock to be removed point by point.

"In 1941, fourteen years after construction began—and at a total cost of $990,000—a new world wonder was unveiled. There stood George Washington, whom Borglum selected because he was 'Father of the Nation'; Abraham Lincoln, 'Preserver of the Union'; Thomas Jefferson, 'The Expansionist'; and Theodore Roosevelt, 'Protector of the Working Man.'

"The figures measure sixty feet from chin to top of head. Each nose is twenty feet long, each mouth eighteen feet wide, and the eyes are eleven feet across. 'A monument's dimensions,' Borglum believed, 'should be determined by the importance to civilization of the events commemorated.'

"Gutzon Borglum died on March 6, 1941, aged 74. The monument was essentially completed. His son, also a sculptor, added the finishing touches."

From *Roadside America*: "The Black Hills can get foggy....Many a tourist Dad has been known to blow his top after driving umpteen miles...only to find he can't see those giant faces, goddammit."

A TV set uses the same amount of energy as an ordinary light bulb.

THE BIRTH OF KLEENEX

Feel a sneeze coming on? If you're like most Americans, you
reach for a kleenex without even thinking about it. But that
wasn't always true. In fact, not so long ago there was no such
thing. Here's how they were invented.

MILITARY SUPPLIES

The Kimberly-Clark Corporation originally designed the product that evolved into Kleenex tissues for *military* use.
• It started in 1914. World War I was being fought in Europe, and the cotton soldiers needed for bandages was starting to run out.
• So Kimberly-Clark devised a product called Cellucotton—an absorbent, soft paper that could be used to dress wounds.
• It was so effective that the army looked for other uses. And they found one: They used it as an air filter for soldiers' gas masks.

PEACETIME PROBLEM

Kimberly-Clark got too enthusiastic about their new material and overproduced it. After the war, they had warehouses full of Cellucotton left over; they *had* to find a new way to sell the stuff.
• Their clever solution: They marketed it as a modern women's tool for cleaning off makeup, and a "sanitary cold cream remover."
• Calling it Kleenex Kerchiefs, they hired movie stars to endorse it as a secret path to glamour. It was a big success.

SURPRISE SOLUTION

But Americans found another use for the product. Kimberly-Clark was inundated with letters that informed them the Kleenex Kerchiefs were great for nose-blowing.
•Men, in particular, wanted to know why Kleenex had to be a woman's product. And women griped that men were stealing their Kleenex to sneeze into.
• During the 1920s, Kimberly-Clark introduced a pop-up box that always left one tissue sticking out of the box, waiting to be grabbed.
• But the question remained—were people buying Kleenex as a cold cream remover, or a nose-blower? A survey showed that 60% of the people used it as the latter. So that's what K-C emphasized, and that's how we think of it today.

ROCK ME, SUE ME

It's not all peace and love in the rock 'n' roll world. It's big bucks...
and as the stakes get higher, the lawsuits get bigger. Here are a few.

G **HOSTBUSTERS**
The "Ghostbusters" theme song, by Ray Parker, Jr. sounded
a lot like Huey Lewis and the News' "I Want a New Drug."
And sure enough, it turns out that the film's producers originally
wanted Lewis, himself, to pen their theme song. When he refused,
they hired Parker and requested something similar to Lewis's hit.
Lewis sued for copyright infringement, and the case was settled out
of court.

HEY, HEY, HEY
The Beatles' version of "Kansas City" was written by Jerry Leiber
and Mike Stoller—or at least that's the way the song was credited
when it came out in 1964. But it turned out the Beatles had recorded a medley of "Kansas City" and "Hey, Hey, Hey," a Little Richard
composition that originally appeared on the B-side of his 1956 hit
"Good Golly Miss Molly." It took Little Richard about 20 years to
figure out what had happened, but when he did—and took it to
court—it paid off in big numbers: $500,000.

MY SWEET LORD
George Harrison's "My Sweet Lord" casually borrowed the melody
of the Chiffons' 1963 hit "He's So Fine," written by Ronald Mack.
One strange aspect of the case: Ronald Mack was dead by the time
his estate pressed charges and won. Another: Although Harrison
had to pay, he was absolved of plagiarism. It was, according to the
judge, "unconscious plagiarism."

STAIRWAY TO GILLIGAN'S ISLAND
Led Zeppelin, the biggest-selling band of the 1970s, were known
among music experts for stealing songs from old blues artists and
then crediting themselves. Their first hit, "Whole Lotta Love," was
virtually a note-for-note recreation of Willie Dixon's "I Need
Love." And "How Much More" was a direct lift of Howling Wolf's
"Killing Floor."

Survey results: Color TV ads are 3-1/2 times more effective than black & white ads.

But when someone messed with one of *their* tunes, it was time for legal action. A San Francisco-based band called Roger and The Goosebumps recorded a hilarious parody of the group's "Stairway to Heaven," matching Zep's melody with the lyrics of the theme song to "Gilligan's Island." Led Zepplin quickly had its lawyers block the song's release. "It was a real blow," said one of the Goosebumps later. "We were getting airplay all over the country—I think we had a hit on our hands." Later, the same band did an equally funny take-off of the Beatles' "Fool on the Hill," called "Fudd on the Hill," sung in an Elmer Fudd voice. Thankfully, the Beatles didn't sue.

SURFIN' USA
The Beach Boys' big hit of 1963 sounded vaguely familiar to Chuck Berry...and it should have; he wrote the melody. Brian Wilson had appropriated it from Berry's 1958 tune, "Sweet Little Sixteen." Berry's publisher sued on his behalf, and won. The result: Berry owns 100% of the rights to both his own tune and Wilson's.

OLD MAN DOWN THE ROAD
The strangest case of an artist being sued for copyright infringement must be the one involvng John Fogerty's 1984 comeback hit, "The Old Man Down The Road."

He was sued for copying himself.

The story: "Old Man Down the Road" bore more than a little resemblence to "Run Through the Jungle," a tune Fogarty had previously written and recorded with Creedence Clearwater Revival, The problem: Fogarty no longer owned the rights to his original song, and there was bad blood between him and Saul Zaentz, the man who did.

Zaentz owned Fantasy Records, the label Creedence Clearwater Revival had recorded on. He and Fogerty had been embroiled in a long, bitter lawsuit over royalties that Creedence said were still owed to them. And when Fogerty included a tune on his solo album (the same one with "Old Man" on it) called "Zaentz Can't Dance," Saul sued him for defamation of character. Fogerty had to change it to "Vanz Can't Dance."

The highlight of the "Old Man" case was Fogerty's appearance in court, where he demonstrated to the jury how he composes tunes. They must have enjoyed it; he won.

LOST IN SPACE

This show still has a cult following; Why? Don't ask us. We've never even been able to figure out why the Robinsons didn't just push that whining SOB Dr. Smith out the airlock and forget him.

HOW IT STARTED

After producing everything from documentaries to comedies in the '50s, filmmaker Irwin Allen discovered kids' science fiction/adventure films in the '60s. He made *The Lost World* (1960), *Voyage to the Bottom of the Sea* (1961), and Jules Verne's *Five Weeks In a Balloon* (1963). All were successful. But special-effects films are hard to finance, so Allen decided to move to TV.

His first effort was a popular 1964 adaptation of *Voyage to the Bottom of the Sea*. His second was to be a live-action version of a comic book called *Space Family Robinson* (Swiss Family Robinson in space). But while Allen was still making the 2-hour pilot in 1964, Walt Disney, who owned the rights to the name, decided that Allen couldn't use it. So Allen changed it to "Lost In Space."

It was supposed to be a serious space adventure show, like "Star Trek" (no kidding), but when Allen showed it to CBS executives for the first time, he got a rude shock. One of the men who was there that day recalls: "Irwin, who has absolutely no sense of humor, thought he was making a very serious program. But in the viewing room, the network executives who were watching the pilot were absolutely hysterical, laughing . . . Irwin got furious and wanted to stop the showing...But his assistant kicked him under the table and whispered, 'Never mind. They love it.'" And they did. CBS bought the show and ran it for 3 years, from 1965 to 1968. Allen went on to make films like *The Poseidon Adventure* and *Towering Inferno*, for which he is known as "The Master of Disaster."

INSIDE FACTS

You Bet Your Life

The man who financed "Lost In Space" was "the one, the only... GROUCHO!" Marx and Irwin Allen were good friends. Groucho included a photo of himself and Allen in his book, *The Groucho-Phile*. The caption: "I taught him everything he knows about 'disaster' pictures. This picture was taken either at his wedding or mine."

Vivien Leigh made only $15,000 for playing Scarlett O'Hara in *Gone With the Wind*.

Saved By the Mail
Dr. Smith (Jonathan Harris) was originally meant to be killed off after 6 weeks. In fact, he was such a "minor" character that his contact stated that he couldn't be billed higher than 7th in the credits! But fan mail was overwhelmingly in favor of keeping him.

Adventures of Zorro
Dr. Smith's popularity was particularly frustrating to Guy Williams (John Robinson), who—guaranteed top billing—assumed he'd be the star. Instead, he rarely got *any* important dialogue. "I must be getting paid more per word than Lawrence Olivier," he groused.

Special Effects
Irwin Allen was notoriously cheap. For example, the dome on the frog alien's space ship in the episode "The Golden Man" was actually a giant champagne glass from a Marilyn Monroe film, salvaged by the director from the 20th Century Fox junk pile. Originally, the space ship in the episode was budgeted at $10,000. But when Allen was told the cost, he hit the roof. "Let the frog walk," he screamed. So the director had to scrounge and get it for free.

TV Robotics
• The Robot (no name) bore a striking resemblance to Robby, the famous robot from the film *Forbidden Planet* (1956). No coincidence. He was created by Bob Kinoshita, Robby's co-designer.
• Lights flashed on the robot in synchronization with his voice. An electronic innovation? No. A little actor was inside, pressing a telegraph key in the left claw as he spoke.
• The actor in the robot saw out via the robot's plastic collar. Viewers couldn't see him in the shell, because he was in black-face.

Phony Numbers
The Robinsons traveled on planet surfaces in a vehicle with the official-looking call numbers "277-2211 IA" painted on it. Actually, the 7 digits are 20th-Century Fox's phone number. And the IA is producer Irwin Allen's initials.

Surprise!
Every member of the cast learned the show was cancelled by reading about it in the newspapers.

The opposite sides of a dice cube always add up to 7.

NOTABLE & QUOTABLE

Memorable comments from memorable personalities.

JOHN WAYNE

- "Westerns are closer to art than anything else in the motion picture business."

- "I don't feel we did wrong in taking this great country away from [the Indians]. There were great numbers of people who needed new land and the Indians were selfishly trying to keep it for themselves."

- [About liberated women] "They have a right to work wherever they want to—as long as they have dinner ready when you get home."

- "There's been no top authority saying what marijuana does to you. I really don't know that much about it. I tried it once, but it didn't do anything to me."

J. EDGAR HOOVER

- "Justice is incidental to law and order."

- "We are a fact-gathering organization only. We don't clear anybody. We don't condemn anybody. Just the minute the F.B.I. begins making recommendations on what should be done with its information, it becomes a Gestapo."

AL CAPONE

- "Don't get the idea that I'm one of those goddamn radicals. Don't get the idea that I'm knocking the American system."

- "Vote early and vote often."

- "When I sell liquor, it's called bootlegging; when my patrons serve it on silver trays on Lake Shore Drive, it's called hospitality."

- "I'm like any other man. All I do is supply a demand."

- "[Communism] is knocking at our gates, and we can't afford to let it in....We must keep America whole and safe and unspoiled. We must keep the worker away from Red literature and Red ruses; we must see that his mind remains healthy."

The leaves of an adult oak tree give off 7 tons of water every day.

DINER LORE

As Richard Gutman said in American Diner: *"One nice thing about a diner is that anyone who shares American values and American ways of doing things can function there."*

ORIGIN OF THE LUNCHWAGON
The year was 1872.
The city was Providence, Rhode Island.
Thousands of late-night factory workers had a problem—every restaurant in town closed promptly at 8:00 p.m., and they couldn't get anything to eat when their shifts let out.

The solution was provided by an enterprising pushcart peddler named Walter Scott. He outfitted a horsedrawn wagon with a stove and storage space and drove around the streets selling sandwiches, boiled eggs, and coffee for a nickel. The wagon only provided shelter for Scott—his customers had to stand out on the street. But it was a welcome service and an instant success. Before long, "after hours lunchwagons" were operating all over town.

INDOOR SEATING
Fifteen years later, an enterprising worker named Sam Jones introduced the first custom-made, walk-in lunchwagon—complete with a kitchen, a counter, and stools. It seated four to five people, and it, was immediately successful. Walk-in lunchwagons became popular all over the Northeast; soon they were being made in factories.

THE DINER EVOLVES
By 1910 dozens of lunchwagons—many of them rundown eyesores—were rumbling around the streets of most New England cities. Although they were only allowed to operate between dusk and dawn, many were staying on the streets until noon—which outraged many "respectable" citizens. Cities began cracking down on them, forcing the wagons off the streets by 10:00 A.M.

Lunchcart owners didn't like the idea of closing up when there was plenty of business around, so they came up with a way to skirt the rules—they just picked a good site where they could set up their lunchcarts permanently. Then they took off the wheels and

The Western hero most often portrayed in films: Buffalo Bill. 2nd place: Billy the Kid.

hooked up to power, water, and gas lines and expanded their kitchens. Now they were officially called "street cafes," and they could operate all day and all night. They were the original 24-hour diners.

DINER FACTS

• The term *diner* originated with manufacturer Patrick J. Tierney, who called his prefab early-1900s restaurants "dining cars." Salesmen shortened them to "diners."

• Tierney was proud that, in 1911, his company built the first diner with an indoor toilet.

• Contrary to popular belief, diners were never converted from railroad dining cars. Rather, in the late '30s manufacturers were so impressed by the streamlined look of modern locomotives that they imitated the style. They called these diners "Streamliners."

• Diners reflect technological advances. When, in the late '30s, materials like stainless steel, Naugahyde, and Formica became available, diner-makers put them to use. So what we call a "classic" diner was actually "state of the art" in its time.

• At their peak in the late '40s, there were some 7,000 diners. Today there are only 2,000.

DINER DIALOGUE (from the film, *Five Easy Pieces*)

Jack Nicholson: "I'd like a plain omelette—no potatoes on the plate—a cup of coffee, and a side order of wheat toast."

Waitress: "I'm sorry, we don't have any side orders here."

Nicholson: "No side orders? You've got bread and a toaster of some kind?"

Waitress: "I don't make the rules."

Nicholson: "Okay, I'll make it as easy for you as I can. I'd like an omelette—plain—a chicken salad sandwich on wheat toast—no mayonnaise, no butter, no lettuce, and a cup of coffee."

Waitress: "A Number Two, chicken salad sandwich—no butter, no mayo, no lettuce, and a cup of coffee. Anything else?"

Nicholson: "Yeah. Now all you have to do is hold the chicken, bring me the toast, give me a check for the chicken salad sandwich, and you haven't broken any rules."

Waitress: "You want me to hold the chicken, huh?"

Nicholson: "I want you to hold it between your knees."

Examining one strand of your hair can enable a scientist to tell your sex, age, and race.

DINER LINGO

Diner waitresses and short order cooks have a language all their own—a sort of restaurant jazz, with clever variations on standard menu themes. Here's a little collection of some of the best.

Burn the British: Gimme an English muffin

Draw one in the Dark: A black coffee

Balloon Juice: Seltzer

An M.D.: A Dr. Pepper

Hold the hail: No ice

Wreck 'em: Scrambled eggs

Sweep the kitchen: A plate of hash

Adam and Eve on a raft: Two poached eggs on toast

A spot with a twist: A cup of tea with lemon

Bossy in a Bowl: Beef stew

A Blonde with Sand: Coffee with cream and sugar

Break It and Shake It: Add an egg to a drink

A Stack of Vermont: Pancakes with maple syrup.

Million on a Platter: A plate of baked beans

A White Cow: A vanilla milkshake

Let it Walk: It's to go

Noah's Boy on Bread: A ham sandwich

A Murphy: A potato

Nervous Pudding: Jello

Paint a Bow-wow Red: Gimme a hot dog with ketchup

Eve with a lid: A piece of apple pie

Burn one, take it through the garden, and pin a rose on it: Gimme a burger with lettuce and onion

Mike and Ike: Salt and pepper shakers

Angels on Horseback: Oysters rolled in bacon and placed on toast

Cow Paste: Butter

Lighthouse: Bottle of ketchup

Hounds on an Island: Franks and beans

Frog Sticks: French fries

Houseboat: A banana split

Wax: American cheese

Fry Two, let the sun shine: 2 fried eggs with unbroken yolks

Throw it in the Mud: Add chocolate syrup

Hug One: Squeeze a glass of orange juice

Life Preservers: Doughnuts

Put out the lights and cry: An order of liver and onions

One from the Alps: A Swiss cheese sandwich

Put a Hat on It: Add ice cream

A Splash of Red Noise: A bowl of tomato soup

Americans watch more TV in January and February than any other time of year.

WILL POWER

A will is the last chance the deceased has to drive the living nuts.
Here are a few true-life examples of slightly offbeat wills.

THE DECEASED: Ms. Eleanor Ritchey, the unmarried granddaughter of the founder of Quaker State Oil (Philip John Bayer).

THE BEQUEST: Ms. Ritchey died in 1968, with an estate worth around $12 million. According to Scott Bieber in *Trusts and Estates* magazine: "Under her will, she left over 1,700 pairs of shoes and 1,200 boxes of stationery to the Salvation Army. The rest of her estate went to the dogs." Real dogs, he means—a pack of 150 strays that Ritchey had adopted as pets. The will set up a trust that permitted the mutts to live in the lap of luxury for up to 20 years. At the end of that period—or on the death of the last of the dogs, whichever came first—the remainder of the estate went to Auburn University.

WHAT HAPPENED: In 1984, Musketeer, the richest dog in America and the last of the original 150, went to that great kennel in the sky. Auburn got its money.

THE DECEASED: Patrick Henry, American patriot.

THE BEQUEST: Everything he owned was left to his wife—as long as she never married again. If she did, she forfeited the whole thing. "It would make me unhappy," he explained, "to feel I have worked all my life only to support another man's wife!"

WHAT HAPPENED: She remarried anyway.

THE DECEASED: Charles Millar, famed Canadian lawyer.

THE BEQUEST: According to Thomas Bedell in *Having the Last Word*, his will "consisted mainly of practical jokes. He willed shares in the Ontario Jockey Club to 2 crusaders against gambling. To 3 men who hated one another, he left equal shares of the same house. And part of his estate was promised to the Toronto mother giving birth to the largest number of children in the decade after his birth."

WHAT HAPPENED: The public either loved or hated it. Newspapers called it "the Stork Derby." Moralists tried to invalidate the will on the grounds that it promoted promiscuity. But in the end, a half a million dollars was split between a quartet of women who had each had 9 kids in the 10 ensuing years.

THE DECEASED: Robert Louis Stevenson, author of *Treasure Island*, etc.

THE BEQUEST: In addition to his normal earthly goods, Stevenson tried to leave his birthday. He willed it to a good friend who'd complained that since she was born on Christmas, she never got to have a real birthday celebration.

THE DECEASED: Felipe Segrandez, the sole survivor of the wreck of the Spanish ship *Santa Cecilia*. At the time he made out his will, he was a castaway on an island somewhere west of Africa.

THE BEQUEST: His will divided his estate between his relatives. It was written in his own blood, sealed in a bottle, and tossed into the ocean.

WHAT HAPPENED: The bottle was found on a South African beach by a prospector and was forwarded to Spanish authorities. Unfortunately, they couldn't execute the will; it was found in 1934, but had been written 178 years earlier, in 1756.

THE DECEASED: An attorney in France.

THE BEQUEST: $10,000 to "a local madhouse." The gentleman declared that "it was simply an act of restitution to his clients."

THE DECEASED: An Australian named Francis R. Lord.

THE BEQUEST: One shilling to his wife "for tram fare so she can go somewhere and drown herself."

WHAT HAPPENED: The inheritance was never claimed.

THE DECEASED: Sandra West, wealthy 37-year-old Beverly Hills socialite.

THE BEQUEST: Her estate was worth about $3 million, most of which she left to her brother—provided he made sure she was buried "in my lace nightgown and my Ferrari, with the seat slanted comfortably."

WHAT HAPPENED: That's how they buried her, surrounding the Ferrari with concrete so no one would be tempted to dig it up and drive it away.

THE DECEASED: A woman in Cherokee County, North Carolina.

THE BEQUEST: She left her entire estate to God.

WHAT HAPPENED: The court instructed the county sheriff to find the beneficiary. A few days later, the sheriff returned and submitted his report: "After due and diligent search, God cannot be found in this county."

THE DECEASED: Edgar Bergen, famed ventriloquist.

THE BEQUEST: $10,000 to the Actor's Fund of America—so they could take care of his dummy, Charlie McCarthy, and put him in a show once a year.

WHAT HAPPENED: They went along with it.

THE DECEASED: A rich, unmarried New Yorker. Died: 1880.

THE BEQUEST: He left everything to his nephews and nieces, with the exception of 71 pairs of pants. He wrote: "I enjoin my executors to hold a public sale at which these trousers shall be sold to the highest bidder, and the proceeds distributed to the poor. No one purchaser is to buy more than one pair."

WHAT HAPPENED: The auction took place. Each person who bought a pair of pants, upon examining their purchase, discovered "a $1,000 bill sewn into a pocket."

THE DECEASED: A merchant.

THE BEQUEST: Quoted in *To Will or Not to Will:* "My overdraft at the bank goes to my wife—she can explain it. My car goes to my son—he will have to go to work to keep up the payments....I want six of my creditors for pallbearers—they have carried me so long they might as well finish the job."

ONE GOOD YAWN DESERVES ANOTHER

Wonder why you cover your mouth when you yawn? Charles Panati did, and here's what he said about it in his book, Extraordinary Origins of Everyday Things.

THE POLITE YAWN

"Today, covering the mouth when yawning is considered an essential of good manners. But the original custom stemmed not from politeness but from fear—a fear that in one giant exhalation the soul, and life itself, might depart the body. A hand to the lips held back the life force."

THE DEADLY YAWN

"Ancient man had accurately observed (though incorrectly interpreted) that a newborn, struggling to survive, yawns shortly after birth (a reflexive response to draw additional oxygen into the lungs). With infant mortality extraordinarily high, early physicians, at a loss to account for frequent deaths, blamed the yawn. The helpless baby simply could not cover its mouth with a protective hand. Roman physicians actually recommended that a mother be particularly vigilant during the early months of life and cover any of her newborn's yawns."

THE CONTAGIOUS YAWN

"Today it is also considered good manners when yawning to turn one's head. But courtesy had nothing to do with the origin of the custom, nor with the apology that follows a yawn. Ancient man had also accurately observed that a yawn is contagious to witnesses. Thus, if a yawn was dangerous to a yawner, this danger could be 'caught' by others, like the Plague. The apology was for exposing friends to mortal danger."

WHAT GOES HERE?

Since we've got a space at the bottom of the page, we'll throw in a recommendation for a favorite bathroom book: *Rules of Thumb*, by Tom Parker. Includes 896 bite-size, bizarre rules for living, about everything from ostrich eggs to "Getting Emotionally Involved."

Genghis Khan is said to have killed over a million people in *one hour* in the year 1221.

THE SHOWER SCENE

*Facts about one of the most chilling
scenes in movie history.*

Alfred Hitchcock has provided filmgoers with some of the cinema's most thrilling moments, but most movie historians agree that in terms of pure shock value, the shower scene in *Psycho* tops the list.

It is probably the most famous single scene in film history.

It's admired for its masterful editing (approximately 65 edits in 45 seconds), its skillful use of music (Bernard Herrman's screeching violins) and its shocking conclusion, where the movie's apparent protagonist (played by Janet Leigh) is suddenly butchered to death in a shower.

• Although there's practically no graphic violence in the scene, it has literally scared some people out of taking showers—including Janet Leigh, who says in her autobiography that *she* refuses to take them anymore.

• Amazingly, Hitchcock later claimed he had made the film as a *joke*.

• The screenplay was adapted from Robert Bloch's novel of the same name in 1959 (by Joseph Stefano, who later created TV's "The Outer Limits"), and was shot on the set of the "Alfred Hitchcock Presents" television series.

FACTS:

Since *Psycho*'s release in 1960, film students have dissected every frame of film in the shower scene. Among the interesting details:

• It took seven days to shoot the 45-second scene.

• By far, the most difficult shot was of Marion Crane's (Janet Leigh's) open-eyed stare as she lay dead outside the shower. At first Hitchcock attempted to get special contact lenses for Leigh, but time constraints prevented it. Instead, Hitchcock used an ingenious three-shot method: (1) a close-up of Leigh's eye from a still photograph, which cuts away to (2) a shower spigot and running water and then back to "live action" of (3) Leigh staring, wide-eyed, on the bathroom floor . . . trying desperately not to blink. It is one of the film's many legends that if you look closely, you can see Leigh blink (Mrs. Hitchcock said she saw it).

- Another legend has it that a stand-in model was used for Leigh—but she denies that. Leigh says the only model used was when her body is carried out in a sheet by police in a later scene.

- The blood washing down the drain was really chocolate sauce.

- Only one shot in the entire shower scene montage shows a knife entering the body and no blood is seen in the shot.

- Some shots use as little as eight frames of film (i.e., one-third of a second).

- Anthony Perkins (as Norman Bates) did not actually act in the scene. He was on Broadway at the time of the shooting, starring in a play; a stand-in filled in as "Mom."

- Mixed-up priorities: According to Hitchcock, studio executives were more concerned about having a toilet flushing onscreen than they were about the implicit violence.

- Janet Leigh refused to let her daughter (actress Jamie Lee Curtis) watch the movie as a child when it appeared on TV.

- Hitchcock got the movie past censors by first submitting a script with many more horrible scenes, knowing that by allowing them to be cut he would get more leverage on the others.

JANET LEIGH ON THE SHOWER SCENE:

"What I was to wear in the shower scene gave the wardrobe supervisor migraines. I had to appear nude, without being nude. She and I pored over striptease magazines, hoping one of their costumes would be the answer. . . . There was an impressive display of pinwheels, feathers, sequins, etc., but nothing suitable for our needs. Finally, the supervisor came up with a simple solution: flesh-colored moleskin. . . . So each morning for seven shooting days and seventy-one setups, we covered my private parts, and we were in business."

"For sundry reasons, we had to do [the scene] over and over. At long last a take was near completion without a mishap. Abruptly I felt something strange happening around my breasts. The steam from the hot water had melted the adhesive on the moleskin, and I sensed the napped cotton fabric peeling away from my skin. What to do?...I opted for immodesty...and made the correct judgment. That was the printed take."

A FOOD IS BORN

*These foods are fairly common, but you've probably
never wondered where they came from. Here
are the answers anyway.*

FROZEN CONCENTRATED ORANGE JUICE. During
World War II, the U.S. government wanted an easy-to-carry,
powdered orange juice for soldiers in the field. They commissioned the Minute Maid Company to develop it, but the effort only
succeeded a few weeks before the war ended—so the powder was
never produced. However, as a by-product of their research, Minute Maid discovered that o.j. could be concentrated and frozen.
When the war was over, they took advantage of the discovery and
marketed it.

McDONALD'S FILET-O-FISH SANDWICH. The first successful non-burger "entree" in McDonald's history was a concession to
organized religion. In the early '60s, the McDonald's in Cincinnati
lost sales every Friday because the large Catholic population
couldn't eat meat—and McDonald's had nothing else to offer. The
owner asked Mac chairman Ray Kroc for permission to expand the
menu. Kroc resisted at first ("Let 'em eat burgers, like everyone
else!"), but ultimately supported research into selling a fish sandwich. McDonald's researchers decided to use codfish, but didn't call
it that for two reasons: One, they were legally allowed to call it the
much classier "North Atlantic Whitefish," and two, Kroc's childhood memories of cod liver oil were too unpleasant. After successful test-marketing, the fish sandwich went on the McDonald's
menu permanently in 1963.

LIFESAVERS. In 1912 a Cleveland candymaker named Clarence
Crane decided to make a mint to sell in the summer. Until then,
most mints were imported from Europe; Crane figured he could cut
the price by making them in the U.S. He had the candy manufactured by a pill-maker—who discovered that his machinery would
only work if it punched a hole in the middle of each candy. So
Crane cleverly called the mints LifeSavers.

There are no living relatives to William Shakespeare.

A-1 STEAK SAUCE. The Royal Chef for England's King George IV (1820-1830) whipped up this sauce as a treat for His Majesty, a devoted epicure. How did George like it? "Absolutely A-1," he reputedly declared. The sauce became so popular around the Court that when the chef—a gentleman named Brand—retired from his position, he started a company specifically to manufacture it. After World War I, an American company licensed it and distributed it in the States. It's still the biggest-selling sauce of its kind.

CAESAR SALAD. The name of this unique salad doesn't refer to the Roman conqueror, but to the man who created it—a Tijuana restaurateur named Caesar Cardini. Here's one account of its origin: "Cardini started several restaurants in Tijuana, Mexico in the early '20s. He devised the salad in 1924 during the Fourth of July weekend at Caesar's Place. He served it as finger food, arranging the garlic-scented lettuce leaves on platters. Later, he shredded the leaves into bite-sized pieces. The salad became a hit with the Hollywood movie stars who visited Tijuana, and soon was a specialty of such prestigious restaurants as Chasen's and Romanoff's."

MAXWELL HOUSE COFFEE. In the 1880s, a young Tennesseean named Joel Cheek became obsessed with the idea of roasting the perfect blend of coffee. After years of experiments, he came up with the blend he liked. Then, in 1892, he persuaded the owners of Nashville's ritzy Maxwell House Hotel to serve it exclusively. Cheek was so encouraged by the clientele's enthusiastic response to the coffee that he named it after the hotel.

BISQUICK. The first instant biscuit mix was inspired by a train ride. In 1930, an executive of General Mills was traveling by train and ordered some biscuits in the dining car. He expected them to be cold and stale, since it was long past the usual dinner hour. But instead, they were hot and fresh—and they arrived almost instantly. He inquired how this was possible, and was told that the bread dough had been mixed in advance and stored in the refrigerator. The executive thought it was a great idea. He worked with General Mills chemists and created a similar product—but one that could be kept in a box, unrefrigerated. It was so popular when it was introduced in the '30s that it revolutionized American baking habits.

The sound of E.T. walking was made by someone squishing her hands in Jello.

PRIME TIME PROVERBS

More words of wisdom from Prime Time Proverbs,
by Jack Mingo and John Javna.

ON EXISTENCE
"I reek, therefore I am."
—**Diane Chambers,**
Cheers

"There's more to life than sitting around in the sun in your underwear playing the clarinet."
—**Lt. Larry Casey,**
Baa Baa Black Sheep

ON THE GOOD LIFE
"I'm a lucky guy—I mean, life has been good to me. I've got a good job, good health, a good wife, and a fantastic barber."
—**Ted Baxter,**
The Mary Tyler Moore Show

ON THE LEGAL SYSTEM
"This is America. You can't make a horse testify against himself."
—**Mr. Ed,**
Mr. Ed

Venus Flytrap: "I'm not gonna sit here and let her lie!"
Lawyer: "You have to. This is a court of law."
—**WKRP in Cincinnati**

ON INDIVIDUALITY
Frank Burns: "Don't you understand? The man is not normal."
Hawkeye Pierce: "What's normal, Frank?"
Frank: "Normal is everybody doing the same thing."
Trapper McIntyre: "What about individuality?"
Frank: "Well, individuality is fine. As long as we do it together."
—**M*A*S*H**

ON WOMEN
"It's been proven through history that wimmin's a mystery."
—**Popeye,**
The Popeye Cartoon Show

ON LOVE
"Love makes you do funny things. It made me get married."
—**Buddy Sorrel,**
The Dick Van Dyke Show

"Love's the only thing in life you've got to earn. Everything else you can steal."
—**Pappy Maverick,**
Maverick

.According to a *Money* magazine poll, women like money more than sex.

THE MINI-SKIRT SAGA

*Today, when practically anything goes in fashion, people have for-
gotten how revolutionary the mini-skirt was in its day. In the mid-
'60s, when it caught on, it was more than a fashion—it was a
philosophy, a political statement, a news event.
Here are some facts to remind you.*

HISTORY.
The mini-skirt was created by an English seamstress named
Mary Quant. As a girl, Mary hated the straightlaced clothes
grown-ups wore. So when she got older, she made unconventional
clothes for herself.

In 1955, she opened the world's first boutique in London, selling
"wild and kinky" handmade clothes, like the ones she wore. She
used bright colors, lots of plastic, and kept hemlines shorter than
normal (though they weren't minis yet). Her fashions caught on
with hip Londoners. They became known as "mod" (for modern)
clothes, and Mary became a local celebrity.

In 1965, young girls in London were beginning to wear their
dresses shorter than ever. Taking a cue from them, Quant began
manufacturing skirts that were outrageously short for the time. She
called them "mini-skirts." They took off like wildfire.

Later that year, respected French designer Andre Courreges
brought the mini-skirt and go-go boots (his own creation) to the
world of high fashion. This made the mini a "style" instead of a "fad"
and inspired influential women—movie stars, models, heiresses—to
shorten their skirts. But the largest American clothing manufacturers weren't sure whether to hop on the mini bandwagon until the
day in 1965 that Jackie Kennedy appeared in public with a shortened hemline. After that, it was full speed ahead.

The mini fad lasted for less than a decade. But it permanently altered the concept of what was acceptable in women's attire, and
helped break down traditional barriers for women in other areas of
society.

The Meaning of the Mini-Skirt, Part I

In 1965, Mary Quant, creator of the mini-skirt, was asked to reveal
the meaning of the mini-skirt. Her reply: "Sex."

The Amazon River basin supplies the world with about 40% of its oxygen.

The Meaning of the Mini-Skirt, Part II
"Without a doubt, the pill bred the mini, just as it bred the topless bathing suit by Rudi Gernreich in 1964. They were intended to prove that women were in control of their destiny and could choose whom they wished to mate with."

—*In Fashion*, by Prudence Glynn

THE MINI-SKIRT — INTERNATIONAL CONTROVERSY
Today, the mini-skirt is a fashion, not a political issue, but in the '60s, it was a major controversy. Here's how some people reacted:
• **In the Vatican:** Women in mini-skirts were not allowed to enter Vatican City.
• **In the Malagasy Republic:** An anti-mini-skirt law went into effect in 1967. Violators were subject to ten days in jail.
• **In the Congo:** In 1967 police arrested three hundred women wearing mini-skirts, which were banned.
• **In Venezuela:** Churches in Caracas put up signs telling people to give up their minis or "be condemned to hell."
• **In Egypt:** Women in minis were subject to a charge of indecent behavior. This law was passed because two women wore mini-skirts in the center of the city and caused a two-hour traffic jam.
• **In Zambia:** Gangs of youths roamed the streets assaulting girls in mini-skirts and forcibly lowering their hemlines. After a week, the war against mini-skirts was declared officially over when women went on television and said they "realized their mistake."
• **In Greece:** Anyone wearing a mini-skirt was jailed.
• **In the Philippines:** A congressman proposed that mini-skirts be banned. But the proposal was withdrawn when a congresswoman threatened to retaliate by outlawing elevator shoes.
• **In Rio De Janeiro:** In 1966, a sixty-three-year-old man on a bus was overcome when a young woman wearing a mini-skirt crossed her legs in the seat next to him. He bit her on the thigh and was sentenced to three days in jail.
• **In the U.S.A.:** Disneyland outlawed mini-skirts—the gatekeepers measured the distance from the woman's knee to her hemline and restricted her entrance until she ripped out the hem.

In most schools during the '60s, if the hem of a dress didn't touch the floor when a girl was kneeling, it was considered a mini, and the guilty party was sent home. "And don't come back until you look respectable, young lady."

Copernicus was the first person to butter his bread.

THE ORIGIN OF DRACULA

Dracula ifirst appeared in 1897 in a book written by Irish author Bram Stoker. Extraordinary Origins of Everyday Things *says:*

The nineteenth-century Irish writer Bram Stoker came serendipitously upon the subject matter for his novel *Dracula* while engaged in research at the British Museum. He discovered a manuscript of traditional Eastern European folklore concerning Vlad the Impaler, a fifteenth-century warrior prince of Walachia. According to Romanian legend, the sadistic Prince Vlad took his meals al fresco, amidst a forest of impaled, groaning victims. And Vlad washed down each course with his victims' blood, in the belief that it imbued him with supernatural strength.

Vlad's crimes were legend. On red-hot pokers, he impaled male friends who had fallen from favor, and women unfaithful to him were impaled, then skinned alive. Imprisoned himself, he tortured mice and birds for amusement. His mountaintop retreat, known as Castle Drakula, suggested the title for Stoker's novel.

Although Stoker had found his model for Dracula, it was a friend, a professor from the University of Budapest, who suggested a locale for the fiction by relating lore of the vampires of Transylvania. The novelist traveled to the area and was…impressed with its dark, brooding mountains, morning fogs, and sinister-looking castles.

Dracula was an immense success when published in 1897, wrapped in a brown paper cover. And the novel was responsible for reviving interest in the Gothic horror romance, which has continued into the present day in books and films.

EEAGH! TWO AWFUL VAMPIRE RIDDLES
"How can you spot a Vampire jockey?"
   "He always wins by a neck."
"Why aren't Vampires good gamblers?"
   "Because they always make sucker bets."

The Empire State Building contains more than 10 million bricks.

CHURCHILL SPEAKS

Words of wisdom from the quotable
Sir Winston Churchill.

"History will be kind to me, for I intend to write it."

"Although I am prepared for martyrdom, I prefer that it be postponed."

"If you have an important point, don't try to be subtle or clever. Use a pile driver. Hit the point once. Then come back and hit it again. Then hit it a third time—a tremendous whack."

"It is a mistake to look too far ahead. The chain of destiny can only be grasped one link at a time."

"In war you can only be killed once, but in politics, many times."

"I have taken more out of alcohol than alcohol has taken out of me."

"A fantatic is one who can't change his mind and won't change the subject."

"Eating words has never given me indigestion."

"I like a man who grins when he fights."

"I am always ready to learn, although I do not always like being taught."

"The inherent vice of Capitalism is the unequal sharing of its blessings; the inherent vice of Socialism is the equal sharing of its miseries."

"A hopeful disposition is not the sole qualification to be a prophet."

"We are all worms, but I do believe I'm a glow worm."

"It is a fine thing to be honest, but it is also important to be right."

"Never turn your back on a threatened danger and try to run away from it. If you do that, you will double the danger. But if you meet it promptly and without flinching, you will reduce the danger by half. Never run away from anything. Never!"

The #1 TV show of 1961 was a Western called "Wagon Train."

WHO WAS THAT MAN?

Some songs leave you wondering who they're about. Here are the
stories behind a few, from Behind the Hits, *by*
Bob Shannon and John Javna.

I WRITE THE SONGS; BARRY MANILOW
Most people associate this tune with Barry Manilow, because
his version sold millions of records. But it actually has nothing
to do with him. He didn't write it—Bruce Johnston, one of the
Beach Boys, did. And Johnston didn't write it about Manilow—or
himself. He was inspired by someone he considers a truly great
songwriter.

Who was that man?
Johnston says: "I guess it's pretty obvious that I wrote the song
about Brian Wilson."

Wilson, the leader of the Beach Boys, really *has* written songs
the whole world sings. For example: "Good Vibrations," "In My
Room," "Fun, Fun, Fun," "I Get Around," "Surfer Girl," "Help Me
Rhonda," and so on. Good choice.

KILLING ME SOFTLY WITH HIS SONG;
ROBERTA FLACK
Roberta Flack didn't write this song; a poet and folksinger named
Lori Lieberman did.

The Story. One evening in 1972, Lori went to L.A.'s Troubador
to see a singer who had earned the nickname "The Hudson River
Troubador" when he sailed from Maine to New York with Pete
Seeger, trying to call attention to pollution. She was impressed by
what she saw and heard. "I thought he was just incredible," she recalled. "He was singing songs that I felt pertained to my life at that
time. I was going though some difficult things, and what he was
singing about made me think, 'Whoa! This person knows me! I
don't understand.' Never having met him, how could he know me
so well? I went home and wrote a poem and showed it to the two
men I was working with at the time."

Those two men, Norman Gimbel and Charles Fox, thought the
poem could be adapted into a great song. They quickly reworked it
and gave it back to Lieberman to record on her own album.

In its original form it was ten minutes long—too long for radio play—so it was edited and released as a single. It got a little airplay, but never sold. It did, however, get included on a tape of music created especially for airline headsets.

How It Became a Hit: On a flight from Los Angeles to New York, Roberta Flack plugged in her personal headphones and began leafing through the in-flight magazine to see what songs were included on the 10 channels of music that were available. Her main interest was to see if any of her recordings were among the offerings. They weren't.

But Flack happened to notice the listing for a song she'd never heard. The title seemed interesting, so she tuned it in. By the time she reached New York she knew she had to record it. "When I heard it," Flack said, "I absolutely freaked. In New York, I started calling people, asking how to find the guys who wrote that song."

Flack felt she had stumbled on an "uncut diamond," a song that she could restructure and improve and make her own. It became the most important project in her life, and she spent eight months on it. "Roberta came out with the most wonderful version," says Lieberman. "Killing Me Softly" was released in January; it became the top-selling song in the nation by February, and won three Grammy awards for Flack.

Who was that man?
The gentle "killer" was folksinger Don McLean. He had just completed his second album, "American Pie," and his rendition of the title song was the performance that inspired Lieberman. McLean says: "After she announced it, somebody called me up and said, 'Hey, somebody's written a song about you.' The first question I asked was, 'Is it any good?' "

YOU'RE SO VAIN; CARLY SIMON

This is probably old news by now, but it's worth repeating. Carly Simon's first big hit created a controversy. As soon as it was released, people began speculating about its subject. Who was "so vain"? Was it Mick Jagger? Her husband, James Taylor?

Who was that man?
Simon wanted to keep an air of mystery around the song, so she was reluctant to reveal her secret. But producer Richard Perry wasn't so shy. "It's about a compilation of men," he said, "but primarily Warren Beatty."

39% of Americans think that the best way to get rich is to win a lottery.

WORDPLAY

More origins of common phrases.

KEEP THE BALL ROLLING
Meaning: To keep things going, to maintain momentum.
Background: Comes from the presidential election of 1840, which was won by Whig party candidate William Henry Harrison. The election campaign included the usual pamphlets, buttons, banners, and one unique item—a giant 6-foot paper ball with all the Whig slogans written on it (e.g., "Tippecanoe and Tyler Too!"). Harrison's supporters took it from town to town, rolling it down the streets shouting "Keep the ball rolling!"

GET UP ON THE WRONG SIDE OF BED
Meaning: To start the day feeling bad, or to wake up in a bad mood.
Background: Reflects a long-standing cultural bias against the left side of the body. The phrase was originally "get out of bed the wrong way"—which meant with your left foot first, or while you were lying on your left side—a sure sign, people believed, that things were destined to go wrong that day. The phrase evolved into "get up on the wrong side of bed."

BEAT AROUND THE BUSH
Meaning: To avoid dealing with the main issue.
Background: In the Middle Ages, people trapped birds for food by dropping a net over a bush and beating the ground around it with a club. As frightened birds perched in the bush tried to fly away, they were caught in the net. Someone who kept beating around the bush after the birds were trapped never got to the point of the activity—actually getting the birds and eating them.

BARK UP THE WRONG TREE
Meaning: To focus on the wrong object or idea.
Background: A hunting term. In Colonial days, pioneers used hounds to trap raccoons and possums. The dogs would chase the animals up trees, then sit and bay at the tree trunk. Occasionally, the hound would get fooled and the hunter would find his pet barking "up" the wrong tree.

On the average, American men carry more cash than women do.

THE FABULOUS '60S

*More miscellany from the pop decade, courtesy of
Gordon and John Javna's great bathroom reader, 60s!*

WAR GAMES
One of the forgotten footnotes of the Vietnam war is the toys it inspired. In 1961 JFK committed our first troops to Vietnam…and in 1962, toys relating to Vietnam began to appear. "We've discovered through dealer interviews and consumer mail that our customers are demanding toys about Vietnam," explained the sales manager of a major toy company. Among the big sellers:

• **The Mattel "Guerilla Gun."** In 1963, Mattel painted its Dick Tracy Submachine guns camouflage green and packaged each one with a poncho, toy hand grenades, and a beret. They immediately sold 2 million of them, twice as many as they had when the product was just a Dick Tracy gun.

• **The Green Beret hobby kit.** Aurora Plastics marketed a plastic assemble-it-yourself model of a Green Beret holding a machine gun and tossing a hand grenade. "Inspired by the great motion picture *The Green Berets*, starring John Wayne," it said on the box. No mention of the real war, though.

• **"Viet Nam, a Game for Interested Americans."** The next best thing to being there—an educational board game for people who liked role-playing.

WHO CARES ABOUT THE CEREAL?
In 1965 kids discovered an animated TV commercial for a brand-new cereal. It actually had a cast of characters the way cartoons did: lovable old Cap'n Crunch, his crew of kids, his faithful pet, Seadog, and the villains, archenemy Magnolia Bulkhead and Jean LaFoot, the barefoot pirate. The kiddie videophiles loved the commercials and, of course, made their parents buy the cereal. It quickly became the most popular new cereal of the decade, giving its manufacturer, Quaker Oats, the sweet taste of success.

What consumers didn't know: Cap'n Crunch was carefully

The sex organ on a male spider is located at the end of one of its legs.

planned out as a TV promotion *before the cereal even existed.* Quaker hired Jay Ward, creator of Bullwinkle, to come up with a cartoon character and produce one-minute commercials—cereal serials—of Cap'n Crunch sailing the high seas, keeping the world safe for breakfast. Then, when they were satisfied with the ads, Quaker produced the actual cereal. It became the best-selling new cereal of the decade.

WHO DUNNIT?

The first James Bond film, *Dr. No*, came out in 1963. But Ian Fleming's books were already selling well in America by then. Here's how it happened: In 1961, a well-known intellectual was asked by a reporter from *Life* magazine to name his favorite books. The man, who was known to read a book a day, quickly supplied a list of 10 of them. Most were scholarly works . . . except one—*From Russia with Love*, a James Bond thriller.

This was the only book on the list that most Americans would even consider buying. And they did. The guy had so much influence that James Bond became an overnight sensation in bookstores.

Who was the man whose list started the Bond craze?

President John F. Kennedy.

MACHINE AGE MAN

They sang it on TV in 1962: "Here he comes, here he comes, greatest toy you've ever seen, and his name is Mr. Machine. . . ." Mr. Machine was a plastic wind-up robot with a top hat, who clunked and whirred, and walked mechanically. Manufactured by the Ideal Toy Company in 1962, he became one of the most popular toys of the early sixties.

But kids and their parents never realized that Mr. Machine was more than a toy—it was actually a comment on the condition of modern man.

It was created by Marvin Glass, a neurotic toy designer who considered himself something of a philosopher. One day Glass was having a typical argument with his ex-wife. Just before she hung up, she screamed at him: "You're nothing but a machine!" Glass pondered the comment. Maybe she was right, he thought. . . . Maybe the 20th century had turned all of us into machines. Inspired, Glass designed his homage to modern life, Mr. Machine.

LUNACY

We've heard enough about moons and Junes to last a lifetime.
But the joke is that some of the old fables about the power of
the moon might actually be true.

MOON CHILD:
  • The average menstrual cycle for women is 29.5 days—
    precisely the same as a lunar month.
  • The human gestation period is 9 months. But whose months?
    The average birth occurs 265.5 days after conception—which
    happens to be the exact equivalent of 9 lunar months.

STUDIES SHOW THAT:
  • More children are born after new and full moons than at any
    other time.
  • More boys are born after a full moon, and more girls are born
    after a new moon.
  • People who are experiencing a lot of stress have an increase in
    pulse rates during a full or new moon.
  • Surgeons have found that around the full or new moons, their
    patients bleed more.
  • When full and new moons occur, more people are admitted into
    mental hospitals and hospital emergency rooms are busier.
  • There's an increase in certain crimes (rape, robbery, assault)
    during a full moon.

THE WORD
  • "Lunacy" refers to the Roman moon goddess, Luna.
  • In ancient times, people thought that exposure to the moon
    could "affect the mind."
  • People were advised not to sleep with moonlight shining on their
    faces, or they would become "moonstruck" (crazy).
  • The word *lunacy* is probably derived from ancient observations
    that during a full moon, mad people became more frenzied.
  • The term *lunatic fringe* was coined by Teddy Roosevelt, who was
    describing some of his followers in the Bullmoose Party during
    the 1912 presidential election.

From the bottom of a well, you can actually see the stars during the daytime.

THE GUMBY STORY

He's the "Clayboy of the Western World," an American icon.
But what does he stand for, and where did he come from?
Now it can be told.

A STAR IS BORN. Gumby was created in the mid-'50s by Art Clokey, a filmmaker who had learned "stop-motion animation" (film is shot one frame at a time and the inanimate subject is moved between shots) at the University of Southern California, working with a world-famous expert.
• After graduating, Clokey experimented with his "stop-motion" techniques in an art film he called *Gumbasia*. The stars of the film were geometric clay forms ("It was cheaper than getting actors") that metamorphized to the rhythm of a jazz soundtrack.
• Clokey took *Gumbasia* to a Hollywood producer, hoping to make feature films. Instead, the producer decided Clokey ought to make a kids' TV show. He put up the money for a pilot, and Clokey created the star—a clay character named Gumby. NBC then commissioned several 6-minute films.
• Gumby made his first appearance on "The Howdy Doody Show" in 1956. Then in March, 1957 he got his own NBC program.
• Beginning in 1958, "The Adventures of Gumby" was offered as a syndicated show. By the mid-'60s, he was everywhere.

GUMBY: PERSONAL DATA
• His name came from a type of sticky clay soil found in Michigan, known as "gumbo."
• The shape of his head was inspired by a photo of Clokey's father. In it, the senior Clokey had a cowlick that looked to his son like "the bump of wisdom that Buddhists have." So Art passed it on to Gumby.
• According to Clokey: "His green color represents the chlorophyll found in plants, while his bluish tint reflects the sky. He's got his feet on the ground and his head in the sky."
• His pal, Pokey, is orange because, says Clokey, "Pokey represents the critical, doubting, more earthy side of life."
• His voice was supplied by Dick Beals. Pokey's voice was supplied by Clokey himself.

In 60 seconds, your blood makes a complete trip through your body.

HIS FALL AND RESURRECTION

Gumby's popularity lasted through the '60s and into the early '70s. But by the late '70s, he was washed up; TV stations had dropped the show, and toymakers had stopped manufacturing Gumby toys.
• Art Clokey was nearly broke. His house was about to be foreclosed on, and the new toy product in which he had invested heavily—something called Moody Rudy—was proving to be a bomb. Worse, his daughter had recently been killed in a car accident. Life was not going Art's way.
• In 1979, he went to Hong Kong to take a look at the Moody Rudy manufacturing facilities. While he was there, he decided to visit Satya Sai Baba, an Indian holy man he'd once seen in a film.
• As journalist Sean Elder describes it: "On that day in 1979, Clokey and his wife, Gloria, were among the faithful hundreds sitting outside Baba's ashram, awaiting...a glimpse of the Master. Once or twice a day Baba would make the rounds, pouring ash from his hand onto objects that the devout held up to be blessed: books, photographs, religious statues. That afternoon, Sai Baba found Clokey in the lotus position, holding a small likeness of Gumby. Ash poured forth from his hand onto Gumby's sloping head, and the master moved on. 'Then I went home,' says Clokey, 'and things began happening.' "

THE GUMBY REVIVAL

• It started at the Pasadena Art Center, where Clokey gave a talk on animation. The Gumby-philes who attended enjoyed it so much that they set up some screenings of Gumby films (remember, it was pre-video, and they hadn't been seen on TV for years) in the auditorium of the Beverly Hills Library.
• This was sold out for two weeks in a row—which prompted the owners of a chain of movie theaters to send Clokey around the country, appearing with his Gumby films. He was a hit everywhere.
• Inspired by the Gumby revival, a couple of cadets painted a Gumby sign and flew it during the 1980 Army-Navy football game. This, in turn, was spotted by the producer of "Saturday Night Live," who decided it would be a kick to dress Eddie Murphy in a Gumby suit. Suddenly Gumby was a star again.
• Clokey is clear about who's responsible for his turn in fortunes—Satya Sai Baba. "He's the epitome of cosmic creation in human form," he explains. "He taught me that Gumby is me, and since we're all alike, Gumby is everyone."

Gumby and his friends are sometimes moved as many as 9,000 times in a Gumby film.

EARTH TRIVIA

*A few fascinating facts about the planet to
help you while away the time:*

The earth isn't round. It's slightly flattened on the top and bottom.

❖

There are over 300,000 miles of coastline on the planet.

❖

The longest mountain range in the world is the Andes, in South America. It is 4525 miles long. Next longest: The Rockies, followed by the Himalayas, the Great Dividing Range in Australia, and the Trans-Antarctic Mountains.

On a mountain, the temperature drops about 3-1/2° for every 984 feet you climb.

❖

The atmosphere extends about 5,000 miles above the earth. It consists of five separate layers: the exosphere, thermosphere, mesosphere, stratosphere, and troposphere.

❖

The troposphere is the life-supporting layer closest to the earth. It is also the smallest—only 10 miles high.

❖

There are about a million earthquakes every year. Most are so small they don't even register.

❖

The deepest lake in the world is the U.S.S.R.'s Lake Baikal. Its size: 30 miles wide by 400 miles long. Its depth: over a mile (approx. 6,360 feet). "It's so deep," says one source, "that all five of the Great Lakes could be emptied into it."

❖

The largest lake (or inland sea) in the world is the Caspian Sea, on the border of Iran and the U.S.S.R.

❖

About 20% of the Earth's surface is desert. However, most deserts are not sand (only about 15% are). Deserts are frequently bare rock or gravel.

The Sahara Desert takes up about 1/3 of Africa. It is almost as big as the continental United States.

❖

If you could take all of the salt out of the ocean and spread it on land, you'd have a five hundred-foot layer of salt covering the Earth's surface.

You can only see a rainbow in the morning or late in the afternoon.

THE STORY OF LAYLA

Several B.R.I.members wrote and asked for the inside story on this classic Eric Clapton tune—one of the most popular rock songs of all time.

Eric Clapton could play the blues as few other guitarists could—a talent which both satisfied and tortured him. Unlike some of his fellow British "bluesmen," Clapton was keenly aware that he was a white musician imitating an essentially black art form. This created a terrible conflict; playing the blues was his first love, but was he really entitled to practice his craft? In order to reconcile the feelings, Clapton became a blues purist. He believed that you had to suffer in order to be able to play the blues—so he was miserable a lot of the time. He was particularly unhappy when he wrote his most famous composition, "Layla."

THE BIRTH OF LAYLA
The real "Layla's" real name was Patti Boyd—or more accurately, Patti Boyd Harrison. She was the wife of Beatle George Harrison when Eric Clapton began pursuing her.

• Harrison first met her on the set of *A Hard Day's Night* in 1964. A stunning nineteen-year-old blonde model, she was only supposed to make a brief appearance in the film and leave; instead, she and George fell in love and eventually married.

• George and Eric were close friends. They'd known each other since the days when the Beatles and the Yardbirds (Eric's group at the time) were becoming popular. As they both became superstars, they hung out together more and more. They even contributed to each other's recordings. Eric played a magnificent solo on "While My Guitar Gently Weeps"; George co-wrote and played on Cream's "Badge." George wrote "Here Comes the Sun" while sitting in Eric's garden; he wrote "Savoy Truffle" specifically for Eric, who was having dental problems but still couldn't resist chocolates. George joined Eric when he toured with a band called Delaney and Bonnie and Friends, etc.

• George didn't realize, however, that over the years Eric had quietly fallen in love with his wife. Eric told Patti (but not George)

Chicken soup was considered an aphrodisiac in the Middle Ages.

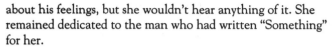

about his feelings, but she wouldn't hear anything of it. She remained dedicated to the man who had written "Something" for her.

• Already a tortured soul, Eric was plunged into despair. In an outburst of emotion, he wrote "Layla." Later, when people asked him who he was singing for, all he would say was, " 'Layla' was about a woman I felt really deeply about and who turned me down, and I had to pour it out in some way."

• You may be wondering how "Patti" became "Layla." The answer: Clapton lifted the name "Layla" from a Persian love story called "Layla and Mashoun." The tale had little similarity to the Eric/Patti/George love triangle. Clapton just liked the title. The song was recorded and released in 1970, but it flopped. The reason: the record was attributed to Derek and the Dominoes; no one knew it was Clapton, so it didn't get airplay.

• Eric, who had poured his heart and soul into the record, threw in the towel. He gave up music and took up heroin. "I basically stayed in the house with my girlfriend for two and-a-half years," he told *Rolling Stone* magazine, "and we got very strung out. Dying from drugs didn't seem to me then to be a terrible thing."

• Ironically, during this low point in his life, "Layla" was re-released and became one of the all-time FM favorites...and then struck gold as a Top 10 single.

• In 1974, Clapton kicked the heroin habit and re-emerged on the music scene with "I Shot the Sheriff," his first #1 song.

• A happy ending for Eric: Patti eventually divorced George and, in a secret ceremony in Tucson, Arizona, in 1979, married Clapton. The ultimate irony: Patti and Eric later joined George in a recording of the Everly Brothers' old hit, "Bye, Bye Love."

UNRELATED MORBID TRIVIA
From Fred Worth's Hollywood Trivia:
• George Reeves, the star of TV's "Superman," was buried wearing the grey double-breasted suit he wore when he played Clark Kent.

• Bela Lugosi, who played the vampire Dracula in many films, was buried in his Dracula cape.

BATMAN ON TV

Holy bonanza! In the summer of 1989, Batman *became one of the biggest-grossing films of all time. But the Batman TV series in 1966 was just as much of a smash on the small screen.*

HOW IT STARTED

Back in 1939, cartoonist Bob Kane created Batman as a stablemate for the popular DC Comics character, Superman. A skilled detective who kept his identity hidden under a cape and mask, this "Batman" hunted down criminals in the night . . . and murdered them. He was an instant smash.

After his comic book success, Batman became a radio series, then made the jump to movie serials in the late '40s.

By 1965, pop art was big and a comic book revival was on, and the time was right for Batman to make a bat-leap onto TV. As it happened, ABC was hard up for anything that would bolster its sagging ratings. So when Douglas Cramer suggested the idea to network executives, they agreed to give Batman a shot. What could they lose? William Dozier, who had never even heard of Batman, was hired to produce the series, and he recruited "the most bizarre thinker I knew," Lorenzo Semple, to develop scripts. Then fate lent a hand. As production for the series was beginning in fall 1965, Columbia Pictures released four hours of old Batman movie serials under the title *An Evening With Batman and Robin*. It played to packed houses at college campuses around the country and ignited "Batmania." Dozier rushed production to take advantage of this good fortune. And Batman premiered in January of 1966. Holy ratings! It shot up to #1 immediately, becoming an instant cult classic.

INSIDE FACTS

Holy Bat-Craze

TV ignited a Batman merchandise boom. In 1966, over 60 manufacturers made more than 500 Batman products and sold more than $60 million worth of them . . . making Batman the biggest fad America had ever seen. Suddenly consumers could buy Batbath bubble soap, Batman peanut butter, Batman greeting cards, Batman pajamas, and so on. The fad was repeated 23 years later, in 1989.

Most American car horns honk in the key of F.

Who Is That Masked Man?
The actors chosen to play the Dynamic Duo were virtual unknowns. Adam West (Batman) had co-starred for a season in a 1961 TV series called "The Detectives," but other than that, had endured 7 years of bit parts in TV shows and Italian Westerns before becoming an "overnight success." Burt Ward (Robin) had even less experience, and was flat broke when he got the part. To celebrate, he and his new bride cashed in 25¢ worth of Coke bottles and bought 8 chicken wings.

Top Priorities
When ABC broke into the middle of a "Batman" episode to announce the emergency landing of the Gemini 8 spacecraft, they were flooded with irate phone calls. Holy priorities! Apparently, Bat-fans cared more about the fictional exploits of the Caped Crusader than the real-life ones of the astronauts.

Follow that Car
The TV Batmobile was a modified Lincoln Continental, customized by George Barris for the show at a cost of $30,000. Despite the impressive fireball that burst from the rear of the car upon ignition, it ran on plain old gasoline.

Guardian Angel
Aunt Harriet, Bruce's kindly old relative, was not in the original comic book. She was added to the Wayne household by Dozier to parry charges of homosexual overtones in the show (3 men living together). "She watches everything," said a network representative.

So Bad, He's Good
In 1966, Frank Gorshin was nominated for an Emmy for his performance as the Riddler, making him the most critically acclaimed villain on TV.

Status
Viewers will spot plenty of familiar faces in "Batman" reruns. "Batman" was the show it was "in" to be "on"; and guest stars included Joan Collins, Milton Berle, Liberace, Vincent Price, Cliff Robertson, Otto Preminger, Zsa Zsa Gabor, Burgess Meredith, et al.

NAZI OR NOT?

These celebrities have been accused of being Nazis. But were they? Or are they just the victims of nasty rumors?

THE ACCUSED: Errol Flynn, swashbuckling screen idol of the '30s and '40s.

THE CHARGE: Flynn actively worked as a Nazi spy.

THE EVIDENCE:
- *Exhibit A*: Flynn was apparently a rabid anti-semite.
- *Exhibit B*: One of Flynn's closest friends, Dr. Hermann Erben, was unmasked as a Nazi spy after the war. He and Flynn traveled extensively together (e.g., during the Spanish Civil War, they went to Spain and posed as journalists), and when Erben was booted out of America by the U.S. Government, Flynn smuggled him back into Mexico.
- *Exhibit C*: During the war, the U.S. Government had Flynn under surveillance, calling him a potential subversive.
- *Exhibit D*: He insisted that the 1941 film *Dive Bomber* be shot on location at the San Diego naval base. His accusers say it was to give "Japanese military planners a look at American defense installations and aircraft carriers."

THE DEFENSE: Flynn died in 1959, and the charge was made 21 years later by author Charles Higham, in his book *Errol Flynn: The Untold Story*.
- Ex-spy Erben denies Flynn had ever worked with him.
- Flynn's Hollywood cohorts scoff at the charges, saying that at worst, Flynn was guilty only of standing by a pal.
- It has been pointed out that although he was watched, Flynn was never picked up by the government
- Flynn's daughters sued Higham for libel. "We're hoping... we might discourage authors like Higham from writing about people who aren't even alive to defend themselves," explained one. The California Supreme Court refused to hear the case.

NAZI OR NOT? The evidence is too thin to convict anyone, but it's an intriguing possibility.

Women are 37% more likely to go to a psychiatrist than men are.

THE ACCUSED: Charles Lindbergh, the first man to fly solo nonstop across the Atlantic. A national hero.

THE CHARGE: Lindbergh was either America's "number one Nazi sympathizer," as many politicians charged, or worse. FDR is quoted as having told Henry Morganthau, his secretary of the Treasury, in 1940: "If I should die tomorrow, I want you to know this. I am absolutely convinced Lindbergh is a Nazi."

THE EVIDENCE:
• *Exhibit A*: In 1938, Lindbergh accepted a medal from Adolf Hitler, and publicly expressed his admiration for Germany.
• *Exhibit B*: Returning to America, he began making speeches in favor of the U.S. staying out of any European conflict at all costs. This was—coincidentally?—a policy priority for the German government as well.
• *Exhibit C*: He became a central figure in the America First Committee (stay out of Europe, take care of America first), tirelessly giving speeches and radio addresses directed not only at keeping America out of World War II, but at preventing the U.S. from supporting Britain.
• *Exhibit D*: When "interventionist" politicians attacked him as a Nazi, his political allies urged him to repudiate fascism and Hitler. He refused to do so.
• *Exhibit E*: Pre-war cables from the German consulate in Washington described his efforts as a wonderful propaganda tool, and urged the Nazi government not to publicly support his position, lest he be branded a traitor.
• *Exhibit F*: In an October, 1941 speech he blamed the British and the Jews for the public pressure to get America into the war. "The leaders of the British and Jewish races…for reasons which are not American, wish to involve us in the war," he said.

THE DEFENSE: When America went to war, Lindbergh wrote in his diary: "I have always stood for what I thought would be to the best interest of this country, and now we are at war I want to take part in it, foolish and disastrous as I think the war will prove to be. Our decision has been made, and now we must fight to preserve our national honor and our national future." He got a job working with Ford Motor Company, developing bomber manufacturing capacity. And in 1944, he went to Germany to help the U.S. study their rocket-building facilities.

NAZI OR NOT? Yes and no. He considered himself a patriotic American and joined in the war effort (even though he disagreed with it). But his sympathies clearly lay with the Nazis. Even in his diaries, he never criticized Hitler or fascism. And the prospect of a Nazi-dominated Europe was a positive one to him; he admired their efficiency and orderliness. When the war was over, he still maintained we should never have become involved. Confronted with the sight of a concentration camp, he merely said it was no worse than America had treated the Japanese, and added: "Judge not, that ye not be judged."

THE ACCUSED: Gary Cooper.

THE CHARGE: Cooper was a " strong Nazi sympathizer." This allegation, too, was made by Charles Higham in his book, *Cary Grant: The Lonely Heart.*

THE EVIDENCE:
• *Exhibit A:* In 1938, Cooper visited Germany.
• *Exhibit B:* While there, he met with high government officials and may even have had a secret meeting with Hitler.
• *Exhibit C:* Hitler's favorite movie was Cooper's *Lives of the Bengal Lancers.*

THE DEFENSE:
• According to Cooper's wife at the time, the charge is "a despicable, bald-faced lie." She says Cooper never went to Germany in 1938.
• Origin of the rumor, according to the ex-wife: she and Gary accompanied her mother and stepfather to Germany in 1939. It was a special favor to FDR, with whom her stepfather was friends.
•Says the ex-wife: "It was shortly after Lindbergh said what he did about the power of the German Air Force. FDR wanted to know about Germany's finances, and my stepfather made contact with a Goering—not Hermann Goering, but his half-brother…to look at some plants."

NAZI OR NOT? The evidence is embarrassingly scanty. Unless more turns up, there's no case at all.

From age 5 to age 15, an American kid will see about 13,500 people killed on TV.

THE BIRDS

Some inside dope on one of Alfred Hitchcock's spookiest films.

Alfred Hitchcock's 1963 film *The Birds* was a milestone: no one had ever tried to work with so many animals at once; and no one has ever used live animals so effectively in a suspense film.

Much of the credit goes to Hollywood's #1 bird expert, Ray Berwick. He was familiar with the Daphne DuMaurier short story on which *The Birds* was based, but never imagined anyone would try to film it. Then, one morning at 6:30, he got a call telling him to be at Hitchcock's office in an hour. He walked in on a *Birds* production meeting, where he was told that $250,000 had already been spent on mechanical birds that didn't work. Could they use live birds? Not even Berwick was sure. But he agreed to try.

BERWICK'S APPROACH

• Although thousands of untrained birds—sparrows, finches, buntings, seagulls, and ravens—were ultimately used, Berwick only trained 100-150 ravens, blackbirds, and seagulls for the film.

• Of the trained birds, only 25 or 30 were well-trained; that's all they needed. Birds, says Berwick, have a tendency to follow leaders, so the well-trained birds lead the others wherever the director wants them to go.

• The small birds weren't trained—and they didn't have to be. In one convincing scene, for example, they were just "dumped down a chimney."

• According to Berwick: Once the wild birds were tame, they lost their fear of humans and actually became "the birds," attacking members of the cast and crew.

• Hitchcock wanted to include an owl among his feathered fiends, but had to cut the owl's scene because it looked comical.

BEHIND THE SCENES

Years after the film was released, Berwick revealed the secret of making seagulls look as though were attacking humans:

• He taught the birds to land on people's heads whenever people were standing still. And each time they performed that stunt

---

If you ate Frosted Flakes as a kid, there's a 50% chance you're still eating them.

successfully, they were fed.

• In the film, the audience saw what *looked* like people running down a street being chased by seagulls; in reality, the seagulls were flying along *with* the people, waiting for the people to stop moving so the birds could perform their trick.

• As soon as the director yelled "Cut!" the actors stopped running and the birds landed on their heads—and received their food rewards.

• **Postscript:** After the film was completed, the seagulls that had been used in the film were taken to the Pacific shore and set free. According to Berwick, trained seagulls will forget what they've been taught in about a week, if no one's working with them. But for the first week after the birds were released, there were strange reports of seagulls landing on people's heads at the beach. No one believed the reports, of course—except the people who'd worked on *The Birds*. And they weren't about to explain it to anyone.

ADVENTURES IN CINEMAGIC

In one carefully crafted scene, co-star Tippi Hedren was rowing across a lake when a seagull seemed to swipe her across the head—leaving her bloodied. Here's how Hitchcock's crew did it:

• They ran two tubes up Hedren's dress: one, which went to her forehead, spurted "blood" ; the other, which went to the top of her head, was attached to an air compressor.

• Then they released the gull, which was one of the birds trained to land on people's heads.

• The gull started to land on Hedren's head. But at the moment it touched her, the air compressor was turned on. The burst of air scared the bird into flying away.

• At the same moment, the "blood" squirted through the other tube, making it seem as though the bird had attacked. A complicated stunt, but clever and effective.

AFTERMATH

Hitchcock and Berwick made a lot of enemies in pet shops wth *The Birds*. After the film was released, sales of pet birds plummeted.

• Turnabout: Years later, Berwick was also responsible for a bird "boom" when he brought Fred the cockatoo to the screen in the TV show "Baretta."

About half the pigs in the world live on farms in China.

STRANGE LAWSUITS

More examples of the American legal system gone slightly nuts.

THE PLAINTIFFS: Michael and Geraldine S., of Bridgehampton, New York.
THE DEFENDANT: The Hampton Day School.
THE LAWSUIT: The S. family was angry that their 6-year-old son Philip, a first-grader, wasn't getting any homework. So they sued the school for $1,500.
THE RESULT: The jury rejected the S.'s claim and "ordered them to hand over the $975 in tuition they had refused to pay the school."

THE PLAINTIFF: Andrew Freese, a 23-year-old silver miner.
THE DEFENDANT: The state of Idaho.
THE LAWSUIT: Freese objected to the slogan on the Idaho license plate, "Famous Potatoes," because it forced him to advertise potatoes against his will. "This imposition has been borne by the long-suffering citizens of Idaho for the last 12 years," he said in his complaint. He added that mentioning only potatoes discriminated against Idaho's other major products, like lumber...and silver.
VERDICT: Unknown.

THE PLAINTIFFS: The family of Tomontra Mangrum, a 15-year-old West Palm Beach girl.
THE DEFENDANT: Marlon Shadd, a 17-year-old West Palm Beach boy.
THE LAWSUIT: Tomontra claimed she was stood up by Marlon on prom night. "I talked to him a few days before, and he said he already had his tux and the tickets," she told reporters. "I was very upset when he didn't show up." Marlon, on the other hand, insisted he'd called off the date a week before the prom. "I told her I fractured my ankle," he said. Tomontra's mother filed suit against Shadd, seeking $49.53 for the cost of the shoes, flowers, and hairdo her daughter had gotten for the prom. Shadd's mother tried to

settle out of court: "I offered her the money. You know what she tells me? She tells me the boy has to be punished."
VERDICT: Pending.

THE PLAINTIFF: Lori C.
THE DEFENDANT: Jack Lee C.
THE LAWSUIT: When Jack met his future bride at a party, he told her his parents had been killed in an auto accident some ten years before. After they were married, Lori "became suspicious when her husband started waving guns around at home. She investigated and found that Jack had shot his parents to death, but was cleared on insanity grounds." She not only sued for divorce, she asked for an additional $20,000 for "emotional distress."
THE VERDICT: Settled out of court.

THE PLAINTIFF: Virginia N., a dental hygenist from Naperville, Illinois.
THE DEFENDANT: James L., her former employer.
THE LAWSUIT: Ms. N. charged that Mr. L. forced his employees to hug him each day before leaving work. She asserted that if she had been informed that to hug and be hugged was part of the job description, she "would not have taken the job." She also said that whenever she tried to "dash from work hugless," her employer complained bitterly. Did she quit or was she fired?
VERDICT: Pending.

THE PLAINTIFF: Randall Dale Adams.
THE DEFENDANT: Filmmaker Errol Morris.
THE LAWSUIT: Adams was convicted of murder in 1977. Ten years later, Morris made a film about the Adams case and as he did, he became convinced that Adams was innocent. The movie, *The Thin Blue Line*, presented the case for Adams's innocence so effectively that he was released from prison. Morris's reward? When Adams got out of jail, he sued the filmmaker for $60,000 for using his story.
VERDICT: Settled out of court. Adams dropped the suit, and Morris agreed that Adams should receive full rights to any further commercial uses—notably films or books—of his life.

PRIME TIME PROVERBS

More words of wisdom from Prime Time Proverbs.

ON CHANGING
"Some of us change, some of us mutate."

—Joyce Davenport,
Hill Street Blues

ON HELPING
New Yorker (Victim):
"Lemme get this straight—
you're saying that you saw me in trouble, so you came over for no reason, with nothing in it for you, and saved my life?"
Good Samaritan: "Yep."
Victim: "You're sick!"

—*Barney Miller*

ON GRATITUDE
Radar O'Reilly: "How can I ever thank you?"
Hawkeye Pierce: "Well, you can give us your firstborn."
B.J. Hunnicut: "And an order of fries."

—*M*A*S*H*

ON NICE GIRLS
Jack Tripper: "She's pure and wholesome and virtuous. Whatever happened to girls like that?"
Janet Wood: "They all go out with guys like you."

—*Three's Company*

Sue Ann Nivens: "Mary, what do you think turns on a man?"
Mary Richards (exasperated): "Sue Ann, I haven't the slightest idea."
Sue Ann: "I know that, dear. I was just trying to make your day."

—*The Mary Tyler
Moore Show*

ON NUCLEAR WAR
Agent 99: "Oh, Max, what a terrible weapon of destruction."
Maxwell Smart: "Yes. You know, China, Russia, and France should outlaw all nuclear weapons. We should insist upon it."
99: "What if they won't?"
Smart: "Then we may have to blast them. That's the only way to keep peace in the world."

—*Get Smart*

ON EXERCISE
"Relaxation helps you live longer. Don't exercise, it could kill you."

—Roger Addison,
Mr. Ed

Not just people: Dogs, too, are either left-handed or right-handed.

SEE EUROPE IN THE U.S.

*Tip from the B.R.I. travel director: Want to see Europe?
Why bother? As fast as you can think up places to visit
overseas, we'll find you a nicer, more sanitary, air-
conditioned domestic version as an alternative.*

THE LEANING TOWER OF PISA

May we suggest a trip to Niles, Illinois.? There, out in front of the local YMCA, is a half-scale replica, with a gift store at the bottom and an observation deck on top. And after you've taken some souvenir photos of your family holding up the Leaning Tower, why not head for a day under the Eiffel Tower? No, not the one in France. Of course, we're referring to the Eiffel Tower at the King's Island Theme Park near Cincinnati, Ohio.

THE STATUE OF DAVID

Why spend 10 billion lira for a cold-water hotel to stay to see this? It doesn't even move, and what else is there to do, once you've seen it? Wouldn't you rather see an exact replica inside Caesar's Palace in Atlantic City, N.J., at the Ringling Brothers Museum of Art in Sarasota, Fla., or in Sioux Falls, S.D., where it is dedicated to Tom Fawich, inventor of the four-door automobile? You bet you would.

THE LAST SUPPER

By all accounts the original Last Supper is peeling and dingy. No need to head to Rome—not only does America have carloads of Last Suppers to see, we've got them made out of such an ingenious variety of materials that even Leonardo himself would've been hard-pressed to match them.
• See one crafted from gourd seeds at the Gourd Museum in Angler, N.C.
• See one made of butterfly wings at the Christ Only Art Gallery, Eureka Springs, Ark.
• There are life-sized versions made of wood at Kissimmee, Florida's Woodcarving Museum, of plaster in Rhyolite, Nev., and a bas-relief in Yucca Valley, California's Desert Christ Park.

• The best one, though, is the larger-than-life stained glass Last Supper in Glendale, California's Forest Lawn Cemetery. This window comes complete with narration...and back-lighting to show the coming of evening to the Holy Land.

STONEHENGE
America has two! There's one in North Salem, N.H., but the best (in the world) is in Mary Hill, Wash. It is full-sized and complete, not just a ruined pile of dusty rocks like the original. And the parking lot is big enough for a car to do "doughnuts" in, something the fun-loving ancient Druids would've appreciated.

THE BLARNEY STONE
With all the trouble in Ireland, you'd be much better off visiting the Blarney Stones in either Shamrock, Texas, or in Irish Hills, Michigan. The latter is heartily recommended, due to its proximity to both the Michigan International Speedway and The Prehistoric Forest dinosaur park. Let 'em match that in Erin.

AFRICA
You can visit Cleopatra's Needle in New York City, Cleopatra's Barge in Las Vegas, and the Rosicrucian Egyptian Shrine in San Jose, California.

• What about actual pyramids? Well, Bedford, Indiana, tried to construct a replica out of limestone (along with a replica of the Great Wall of China) but ran out of funds. But don't pack your bags for Giza yet. Not before you visit the aptly designed Pyramid Supper Club in Beaver Dam, Wisconsin, and sample their specialty after-dinner drink, the "Yummy Mummy."

• After drinks in Wisconsin, why not travel to the Oyotunji African Village near Sheldon, S.C.? There, King Adefunmi I, Ooni of Life, will treat you to a splendid afternoon of traditional Nigerian garb and customs. And remember this: If happy exhaustion catches up with you after your long day, it won't be from a tsetse-fly bite.

GREECE
Tourist disappointment with polluted Athens is well-chronicled. But don't whine about missing history, when a trip to Nashville, Tennessee, will place you in front of a full-scale, clean version of

the Parthenon. And in Greece you can't visit Loretta Lynn's Dude Ranch and motocross attractions after your day of pointless rubble-rousing.

• If that doesn't sate your Grecian yearning, spend the weekend at the Greek Spongers' Village in Tarpon Springs, Florida.

INDIA
From the quiet rolling hills of West Virginia, suddenly there bursts forth the spectacular Hari Krishna Palace of Gold in the town of New Vrindavan. This tremendous palace recreates the mystical buildings and gardens of India—sans untouchables—in a truly fabulous manner. Now you know what gets done with all that money the Krishnas raise in airports.

• The illusion of India is not yet complete, the Krishnas say, but will be by the time they finish the adjoining Krishnaland theme park, complete with live elephants to transport guests from the Temple of Understanding to the Diety Swan Boat rides. All this is forecast to cost $50 million.

DENMARK
There are a number of "little Denmarks" in the United States, but there is none better than Solvang, Calif. Danish windmills and thatched roofs appear as one drives through the warm countryside of Southern California. Is Solvang better than Denmark? Is Denmark 30 minutes from the beautiful beaches of Santa Barbara? Does Denmark have MTV? Case closed.

SWITZERLAND
Sugarcreek, Ohio, and the surrounding towns one up this land of neutral nebbishes. If Switzerland is so proud of its cheeses, how come they don't have the world's largest cheese wheel, like they do at Heine's Place (in nearby Berlin, Ohio)? And don't believe the Swiss travel brochures if they tell you that Switzerland is the home of the world champion of Steinstossen, or stone-tossing, because he lives in Sugarcreek. (Stone-tossing is a big deal in Switzerland. Isn't that exciting?) Sugarcreek has gas stations that look like ski chalets, the world's largest cuckoo clock and, if that weren't enough, John F. Kennedy's Navy footlocker is exhibited in the town museum.

Every time Beethoven sat down to write music, he poured ice water over his head.

MORE FAMOUS CHEATERS

*The culprits here are a small-time trio of crooks
and a big-time corporation.*

CULPRITS: Clifford Irving and friends.

CIRCUMSTANCES: In 1971, billionaire Howard Hughes was the most famous recluse alive. For fifteen years he had refused to give interviews, refused to be photographed, refused even to be seen in public. So when a little-known author named Clifford Irving stepped forward as co-author of Hughes's authorized autobiography, it created a sensation. Irving had proof—letters scrawled in Hughes's own handwriting, checked and verified by the world's leading handwriting experts, attesting to the fact that the project was genuine.

Life magazine paid Irving an enormous sum for the magazine rights. "We've checked this thing out. We have proof," a Time, Inc. spokeman declared. Then McGraw-Hill gave Irving $650,000 for the right to publish the book, and the author delivered a 1050-page manuscript with Hughes's own notes in the margins.

Then the scheme fell apart. Irving had guessed that Hughes would remain aloof rather than becoming embroiled in a messy public confrontation. But he guessed wrong. In 1972 Hughes publicly disavowed the book; at the same time, Swiss authorities found out that Irving's wife, Edith, had been depositing checks made out to Hughes. Further investigation revealed that while Irving was in Mexico supposedly interviewing the rich hermit, he was actually having an affair with a German actress.

VERDICT: The Irvings and an accomplice named Dick Suskind were arrested and tried on various charges, ranging from conspiracy to breaking Swiss banking laws. They were convicted.

AFTERMATH: First of all, they had to give the money back. Then Clifford served 17 months in prison; he was paroled in 1974. Edith served 2 months in a U.S. jail and 14 in a Swiss one. Suskind served 5 months. When it was over, the Irvings got a divorce. Edith

---

More Hollywood films have been made about boxing than about any other sport.

remarried and moved to Spain. Suskind moved to Spain, too. Irving moved to Easthampton, Long Island and started writing again. In 1982 he published a moderately successful novel called *Tom Mix and Pancho Villa*.

CULPRIT: General Motors, America's auto manufacturing giant.

CIRCUMSTANCES: In the '30s, General Motors was looking for ways to expand its bus manufacturing business. So, along with Greyhound, Standard Oil, Firestone Tires, and several other corporations, they formed a company to buy municipal streetcar systems and dismantle them.

They started in 1932 with a few small urban public transportation systems—the streetcar lines in Kalamazoo, Michigan; Saginaw, Michigan; and Springfield, Ohio. When that worked, they moved on to bigger cities.

In 1936, they "engineered the conversion of New York City's stretcars to GM buses." Later, they moved on to Los Angeles.

As anti-trust lawyer Bernard Snell tells it: "In December 1944, [a company] financed by GM and Standard Oil...purchased the local system, scrapped its electric transit cars, tore down its power transmission lines, ripped up the tracks, and placed GM diesel buses fueled by Standard Oil on Los Angeles' crowded streets."

VERDICT: "In April of 1949," says *Environmental Action*, "a Chicago federal jury convicted GM of criminally conspiring with Standard Oil and Firestone to replace electric transportation with buses and to monopolize sale of buses. GM was fined $5,000."

AFTERMATH: While once there was a "vibrant public transportation" system of non-polluting electric trolleys and streetcars in America, we now have buses spewing tons of carbon monoxide into the air, doing their part to make urban air unbreathable. And, of course, General Motors has a lucrative bus business.

Footnote: The head of GM once said, "What's good for General Motors is good for America." Would he still think so? By the summer of 1989, Los Angeles—with its abnormally heavy dependence on cars—had the worst quality air in the U.S. It was so bad that L.A. was forced to adopt an emergency plan to cut down on pollution. Ironically, the measures suggested included: "Cleaner-running buses," and "cleaner fuel for all buses." Plus: "The use of electric cars will be encouraged."

A common housefly's life span is only two weeks.

FOOTBALL NAMES

*Football fans know these names by heart. But they probably don't
know how the teams got them. Here are the stories behind some
famous names; info from* Name That Team!

Los Angeles Rams. When they were founded in Cleveland in
1937, the team's owner resisted public pressure to call his
club the Indians, after the local baseball team. Instead, he
named them after a college football team—the Fordham Rams. In
1945, the Rams became the first N.F.L. franchise to switch cities
when they moved to L.A.

Cleveland Browns. When the Rams left Cleveland, a new N.F.L.
franchise took its place, and a contest was held to pick a new name.
The winner was the "Panthers" …but the owners found out there
was already a semipro Ohio football team called the Panthers—and
they stunk. So another contest was held. This time the winner was
"Brown Bombers," inspired by boxing champion Joe Louis. The
name was then shortened to "Browns," probably because the
coach's name was Paul Brown.

Houston Oilers. The owner of the team made all his money in oil,
and picked the name "for sentimental reasons."

Los Angeles Raiders. Originally located in Oakland, California,
the team was first called the "Metropolitan Oakland Area Football
Club." That was too unwieldy, so the Oakland Chamber of Com-
merce held a contest to find a new one. The winner: the "Oakland
Senors." The team's reaction: "Forget it." The owners came up with
"Raiders" on their own.

Green Bay Packers. The club was named for the Indian Packing
Company, which sponsored the team when it was formed in 1919.
Ironically, the company went out of business during the Packers'
first season. But the team was a success; they joined the N.F.L. two
years later.

New Orleans Saints. The team was admitted to the N.F.L. on November 1, 1966—which happens to be All Saints' Day. But the team probably got its name from the classic New Orleans jazz tune, "When the Saints Go Marching In."

Philadelphia Eagles. When they first began playing, in 1924, they were a pathetic club called the Frankford Yellowjackets (Frankford was the section of Philly they played in). The team went belly-up during the Depression, and two local businessmen bought it for $2500. F.D.R. had just been elected President; his two major economic programs—the New Deal and the National Recovery Act—used an eagle as their symbol. The team's new owners adopted the New Deal eagle as their symbol, too.

Phoenix Cardinals. Originally the Chicago Cardinals. They got their name when the team's owner bought a batch of second-hand jerseys from the University of Chicago. Someone commented they looked like the University's maroon shirts, and the owner replied defensively that they weren't maroon—they were "cardinal red." The name stuck.

Washington Redskins. They started out as the Duluth (Minnesota) Eskimos in 1928. In 1932, because they were having a tough time surviving, they moved to Boston. Their new home was the stadium owned by baseball's Boston Braves (now the Atlanta Braves), so they changed their name to the Boston Braves as well. But the arrangement didn't work out; the following season, the football team moved across to Fenway Park, home of the Boston Red Sox. To avoid offending the Red Sox (by keeping the name of the local rivals), the football team changed its name from Braves to Redskins. In 1938, the Redskins moved to Washington.

New York Giants. When the team was formed in 1925, they played in the Polo Grounds—home of the New York Giants baseball team. Owner Timothy Mara was a Giants fan already, so he named his team after them.

Chicago Bears, Detroit Lions, and **New York Jets.** All derived their names from local baseball teams—the Chicago Cubs, Detroit Tigers, and New York Mets.

Amazing garden: 50% of all species of flowers in the world are found in South America.

VONNEGUT SAYS...

*A few thoughts from novelist
Kurt Vonnegut, Jr.*

"What passes for culture in my head is really a bunch of commercials."

"Laughing or crying is what a human being does when there's nothing else he can do."

"It strikes me as gruesome and comical that in our culture we have an expectation that a man can always solve his problems. This is so untrue that it makes me want to laugh—or cry."

"People don't come to church for preachments, of course, but to daydream about God."

"The canary bird in the coal mine theory of the arts: Artists should be treasured as alarm systems."

"People need good lies. There are too many bad ones."

"Thinking doesn't seem to help very much. The human brain is too high-powered to have many practical uses in this particular universe."

"We are healthy only to the extent that our ideas are humane."

"Beware of the man who works hard to learn something, learns it, then finds himself no wiser than before."

"Any reviewer who expresses rage and loathing for a novel is preposterous. He or she is like a person who has put on full armor and attacked a hot fudge sundae."

"I can think of no more stirring symbol of man's humanity to man than a fire engine."

"There is no reason why good cannot triumph as often as evil. The triumph of anything is a matter of organization. If there are such things as angels, I hope they are organized along the lines of the Mafia."

"Say what you will about the sweet miracle of unquestioning faith. I consider a capacity for it terrifying."

"We are what we pretend to be."

The $ Barometer: *Citizen Kane,* considered the best movie ever made, was a box office flop.

96 TEARS

*"96 Tears" is as popular today as it was when it was first released
in 1966. Here's the story behind the song, from* Behind the Hits.

One of the all-time classic rock tunes is a simple song called
"96 Tears." The band responsible for it, Question Mark
and the Mysterians, were the embodiment of a number of
rock phenomena: They were the ultimate "garage band"; they were
living proof that anyone could be discovered and become a star;
and finally, they were the classic one-hit wonder, a band that
zoomed to the top and suddenly disappeared.

THE MYSTERY

Maybe you had to be there to appreciate this, but part of the excitement about "96 Tears" when it originally hit the airwaves in
1966 was trying to figure out who'd recorded it. They called themselves "Question Mark and the Mysterians." But who were they,
really? Why wouldn't they reveal their true identities? It gave the
deejays something to talk about when they played the record
("Friends, I have it on authority that Question Mark is actually
Bob Dylan"), and it lent a little glamour to an otherwise ordinary
garage-band tune. As a matter of fact, it's more interesting not to
know who recorded "96 Tears." Does the name Rudy Martinez
mean anything to you? That's Question Mark's real name.

BACKGROUND

The band's members were actually five young guys from Mexico
whose families had all migrated to work in Michigan's Saginaw
Valley. They took their group name from a Japanese alien-invasion
movie, and they adopted their pattern of secrecy from their lead
singer. Rudy always sported dark glasses and called himself "Question Mark." Early in the band's career, he wanted everyone else to
go incognito, too; he suggested that the group be called XYZ, and
that each member be referred to only by initials. Maybe he'd seen
too many James Bond movies.

The band played around the Saginaw area for a few years in the
mid-'60s, developing a repertoire that included an original number
called "Too Many Teardrops," a poem that Rudy had written and

set to very simple music. The rest of the group liked the tune, but not the title. They wanted to call it "69 Tears." But they decided they'd never get it onto the radio with a title like that. So they eventually began calling it "96 Tears" instead.

THEIR BIG BREAK
Like millions of other garage bands in the '60s, Question Mark and the Mysterians wanted to make a record. But no big label would talk to them, so they contacted a woman named Lilly Gonzales, who owned a little outfit in Texas called Pa-Go-Go Records. They told her they had some good songs, and she set them up with a recording session in a Bay City, Michigan, studio. (Actually, it wasn't a real studio—it was a converted living room).

They hauled their instruments—guitar, bass, drums, and Farfisa organ—to the studio, and played a few tunes. Then Pa-Go-Go pressed 500 records and sent them back to the band to distribute to deejays in the area.

The boys carried their discs around, asking jocks to listen…and surprisingly, several did. Particularly Bob Dell at WTAC in Flint and Tom Shannon at CKLW in Detroit, who played "96 Tears" regularly.

Then a funny thing happened. Executives at a national label that was almost bankrupt, Cameo Records, heard "96 Tears" on CKLW, and picked it up for distribution. They began selling it in other parts of the country. And suddenly, it took off. The song was recorded in February. By October, seven months later, it achieved the ultimate rock 'n' roll fantasy—#1 in America.

A PERFECT ENDING
The band broke up, according to lead guitarist Robert Balderrama, because its anonymous lead singer, Question Mark, "was on kind of an ego trip." Figure that one out.

IRRELEVANT ASIDE
In 1989, the Federal government financed a study on tuxedos to find out how to tax them. In a 54-page report, they revealed thought-provoking data like: "There are two major types of tuxedos—basic black tuxedos and fashion tuxedos." Their "principal findings" were that a rental tux lasts an average of 1.9 years, while the privately owned tux might last as long as 3.7 years.

John Wayne appeared in 153 movies. In all but 11 of them, he was the star.

THE ORIGIN OF FRANKENSTEIN

The original Frankenstein's monster wasn't Boris Karloff—it was (believe it or not) a character created by a 19-year-old author named Mary Shelley...more than 170 years ago.

BACKGROUND

In the summer of 1816, 19-year-old Mary Wollstonecraft Shelley and her 24-year-old husband, the poet Percy Bysshe Shelley, visited Switzerland. "It proved a wet, uncongenial summer," she wrote some 15 years later, "and incessant rain often confined us for days to the house."

To pass the time, the Shelleys and their neighbors—28-year-old Lord Byron, his 23-year-old personal physician, and his 18-year-old lover—read German ghost stories aloud. They enjoyed it so much that one day, Byron announced, "We will each write a ghost story." Everyone agreed, but apparently the poets, unaccustomed to prose writing, couldn't come up with anything very scary.

Mary was determined to do better. "I busied myself to think of a story," she recalled, "One which would speak to the mysterious fears of our nature and awaken thrilling horror." Yet she couldn't come up with anything. Every morning, her companions asked: "Have you thought of a story?" "And each morning," she wrote later, " I was forced to reply with a mortifying negative."

A FLASH OF INSPIRATION

One evening Mary sat by the fireplace, listening to her husband and Byron discuss the possibility of reanimating a corpse with electricity, giving it what they called "vital warmth."

The discussion finally ended well after midnight, and Shelley retired. But Mary, "transfixed in speculation," couldn't sleep.

"When I placed my head on the pillow," she recalled, " I did not sleep, nor could I be said to think. My imagination, unbidden, possessed and guided me, gifting the successive images that arose in my mind with a vividness far beyond the usual bounds of reverie. I saw—with shut eyes but acute mental vision—I saw the pale student of unhallowed arts kneeling beside the thing he had put together....I saw the hideous phantasm of a man stretched out, and

---

The only manmade structure you can see from outer space is the Great Wall of China.

then, on the working of some powerful engine, show signs of life and stir with an uneasy, half-vital motion.

"Frightful must it be; for supremely frightful would be the effect of any human endeavor to mock the stupendous mechanism of the Creator of the world. His success would terrify the artist; he would rush away from his odious handiwork, horror-stricken. He would hope that, left to itself, the slight spark of light which he had communicated would fade; that this thing would subside into dead matter; and he might sleep in the belief that the silence of the grave would quench forever the transient existence of the hideous corpse which he had looked upon as the cradle of life. He sleeps; but he is awakened; the horrid thing stands at his bedside, opening his curtains, and looking on him with yellow, watery eyes...."

THE PERFECT HORROR STORY

At this point, Mary opened her eyes in terror—so frightened that she needed reassurance it had all just been her imagination. She gazed around the room, but just couldn't shake the image of "my hideous phantom." Finally, to take her mind off the creature, she went back to the ghost story she'd been trying to compose all week. "If only I could contrive one," she thought, "that would frighten people as I myself had been frightened that night!" Then she realized that her vision was, in fact, the story she'd been reaching for.

As she recounted: "Swift as light and as cheering was the idea that broke in upon me. 'I have found it! What terrified me will terrify others; and I need only describe the spectre which had haunted my midnight pillow.' On the morrow I announced I had thought of a story. I began the day with the words, 'It was on a dreary night in November,' making only a transcript of the grim terrors of my waking dream."

THE NOVEL

The first version of Frankenstein was a short story. But Mary's husband encouraged her to develop it further, and she eventually turned it into a novel. It was published anonymously in 3 parts in 1818. "Mary," notes one critic, "did not think it important enough to sign her name to the book....And since her husband wrote the book's preface, people assumed he had written the rest of the book as well....It was not until a later edition of *Frankenstein* that the book was revealed as the work of a young girl."

HOW PANTYHOSE HATCHED

Today, you can find pantyhose in every supermarket, clothes store, department store, drug store, and so on. Surprisingly, they've only been around since the mid-'60s.

In the early '60s, women were still wearing traditional stockings with garter belts, as they had since 1939, when DuPont first introduced nylons.

But as the mini-skirt caught on, stockings became impossible to wear. Whenever a woman sat down, the tops of her stockings showed. It was embarrassing. But what could she do instead?

Hosiery manufacturers looked desperately for a solution to the problem. They tried all kinds of bizarre things—stocking glue (roll it onto the top of your leg, and the stocking will stick there—no garters needed), decorating the tops of the stockings (so it looked like they were meant to be seen), even girdles with stockings already attached. But the only alternative that really made sense was a new kind of sheer tights called pantyhose. And they were much more expensive than stockings. Would women pay for them?

Enter Mary Quant, the creator of the mini-skirt. She added patterns to tights and—accompanied by a huge publicity campaign—introduced them as an integral part of the mini-skirt outfit. It was not only the solution to embarrassing stocking problems, she said, but an essential element of the "mini-look." Since it was in fashion, woman gladly paid the price.

Once the market for pantyhose was established, manufacturers developed ways to cut prices. Soon, undecorated pantyhose were cheaper than traditional stockings, and—since they were more convenient—they quickly replaced the old-fashioned kind. By the early '70s, 95% of all women's hosiery sold was pantyhose.

FASHION FLOP: In the mid-'60s, Coty tried cashing in on the colored pantyhose craze by offering "Body Paint." Why bother wearing expensive pantyhose, they asked, when you can paint your legs? The "mini, kicky, bare-as-you-dare fashion" was packaged in a paint can, and came complete with a roller and paint tray. There were four colors: Blue, green, mauve, or "flesh." It bombed.

Plywood emits formaldehyde—it's one of the home's biggest indoor polluters.

BY GEORGE!

George Burns was always a popular performer. But by lasting longer than his compatriots, he's become an elder statesman, too.

"Too bad that all the people who know how to run the country are driving taxicabs and cutting hair."

"By the time you're eighty years old, you've learned everything. You only have to remember it."

"I must be getting absent-minded. Whenever I complain that things aren't what they used to be, I forget to include myself."

"The most important thing in acting is honesty. If you can fake that, you've got it made."

"I don't believe in dying—it's been done. I'm working on a new exit. Besides, I can't die now—I'm booked."

"I smoke cigars because at my age, if I don't have something to hold onto, I might fall down."

"Retirement at 65 is ridiculous. When I was 65, I still had pimples."

"Happiness? A good cigar, a good meal, a good cigar, and a good woman—or a bad woman; it depends on how much happiness you can handle."

"If you live to the age of a hundred, you've got it made, because very few people die past the age of a hundred."

"I don't worry about getting old. I'm old already. Only young people worry about getting old."

"I was married by a judge. I should have asked for a jury."

"Happiness is having a large, loving, caring, close-knit family in another city."

"Critics are eunuchs at a gang-bang."

"To be perfectly honest, I don't think acting is very hard. They say the most important thing to be able to do is laugh and cry. Well, if I have to cry I think of my sex life, and if I have to laugh, I think of my sex life."

THE THREE STOOGES

There's nothing like the sound of a good "Nyuk, nyuk, nyuk" to make a Three Stooges fan smile. Even if you don't like them, you have to be impressed by their enduring popularity.

HOW THEY STARTED. There are so many different stories about the Stooges' origin that it's hard to know which is correct. Probably none of them. Anyway, here's one that sounds good.

• There was a vaudevillian named Ted Healy, a boyhood friend of Moe and Shemp Horwitz. One night in 1922, some acrobats working for him walked out just before a show. Desperate, he asked Moe to fill in temporarily, as a favor.

• Moe, in turn, got his brother Shemp out of the audience, and the 3 of them did an impromptu routine that had the audience in stitches. Moe and Shemp loved the stage, so they changed their names from Horwitz to Howard and hit the road with their friend as Ted Healy and the Gang (or Ted Healy and his Stooges, depending on who tells the story).

• In 1925, the trio was on the lookout for another member and spotted Larry Fine (real name: Louis Feinberg) playing violin with the "Haney Sisters and Fine." Exactly why they thought he'd be a good Stooge isn't clear, since he'd never done comedy before, but he joined as the third Stooge anyway.

• They traveled the vaudeville circuit for years under a variety of names, including Ted Healy and his Racketeers, his Southern Gentlemen, his Stooges, etc. Then they wound up in a Broadway revue in 1929, which led to a movie contract.

• In 1931, Shemp quit and was replaced by his younger brother, Jerry. At the time, Jerry had a full head of hair and a handsome mustache—but Healy insisted he shave them both off...hence the nickname "Curly."

• Three years later, after a bitter dispute, the boys broke up with Healy. They quickly got a Columbia film contract on their own, and The Three Stooges were born.

• Over the next 23 years, they made 190 short films—but no features. For some reason, Harry Cohn, head of Columbia Pictures, wouldn't allow it (despite the Stooges' popularity and the fact they

---

J. Paul Getty—at one time, the richest man in the world—had a pay phone in his mansion.

were once nominated for an Oscar).
• Between the '30s and the '50s, the Stooges made four personnel changes: In 1946, Curly suffered a stroke and retired; Shemp then returned to the Stooges until his death in 1955; he, in turn, was replaced by Joe Besser (Joe) and Joe DeRita (Curly Joe).

INSIDE FACTS.

Two-Fingered Poker
One day backstage in the '30s, Larry, Shemp and Moe were playing cards. Shemp accused Larry of cheating. After a heated argument, Shemp reached over and stuck his fingers in Larry's eyes. Moe, watching, thought it was hilarious...and that's how his famous poke-in-the eyes routine was born.

Profitable Experience
By the mid-'50s, the average budget for a Three Stooges' episode—including the stars' salaries—was about $16,000. Depending on the time slot, Columbia Pictures can now earn more than that with one showing of the same film...in one city.

So What If He's Dead?
The last four Stooges episodes featuring Shemp were filmed after he died. The films' producer, Jules White, brought in a Shemp "double" who was only seen from behind.

The Stooges' Resurrection
By the mid-'50s the demand for short films had petered out. So in 1957, Columbia unceremoniously announced they weren't renewing the Stooges' contracts. Moe and Larry were devastated. After 23 years, what else could they do? Moe was rich from real estate investments, but Larry was broke—which made it even harder. They decided to get a third Stooge (Curly and Shemp were dead) and go back on tour. Joe DeRita, "Curly Joe," was selected. They started making appearances in 3rd-rate clubs, just to have work.

Meanwhile, Columbia, looking for a way to get a few bucks out of its old Stooge films, released them to TV at bargain prices. They had no expectations, so everyone (particularly Moe and Larry) was shocked when, in 1959, the Stooges emerged as the hottest kids' program in America. Suddenly the Stooges had offers to make big-time personal appearances and new films. And they've been modern American cult heroes ever since.

A BIZARRE GENIUS

Great geniuses are often said to be "born ahead of their time."
William James Sidis, on the other hand, seems to have been born
out of his time completely; on the wrong world, in the wrong
dimension. Perhaps someday the world will understand
Sidis's strange genius. Probably not.

William James Sidis was born in 1898. His father, Boris Sidis, taught psychology at Harvard and was considered one of the foremost psychologists of his day. Boris argued that traditional approaches to childrearing obstructed the learning process. The elder Sidis was determined not to make that mistake with his son.

• He started by stringing words together with alphabet blocks above the child's crib.

• He eschewed the usual "googley-goo" babytalk that adults lapse into around infants, speaking instead to the child the same way he would speak to an adult. If the boy showed any interest in a subject, Boris encouraged his curiosity and study.

The effect of all this on the boy was astounding. By the time he was two, Willie was reading literature meant for adults; by age four he was typing letters in French and English; at age five he wrote a treatise on anatomy and dazzled everyone with a mathematical expertise few adults could match.

HIGHER EDUCATION
William Sidis graduated from Brookline High School when he was eight years old. When he applied to Harvard, the entrance board suggested he take a few years off to let his personality catch up to his intellect.

• Willie spent the time between high school and college reading books in French, German, Latin, Greek, Russian, Turkish, and Armenian.

• The boy entered Harvard at age eleven, becoming the youngest student ever to attend the school.

• Later that year, he gave a speech in front of the Harvard Mathematical Society on the subject of "Four-Dimensional Bodies." After the speech, Professor Daniel Comstock of MIT told reporters that

---

The first baseball team to put numbers on their uniforms: the N.Y. Yankees, in 1929.

the boy would someday be the greatest mathematician of the century.

DOWNHILL
From that moment on, William Sidis's world was never the same. Reporters followed his every move. He was a celebrity. His classmates treated him differently.

• The boy kept to himself, walking to his classes alone.

• At some point, Sidis realized his intellect was not admired—it was stared at. He wasn't merely intelligent—he was a freak.

• Within a year, at age 12, he suffered a nervous breakdown. He was taken to his father's Psycho-therapeutic Institute and treated.

• A few months later, Willie was back at Harvard, studying as diligently as ever. He graduated cum laude at the age of sixteen.

• In 1918, he began teaching mathematics at Rice University in Texas. But the annoyance of constant media attention finally took its toll. Quitting his teaching post, the young man moved back to Boston and, after a notorious arrest at a socialist march, disappeared from sight.

• In 1924, a reporter found him in New York City, working in a Wall Street office for menial pay. Sidis told the reporter that he was not the boy-wonder he once was. (Although this was probably not true. At one point, Sidis's knowledge of mathematics led him to completely rework his employer's statistical tables in his spare time, for amusement.) He wanted anonymity and a menial job that made no demands on him. Soon afterwards, he dropped out of sight again.

A STRANGE OBSESSION
• As an adult, Sidis had one great passion, a passion that has intrigued psychologists and writers for years. Sidis spent hours every day in search of streetcar transfers. He would chase them through windy lots, chisel them from icy sidewalks, and rescue them from rainy gutters. During his lifetime, he collected over two thousand of them, all different.

• In 1926, he published a book on the subject of his hobby. The book, *Notes on the Collection of Transfers*, is—to say the least—esoteric. Sidis filled it with page after page of detailed information on how the transfers are interpreted, how to use them to their best advantage, and techniques used by the devoted "peridromophile" (his term for someone who collects streetcar transfers) to find abandoned transfers.

- For those with merely a passing interest in the subject, he provided a chapter of bad streetcar jokes.

- Sidis used the pseudonym "Frank Folupa" to throw the press off the track, but it did not work. The book was quickly ascribed to him and once again, Sidis had to flee from the curious eyes of the press, losing himself in the crowded streets of New York City.

- Sidis managed to stay out of view for many years after that. In 1937, a writer working for *The New Yorker* magazine found him in a rundown rooming house in South Boston.

- Sidis told the reporter that he was no longer a mathematical genius. "The very sight of a mathematical formula," he claimed, "makes me physically ill." When the *New Yorker* article appeared, Sidis sued for invasion of privacy. Acting as his own attorney, Sidis offered to take an I.Q. test to prove just how normal he was. The suit was thrown out of court.

- Again the world forgot about him—until 1944, when, at the age of 46, William James Sidis died of a cerebral hemorrhage.

No one can explain his life. But one thing is certain: he knew more about streetcar transfers than anyone in history. And for this, we salute him.

ANOTHER "UNUSUAL" COLLECTOR

George Wahlert, of New York, has what he believes to be the world's largest collection of Apollo 11 memorabilia. He hasn't got any moon rocks or lunar modules yet, but he does have stamps, plates, mugs, cups, plaques, medals, flags, towels, curtains, T-shirts, hats, pencils, spoons, watches, clocks, models, lunchboxes...and even a bedspread—all commemorating the first flight to the moon.

How did George become hooked on the subject? Apollo 11 landed on the moon on his birthday.

Now he has enough stuff to fill a museum.

Would he like to go to the moon someday? He already has his Pan Am ticket.

He even bought two acres of moon land, and has a moon deed to prove it. "There's probably a lunar rover parked on my property right now," he says.

When they grow up: 1 in 100 American boys, and 1 in 150 girls, will become lawyers.

MACK THE KNIFE

A classic tune with a classy history. From Behind the Hits,
by Bob Shannon and John Javna.

Bobby Darin's version of "Mack the Knife" was the #1 song of 1959. But few people who enjoyed it then—or have since—had any idea of its strange 30-year history.

THE SHARK BITES...
"Mack" debuted in Germany in 1929, in the Kurt Weill / Bertolt Brecht production of the *Threepenny Opera*, a scathing social commentary with parallels to the rise of Adolf Hitler. It was then known as "The Ballad of Mac the Knife" and was a song about MacHeath, the central character of the play. It was quite candid about Mac's bloody escapades.

The Nazis didn't particularly like Weill; he, Brecht, and Weill's wife, Lotte Lenya—who had created the role of Jenny in the original play—fled to the United States.

NEVER A TRACE OF RED
But it wasn't until the early '50s that the *Threepenny Opera* was performed here—and when it was, "The Ballad of Mac the Knife" became a very different song. In the conservative atmosphere of the times, the German lyrics were considered too violent to be translated literally. So an American named Marc Blitzstein was assigned to rewrite it.

MACKIE'S BACK
By 1956, millions of Americans had heard the melody of "Mac the Knife"...but they still hadn't heard either the German *or* American version of the lyrics—because the Dick Hyman Trio had recorded it as an instrumental. Hyman called it "Moritat," and it sold over a million copies.

Around that time, Louis Armstrong also recorded it, using Blitzstein's lyrics. But when Satchmo sang the song, he made a mistake in the list of characters near the end; he added singer/actress Lotte Lenya's name to the roll-call of ladies who'd succumbed to "Mackie." It was this version that got to Bobby Darin.

According to polls, America's all-time favorite foreign movie star is Brigitte Bardot.

DARIN'S "MACK" ATTACK

An up-and-coming rock 'n' roll singer who had already scored with "Splish Splash," "Queen of the Hop," and "Dream Lover," Darin was hesitant about "Mack the Knife." He recorded it as part of an album called "That's All," but never envisioned it as a single. His friend Dick Clark agreed, telling Darin that it could never be a hit—it was too different. Besides, about twenty different versions of the song had already been recorded in 1956.

But Darin didn't have the last word on the subject. His record label, Atco, decided to release it as a single over his objections. To his surprise, "Mack the Knife" rocketed up the charts immediately. It was not only the most popular record of the year—selling over two million copies—but also won the Grammy for "Record of the Year." Darin was named "Best New Artist," although he'd been around the Top 10 for a while, and the song transformed him into a Frank Sinatra-type entertainer.

MACKIE'S BACK...AGAIN

In all, between 1956 and 1960 "Mack the Knife" appeared in the Top 40 seven times. The most memorable of these was the last one, by Ella Fitzgerald. Her version—a tribute to Satchmo and Darin—was recorded live at a concert in Berlin, and she forgot the words. It wasn't a problem, though. Ella is one of the all-time great improvisers, and the Germans had no idea what the English meant. She just made up the lyrics, which was all anyone had been doing since the original English translation anyway.

• **Final note:** The song keeps going and changing. In the late '80s, Frank Sinatra attempted a version of "Mack the Knife." He didn't start with Weill's, or Armstrong's or Darin's version, though—instead, he copied Ella's.

ABOUT BOBBY DARIN:

• His real name was Walden Robert Cassotto.
• He picked the named "Darin" out of a phone book.
• While he was a scuffling young singer, he and Connie Francis fell in love. Her father chased him away. She never got over it; Darin went on to marry teenage heartthrob Sandra Dee.
• Darin's first big hit, "Splish Splash," was written by the mother of a popular New York deejay, Murray the K.
• His congenitally weak heart gave out in 1973; he died at age 37.

The oldest tree in the world is the macrozamia tree of Australia. It lives for 7,000 years.

BODY PARTS

Some interesting facts about the human body.

How much blood is running through your body right now? If you're an average person, about 6 quarts.

☞

If you've got a normal head of hair, you have about 100,000 hairs on it.

• But if you're a redhead, you've probably got only about 90,000. For some reason, redheads have less hair than other people.

• Blondes, on the other hand, have more hair on their heads.

☞

Your brain weighs 3 pounds. It contains 14 billion cells.

☞

A human hair grows at an average rate of 8 inches a year.

☞

At birth, an infant has 350 bones.

• As the child grows, many bones fuse with other bones.

• So by the time the child is grown, his or her body contains only 206 bones (give or take a few—not every bone does what it's supposed to).

☞

Your heart will probably beat 36 million times this year.

Your eye measures about an inch in diameter.

• It weighs around a quarter of an ounce.

• If you're a man, your eyes are slightly bigger than the average woman's.

☞

If your sense of smell isn't working, you can't taste an onion.

☞

The normal adult has 656 muscles.

• 42% of an average male's body weight is muscle.

• 38% of an average female's body weight is muscle.

☞

As an infant grows, the body part that grows least is the eye. While the rest of an adult body is 20 times bigger than it was at birth, the eye is only 3-1/4 times bigger.

☞

The average adult gets 7-1/2 hours of sleep every night.

• As we age, we need less sleep—until we hit our 60s, when the need starts to increase again.

LILY TOMLIN SAYS...

Comments from a great comedienne.

"No matter how cynical you get, it's impossible to keep up."

"There will be sex after death; we just won't be able to feel it."

"The trouble with the rat race is that even if you win, you're still a rat."

"For fast acting relief, try slowing down."

"If truth is beauty, how come no one has their hair done in the library?"

"Why is it when we talk to God, we're said to be praying—but when God talks to us, we're schizophrenic?"

"If you read a lot of books, you're considered well-read. But if you watch a lot of TV, you're not considered well-viewed."

"The best mind-altering drug is truth."

"If something's true, you don't have to believe in it."

"You are what you think.... Geez, that's frightening."

"Sometimes I worry about being a success in a mediocre world."

"I had a friend who was getting married. I gave her a subscription to *Modern Bride*. The subscription lasted longer than the marriage."

"If love is the answer, could you rephrase the question?"

"What most distinguishes us humans from lower animals is our desire to take drugs."

"Sometimes I feel like a figment of my own imagination."

"We're all in this alone."

"What goes up must come down...but don't expect it to land where you can find it—Murphy's Law applied to Newton's."

"Our ability to delude ourselves may be an important survival tool."

"LET'S DO THE TWIST"

Looking back 30 years, past slam-dancing and Flashdancing and Dirty Dancing, it's hard to believe how significant—and scandalous—the tame Twist was when it first appeared. It's considered nostalgic fun today, but it was a powerful force in its time. It helped change American society in the '60s, and its impact is still being felt. Here's a quick retrospective.

ITS ORIGIN

Everyone knows that "Mr. Twister" is Chubby Checker. "You know," he said, "I taught the world how to dance as they know it today. I'm almost like Einstein creating atomic power. Whatever dances came after the Twist, it all started here."

But "The Twist" was not originally done by Chubby Checker. The original version was written and recorded by a rhythm and blues performer named Hank Ballard.

• In the '50s, Ballard was a popular R&B singer who toured with his band, the Midnighters. The band often danced while they played, and one night . . . . "I was just watching them go through their routines, seeing them twisting their bodies," Ballard recalls, "and the lyric just came to me—'Twist.' " He wrote the rest of the lyrics to go along with their movements, taking the melody from an old R&B song, "What'cha Gonna Do."

• In 1959 he recorded the song and it was released as the flip side of "Teardrops on My Letter." He thought it should be the hit side, but couldn't convince his record company. "They thought it was just another mediocre record," he sighs.

• Ballard and his group tried to popularize the dance as they toured the country, and when they got to Baltimore it finally caught on. There, a deejay named Buddy Dean (who hosted a TV dance party) watched Baltimore teenagers Twisting up a storm. "He saw these kids doing the dance," says Ballard, "so he called up Dick Clark and told him to come over and see them."

• Clark, hosting "American Bandstand" in nearby Philadelphia, liked what he saw. He played the song on his show, and was impressed by the audience response, so he offered Ballard a chance to introduce the dance on "Bandstand." It would have been Ballard's big break, but it fell through. Instead, Clark got someone to do a new version. "He was trying to find someone to emulate my voice," Ballard says.

ENTER CHUBBY CHECKER

Clark found just the right person—Ernest Evans, an expert at mimicking other singers. Ernest changed his name to Chubby Checker at the suggestion of Clark's wife ("He looks just like a little Fats Domino—let's call him Chubby Checker"), and the new version of "The Twist" was released.

• Chubby copied Ballard's version exactly—it's almost impossible to tell the difference between them.

• With Dick Clark pushing it, Checker's record became a #1 smash in 1960, and the dance became a teenage craze. Then, like all fads, it died down.

• In 1962, however, adults discovered it. Society celebs like Zsa Zsa Gabor were photographed twisting at the Peppermint Lounge . . .and suddenly the dance was bigger than ever. Chubby's version of "The Twist" zoomed back up the charts to #1 again. It is still the only record ever to reach #1 in two different years. It was on the charts for 8 months, longer than any other #1 record in history.

• Twist records were released by the carload. Joey Dee and the Starliters hit #1 with "The Peppermint Twist"; young Rod McKuen sang "Oliver Twist"; Ray Charles put out a Twist album; Chubby did "Let's Twist Again"; Sam Cooke did "Twistin' the Night Away"; even Frank Sinatra got into the act. Everyone in America, it seemed, was doing the Twist. Except Hank Ballard.

AS A DANCE

The "Twist" made social dancing accessible to everyone; it was the first dance that anybody—young or old, athletic or uncoordinated, etc.—could do. There was nothing special to learn, no need to take lessons, and no need to practice. Instructions for the Twist could be summed up in one sentence. "It's like putting out a cigarette with both feet," explained Chubby Checker, "and coming out of a shower and wiping your bottom with a towel to the beat of the music. It's that simple."

• It was the first modern dance that people did without touching each other. Practically every popular dance since 1960 (except

A monkey was once tried and convicted for smoking a cigarette in South Bend, Indiana.

disco) is a direct outgrowth of the Twist.

• And finally, after howling about the immorality of rock 'n' roll in the late '50s, parents gave up their protests in 1962 and joined in . . .doing the Twist. It was the first time adults accepted rock. Until then, it was associated with juvenile delinquency.

AS A MERCHANDISING BOOM

While the Twist was *the* popular dance, Twist merchandise sold like hot cakes. You could get "twist" anything.

• Clothes became "Twist clothes" if you put fringes on them (fringes would fly out when you twisted);

• A "Twister chair" was so twisted that you couldn't sit on it;

• "Twist cigars" (bent stogies) were available;

• You could even eat a misshapen hot dog called a "Twistfurter." "The Twist has now danced its way onto the dinner table," announced its manufacturer.

AS A SCANDAL. Some examples of the international furor caused by the Twist:

1961: The Associated Press reported a scandalous scoop. "Under a secret service guard," AP claimed, "Mrs. Jacqueline Kennedy slipped out of Palm Beach last night and for an hour and a half danced the Twist in a Fort Lauderdale nightclub." AP turned out to be wrong—Jackie was home all night. AP had to publish a public apology. . .its first since it announced the end of World War II prematurely.

1962: Tampa, Florida, banned the Twist in its community centers.

1962: The United Arab Republic banned the Twist.

1962: Red Chinese newspapers castigated "ugly displays" of young people doing the Twist in Maoming Cultural Park in China.

1962: The Twist was banned by the Buffalo, New York, diocese in parish, school, and Catholic Youth Organization events.

1962: The South African foreign minister deplored the fact that South African youth were doing the Twist, calling it a "strange god from the United States."

1963: The Twist was East Germany's most popular dance, despite the fact that the Communist Party had denounced it.

1963: The South Vietnamese government said the Twist "was not compatible with the anti-Communist struggle," and banned it.

There have been 69 movies featuring the character Zorro.

MUHAMMAD ALI SPEAKS

The great boxer was also known as a talker.
A few of his comments:

"Pleasure is not happiness. It has no more importance than a shadow following a man."

"Everybody's negotiable."

"I'm so fast I could hit you before God gets the news."

"When you're as great as I am, it's hard to be humble."

"A nation is only as good as its women."

"My toughest fight was with my first wife."

[Explaining his retirement] "There are more pleasant things to do than beat up people."

"I'll beat him so bad he'll need a shoehorn to put his hat on."

"There are no pleasures in a fight, but some of my fights have been a pleasure to win."

"It's just a job. Grass grows. Birds fly. Waves pound the sand. I beat people up."

"I'm not only the greatest, I'm the double greatest."

"When you can whip any man in the world, you never know peace."

"No one knows what to say in the loser's room."

"Wars on nations change maps. Wars on poverty map change."

"The man who views the world at 50 the same as he did at 20 has wasted 30 years of his life."

"I fear Allah, thunderstorms, and airplane rides."

"I'm one black man who got loose."

"Christianity is a good philosophy if you live it, but it's controlled by white people who preach it but don't practice it. They just organize it and use it any which way they want to."

"I just *said* I was the greatest—I never thought I was."

At one time, Hawaiian women were forbidden by law to eat coconuts.

AMERICA'S NOSTRADAMUS

*If you read the National Enquirer at the checkout counter of
your local supermarket, you've seen that people like Jeanne Dixon
are always trying to predict the future. They rarely get it right, of
course. But in 1900 John Watkins did. In an article written for
The Ladies' Home Journal, he looked a century into the future
and foresaw subways, air-conditioning, Satellite TV, and lots
more. No one has ever come close to this prognosticating feat—
except maybe Nostradamus. Here's a small excerpt
from Watkins' amazing 1900 article.*

BACKGROUND. John Elspeth Watkins was a Philadelphia newspaperman whose predictions were recently redis-
covered by two Indiana professors. They call him "The
Seer of the Century," and note that he was lucky enough to see
many of his predictions come true before dying in the '40s.

What's amazing about these predictions? Remember what was
going on in 1900: Production on primitive autos had just begun;
they were still just a novelty. People lived in squalor and ill health,
and died young. There was no such thing as an airplane. There was
no radio; the first feature movie hadn't yet been made; the telephone had been invented a scant 25 years earlier. It was a whole
different world—yet somehow, Watkins described ours in detail.

"These prophecies," he wrote in his introduction, "will seem
strange, almost impossible."

It's a fascinating measure of how things have changed to realize
that our way of life seemed like science fiction to the average
American of 1900.

EXCERPTS FROM WATKINS' PREDICTIONS

"Man Will See Around the World. Persons and things of all
kinds will be brought within focus of cameras connected electrical-
ly with screens at opposite ends of circuits, thousands of miles at a
span. American audiences in their theatres will view upon huge
curtains before them the coronations of kings in Europe or the
progress of battles in the Orient. The instrument bringing these
distant scenes to the very doors of people will be connected with a
giant telephone apparatus transmitting each incidental sound into

---

For every hour you listen to the radio, you hear approximately 11,000 spoken words.

its appropriate place. Thus the guns of a distant battle will be heard to boom when seen to blaze, and thus the lips of a remote actor or singer will be heard to utter words or music when seen to move."

"The American Will Be Taller by from one to two inches. His increase in stature will result from better health, due to vast reforms in medicine, sanitation, food, and athletics. He will live fifty years instead of thirty-five as at present—for he will reside in the suburbs."

"Hot and Cold Air from Spigots. Hot or cold air will be turned on from spigots to regulate the temperature of a house as we now turn on hot or cold water from spigots to regulate the temperature of the bath....Rising early to build the furnace fire will be a task of the olden times. Homes will have no chimneys, because no smoke will be created within their walls."

"No Mosquitoes nor Flies. Boards of health will have destroyed all mosquito haunts and breeding grounds, drained all stagnant pools, filled in all swamp-lands, and chemically treated all still-water streams. The extermination of the horse and its stable will reduce the house-fly."

"Ready-Cooked Meals Will Be Bought from establishments similar to our bakeries of today. Such wholesale cookery will be done in electric laboratories...equipped with electric stoves, and all sorts of electric devices, such as coffee-grinders, egg-beaters, stirrers, shakers, parers, meat-choppers, meat-saws, potato-mashers, lemon-squeezers, dishwashers, dish-dryers and the like. All such utensils will be washed in chemicals fatal to disease microbes."

"There will Be No Street Cars in Our Large Cities. All traffic will be below or high above ground when brought within city limits. In most cities it will be confined to broad subways or tunnels, well lighted and well ventilated, or to high trestles with "moving-sidewalk" stairways leading to the top. These underground or overhead streets will teem with automobile passenger coaches and freight wagons, with cushioned wheels. Subways or trestles will be reserved for express trains. Cities, therefore, will be

The Boy Scouts were founded in 1910.

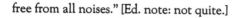

free from all noises." [Ed. note: not quite.]

"Photographs Will Be Telegraphed from any distance. If there be a battle in China a hundred years hence snapshots of its most striking events will be published in the newspapers an hour later. Even today photographs are being telegraphed over short distances. Photographs will reproduce all of Nature's colors."

"Automobiles Will Be Cheaper Than Horses are today. Farmers will own automobile hay-wagons, plows, harrows, and hay-rakes. A one-pound motor in one of these vehicles will do the work of a pair of horses or more....Automobiles will have been substituted for every horse vehicle now known....The horse in harness will be as scarce, if, indeed, not scarcer, then as the yoked ox is today."

"Everybody Will Walk Ten Miles. Gymnastics will begin in the nursery, where toys and games will be designed to strengthen the muscles. Exercise will be compulsory in the schools. Every school, college, and community will have a complete gymnasium....A man or woman unable to walk ten miles at a stretch will be regarded as a weakling."

"There Will Be No Wild Animals except in menageries. Rats and mice will have been exterminated. The horse will have become practically extinct....The automobile will have driven out the horse. Cattle and sheep will have no horns. They will be unable to run faster than the fattened hog of to-day. Food animals will be bred to expend practically all of their life energy in producing meat, milk, wool, and other by-products. Horns, bones, muscles and lungs will have been neglected."

"Submarine boats submerged for days will be capable of wiping a whole navy off the face of the deep. "

"To England in Two Days. Fast electric ships, crossing the ocean at more than a mile a minute, will go from New York to Liverpool in two days. The bodies of these ships will be built above the waves. They will be supported upon runners, somewhat like those of the sleigh. These runners will be very buoyant. Upon their undersides will be apertures expelling jets of air. In this way a film of

---

Until 1857, foreign coins were considered U.S. money if they were made of a precious metal.

air will be kept between them and the water's surface. This film, together with the small surface of the runners, will reduce friction against the waves to the smallest possible degree." [Ed. note: Wow! He's predicting hydrofoils.]

"Telephones Around the World. Wireless telephone and telegraph circuits will span the world. A husband in the middle of the Atlantic will be able to converse with his wife sitting in her boudoir in Chicago. We will be able to telephone to China quite as readily as we now talk from New York to Brooklyn. By an automatic signal they will connect with any circuit in their locality without the intervention of a 'hello girl.' "

"Automatic instruments reproducing original airs exactly will bring the best music to the families of the untalented. In great cities there will be public opera-houses whose singers and musicians are paid from funds endowed by philanthropists and by the government. The piano will be capable of changing its tone from cheerful to sad. Many devices will add to the emotional effect of music."

"How Children Will Be Taught. A university education will be free to every man and woman. Several great national universities will have been established. Children will study a simple English grammar adapted to simplified English, and not copied after the Latin. Time will be saved by grouping like studies...Medical inspectors regularly visiting the public schools will furnish poor children free eyeglasses, free dentistry, and free medical attention of every kind. The very poor will, when necessary, get free rides to and from school and free lunches between sessions." [Ed. note: An incredible, revolutionary concept in 1900.]

"Oranges...in Philadelphia. Fast-flying refrigerators on land and sea will bring delicious fruits from the tropics and southern temperate zone within a few days. The farmer of South America, South Africa, Australia, and the South Sea Islands, whose seasons are directly opposite to ours, will thus supply us in winter with fresh summer foods which cannot be grown here. Scientists will have discovered how to raise here many fruits now confined to much hotter or colder climates."

All the Zodiac symbols are animals, except one—Libra.

LEAVE IT TO BEAVER

*The Cleavers and their clan are classic TV creations—from June,
who wore pearls while she vacuumed…to the rotten Eddie Has-
kell…to Beaver Cleaver, the quintessential '50s innocent.*

HOW IT STARTED.
By 1957, shows like "The Danny Thomas Show" and "Father Knows Best"—sitcoms that portrayed modern American family life from an adult point of view—were hits. But Bob
Mosher and Joe Connelly, who'd written together since 1942 (their
major credit was over 1500 "Amos 'n' Andy" TV and radio scripts)
came up with a new twist—a family sitcom that centered on the
kids, not the parents. They called the program "Wally and Beaver"
and modelled the characters after their own children. The stories
they proposed were based on real-life occurrences in their own
households.

When the pilot was filmed in 1957, it featured a slightly differ-
ent cast than the one America eventually came to know: Barbara
Billingsley (June) and Jerry Mathers (Beaver) were in it, but Hugh
Beaumont (Ward Cleaver) and Tony Dow (Wally) were not.

CBS liked it anyway, and bought it for the 1957-58 season.
Beaumont and Dow were hired to join the permanent cast, and
production began.

However, the producers made one last change—they gave their
show a new title. "Wally and the Beaver" didn't work, they said,
because "it sounded like a show about a boy and his pet." Instead,
they appropriated the title of a 1954 sitcom, "Leave It to Larry,"
and altered it slightly.

"Beaver" ran from 1957 to 1963. Surprsingly, though, it was
never a huge hit. In its six seasons on the air, it didn't place among
the Top 25 shows of a year even once.

INSIDE FACTS
Meet the Beave
At age 8, Jerry "Beaver" Mathers was already a professional actor,
with TV appearances and a major film role (in Alfred Hitchcock's
The Trouble With Harry) under his belt. But he was so fidgety when
he was auditioning for the role of Beaver that the producers asked

---

World's record: A New York man carried a milk bottle on his head continuously for 24 miles.

him what the trouble was. He blurted out: "I gotta go to my scout meeting." Rather than disqualifying him, that won Jerry the job. His honesty and "little boy" qualities were exactly what they were looking for in their main character.

Big Boys Don't Cry

After the pilot, "Beaver's" producers began searching for a new actor to play Ward. One day, Jerry Mathers was called in to read with Hugh Beaumont, who'd befriended him when they co-starred in a religious film. In one scene, tears had been required, but Jerry just couldn't do it. Beaumont gave the boy invaluable advice: "Cover your face with your hands and laugh—it'll sound the same." It worked. So now, here was the man who'd been so kind to him, reading for the part of his father. When Jerry got home that night, he prayed Beaumont would get the part of Ward. And he did.

Those Pearls

June Cleaver caused a nation of TV-viewing kids to wonder why their moms didn't wear pearls while doing the laundry, too. The secret: Barbara Billingsley wore them in each episode not for aesthetics or even character development, but because the ex-model had a very skinny neck.

But Don't Flush It!

The first "Beaver" episode ever filmed, "Captain Jack," wasn't the first one aired—because it was censored! It included scenes of Wally and Beaver keeping a pet alligator in their toilet tank, and showing a toilet on camera was against CBS policy. It was finally shown as the 4th episode.

Monstrous Copy

After "Beaver," Mosher and Connelly created another family sitcom—"The Munsters"! Oddly enough, several "Munsters" episodes re-worked Beaver plots, with child werewolf Eddie Munster filling in for the Beave.

Historic Coincidence

Two events make Oct. 4, 1957 a historic date to remember: on that day, both "Leave It to Beaver" and Russia's first satellite, Sputnik 1, were launched.

THE GREAT ROCKEFELLER

John D. Rockefeller, one of the most famous Americans who ever lived, is a hero to some, a villain to others. Here are some facts about his life that you may not have heard before, excerpted from Everybody's Business.

HIS PARENTS

"Rockefeller, born in 1839, seems to have inherited his character in equal portions from his con artist father and his stern, Calvinist mother."

The Father: "William Avery Rockefeller, was a tall, effusive, barrel-chested man who amassed great sums of money first by flimflamming the Iroquois Indians near his home in upstate New York and later by selling patent medicines, including an elixir he claimed could cure cancer."

• "He gave medical consultations to the gullible country folk for $25—a good two months' wages."

• "In 1849 he was indicted for the rape of a young woman who had worked in the Rockefeller household...."

• "He moved his family to Cleveland in 1853 so that he could take advantage of the settlers streaming west in covered wagons with their life savings."

• "He often went away for long periods, and finally he disappeared altogether. Years later, a reporter working for Joseph Pulitzer discovered that the elder Rockefeller survived to the age of 96 and spent his last 40 years living under an assumed name in South Dakota in a bigamous marriage with a woman 20 years his junior."

The Mother: "The task of setting the children on the path of righteousness fell to the mother, Eliza Davison Rockefeller, described as a 'thin, hatchet-faced woman with flaming red hair and equally stark blue eyes.' "

• "A devout Baptist, she studied the Bible and filled young John with maxims he carried through life, such as 'Willful waste makes woeful want.' "

ROCKEFELLER GOES INTO BUSINESS

"Upon graduating from high school in 1855, Rockefeller chose to

---

Speed demon: A squid can swim up to 35 miles per hour.

go into business rather than to college."

• "He got a job as a bookkeeper with a Cleveland commodity merchant for $3.50 a week—10% of which he faithfully donated to the Baptist church."

• "After three years he had saved $800 and he decided to start his own commodity business with a partner, Maurice Clark."

• "Needing another $1,000, he turned to his father, who had promised each of his children that amount when they turned 21. John was only 19-1/2, but his father agreed to lend him the money at 10% interest until he came of age. 'I cheat my boys every chance get,' the father liked to say. 'I want to make 'em sharp.' "

ROCKEFELLER DISCOVERS OIL

"Commodity prices rose sharply during the Civil War, and the new firm of Clark & Rockefeller made impressive profits. But a development even more far-reaching than the war was emerging around Titusville, Pennsylvania, where Edwin Drake had drilled the world's first successful oil well in 1859."

• "Oil was established as the cheapest, most efficient of illuminants, and...quickly started to replace candles and whale oil. The 'oil regions' sprouted derricks overnight, and dozens of refineries sprang up, first in Pittsburgh and New York and then...Cleveland."

• "In 1863 an acquaintance of Clark came to the partners with a proposition to start a refinery. Rockefeller dipped into his savings and invested $4,000 as a silent partner. At first he saw it as an unimportant sideline, but as the oil boom continued he began to devote more of his attention to it. In 1865, at the age of 26, he bought out the others and took control of the business."

• "His refinery was already the largest in Cleveland, and he was determined to expand. Around this time a startled bystander happened to see Rockefeller in his office, jumping into the air, clicking his heels, and rejoicing to himself, 'I'm bound to be rich! Bound to be rich! Bound to be rich!' "

ROCKFELLER DESTROYS HIS COMPETITION

"Rockefeller now set out to control the oil industry. He realized that the big money in oil would not be made at the well, since prices collapsed every time someone struck a new find."

• "The key to his success, Rockefeller saw, was to control the refining and transportation of oil. Borrowing heavily from Cleveland banks, he expanded his refining capacity and leased all the available tank cars from the railroads, leaving his competitors with no way to ship their oil out of Cleveland."

• "Next he negotiated an agreement with the Lake Shore Railroad to give him secret rebates on the crude oil he shipped from the oil regions to Cleveland and the refined oil he sent from Cleveland to the East Coast....With his freight advantage secure, Rockefeller formed a new company in 1870, called Standard Oil."

• "In the same year several railroads came up with a new plan: they would secretly combine with the largest refiners in each major refining center, to the benefit of both parties. Freight rates would go up, but the refiners in the scheme would get their money back through rebates on their shipments and additional 'drawbacks' on the shipments of other refiners who were not in on the arrangement. Rockefeller saw it as a way to get rid of his bothersome competitors in Cleveland: they could either collapse their businesses into his, in exchange for stock, or they would be bankrupted by the rebate scheme."

BROTHERLY LOVE

"Rockefeller's younger brother, Frank, was a partner in a firm competing with Standard Oil. John D. told him: 'We have a combination with the railroads. We are going to buy out all the refiners in Cleveland. We will give everyone a chance to come in....Those who refuse will be crushed. If you don't sell your property to us, it will be valueless.' Frank did not sell, and he went bankrupt. He remained bitter for the rest of his life and eventually moved his two children's bodies from the family burial plot in Cleveland so they would not have to spend eternity in the company of John D. Rockefeller."

GOOD MR. ROCKEFELLER

"Rockefeller looked back on this period with great piety. 'The Standard was an angel of mercy,' John D. told a biographer late in life. It was a situation, he explained, of 'the strongest and most prosperous concern in the business...turning to its less fortunate competitors...and saying to them, "We will stand in for the risks and hazards of the refining business....Come with us, and we will do you good." ' "

Men live longest in Japan (79.7 years). 2nd place: Norway (79.4 years).

ROCKEFELLER WANTS IT ALL

"Within three months, Rockefeller bought up all but 3 of his 25 competitors in Cleveland. Standard Oil controlled one-quarter of the nation's refining capacity, but he was not satisfied. "

• "Rockefeller raised his sights and convinced more independent refiners in New York, Philadelphia, Pittsburgh, and the oil regions to come into the Standard combine. He did it with such secrecy that almost no one knew about his oil monopoly until it was a fait accompli."

• "By 1880 Rockefeller was refining 95% of the nation's oil."

• "At the time, American companies were prohibited from owning shares in other companies in other states. To get around this restriction, Rockefeller devised an 'oil trust,' which owned shares in each of the component companies—pretending all the while that the companies were independent."

• "He lavished bribes and 'deals' on state legislators."

• "He drove his competitors out of business by undercutting their prices until they gave up, and he expanded his power by buying oil-fields across the country."

CHANGING HIS IMAGE

Rockefeller was one of the most powerful men in the world when, in a 1911 anti-trust action, the Supreme Court forced Standard Oil to divide itself into into 31 different companies—but it wasn't as big a blow as it seemed to the public—because behind the scenes, Rockefeller held the bulk of the stock in all of them.

• With the aid of a publicist named Ivy Lee, the Rockefellers began a concerted effort to change his image. The Rockefeller Foundation was created; at Lee's behest, Rockefeller began giving away nickels (to children) and dimes (to adults) on the street; newspapers were encouraged by Lee to cover John D.'s golf games instead of his business practices.

• The effort was so effective that when he died in at age 97, John D. Rockefeller was known as a philanthropist by most Americans.

• His obituaries did little to contradict the image. Ivy Lee had seen to it that they were rewritten to include only data supplied by an "authorized" biographer.

About 70% of Americans who go to college do it just to make more money.

ELEMENTARY, MY DEAR STEVE

Once again, here's the famous woman sleuth, Leslie Boies, with a few simple mysteries for you to solve. Answers on page 223.

Leslie Boies, beautiful blonde detective, was reading a report on the "Penge Bungalow Case" to her faithful companion, Steve.

"Mrs. Krojanker was making biscuits in the kitchen and accidentally dropped her diamond ring into some coffee," she read. "Strangely enough, though, the diamond didn't get wet."

"Wait a minute," Steve interjected. "How is that possible?"

"It's elementary, Steve," Leslie replied.

What happened?

2. "You know, Steve," Leslie said, "Once, I was captured and almost bumped off by my arch-enemy, Fritz von Springmeyer."

Steve was surprised. "I didn't know that."

"Yes, the only thing that saved me was his gang's code of honor. They had a tradition—they always gave their captives an even chance to escape death. They took two pieces of paper, wrote "death" on one and "freedom" on the other. Then they told me to pick one. Now, I knew that that von Springmeyer couldn't afford to let me live, so he'd probably written "death" on both papers. But I thought fast, and they had to free me."

Steve was stumped. "How'd you, do it, Les?"

How *did* she do it?

3. Leslie and Steve were having coffee, discussing Leslie's latest case. The famous detective happened to glance down and saw there was a fly in her coffee.

"Yuck! Waiter!" she called, "Take this coffee away and bring me a fresh cup."

The waiter took her coffee away, and returned with more.

Leslie took a sip. Then she exploded angrily—"Waiter, this is the same cup of coffee I had before!"

How did she know?

It is illegal to own pets in China.

THE NUT BEHIND GRAPE NUTS

To appreciate this story, first read "The Birth of a Flake" on page 63. Then come back and read this.

One of the guests in John Kellogg's Battle Creek sanitarium (The San) was a feeble 37-year-old named Charles W. Post, who arrived there in 1891. His story is told in the strangely fascinating book, *The New Nuts Among the Berries:*

Born in Springfield, Illinois in 1854, Post had wandered in search of success until, at age 37, he had become a well-to-do real estate salesman and blanket manufacturer in Fort Worth, Texas. He had also become a sick man, although we do not know the nature of his illness.

We do know that Dr. Kellogg promptly put Post in a wheelchair, and that after a few months Post hadn't enough cash left to remain a San resident; he had to become an outpatient. So he and his wife and daughter lived in a rented room in town, while Mrs. Post sewed suspenders to pay her husband's medical bills.

By the end of 9 months, Post was getting desperate. He still felt sick, and now he was destitute to boot. He pleaded with Dr. Kellogg to keep him on as a patient. He had spent quite a little time around the San's experimental kitchen. He knew that Kellogg had a new cereal coffee, called Minute Brew, and begged to help promote and sell the coffee in exchange for treatment and a little share of the profits. Post was coldly refused. John Harvey was not a loose man with money. And he did not believe in sharing profits with anyone....Why take Post in?

So Post studied the powers of the mind, took up Christian Science, determinedly repeated to himself, "I am well," got out of his wheelchair and went to work. He had studied the economics of The San and liked what he saw. So with his gift of persuasion, he raised some money and by 1892 established his small La Vita Inn on a

In Alabama, a man was once tried and convicted for wearing a false mustache to church.

plot of 10 acres. Here diet and mental healing were combined, and at prices much lower than those of The San. Meat was allowed to lure those who wanted it. But despite these and other inducements, Mrs. Post still had to go on sewing suspenders.

Post got some of Kellogg's overflow, some of his malcontent clients, and some of his employees. He talked up his own powers to heal with faith and hypnosis. But things were still so slow that he went back to Kellogg and offered to pray for San patients for only $50 a week. The answer was the usual no.

So now Post began writing a book—*I Am Well! The Modern Practice of Natural Suggestion as Distinct from Hypnotic or Unnatural Influence*.....The book featured amazing stories of instant cures—no waiting around for months and taking all those enemas. In some cases of bad teeth, dyspepsia, or troubled bladder, one could hope for same-day service. He also knocked out a pamphlet, *The Road to Wellville*, which he gave away. In both the book and the pamphlet he criticized Kellogg, making the Doctor his certain enemy.

Later on, the San magazine, *Good Health*, would say that Post had spent a lot of time around the San kitchen. The clear implication was that Post had borrowed some of the formulas for his products. *Good Health* quoted Kellogg as saying, "Let him see everything that we are doing. I shall be delighted if he makes a cereal coffee and wish him every success. The more he sells of it the less coffee will be consumed, and this will be of great benefit to the American people."

In January of 1895, the year Dr. Kellogg discovered and launched the cereal flake, C.W. Post put out [a coffee substitute he called] Postum Cereal Food Coffee. The original marketing tool was a handcart which was pushed through the town of Battle Creek.

Soon Post took samples to Grand Rapids, Michigan. Almost without capital, he told wholesale grocers they could pay him if and when they sold their Postum. He talked newspapers into ad credit on the strength of the line, "It Makes Red Blood." By the end of the year, his sales amounted to over $250,000. In three years, they tripled.

American law: Less than 50% of the lawsuits filed actually go to court.

Steadily Post opened wider and wider markets, using ads for which he invented such ailments as "coffee neuralgia" and "coffee heart." Postum could cure them, he said. "Lost Eyesight Through Coffee Drinking" was another of his gambits. And they worked; 50 years later Postum was still being sold as the answer to "coffee nerves." He ploughed a fortune into advertising, using every cent of profit and borrowing more. He began to take ads in the New York Magazine of Mysteries, offering spot cash to get testimonials of cures.

Largely because sales of Postum fell off in summer, Post came up with a cereal to try and take up the warm-weather slack....It was broken into rock-hard bits crumbled from sheets of baked wheat. He called it Grape Nuts, and he pulled out all the stops to announce its curative properties. According to ads which first ran in 1898, it was almost a specific for appendicitis. It tightened up loose teeth, fed the brain through what was implied to be almost a direct pipeline, and quickly disposed of tuberculosis and malaria. Of course, it worked better when consumed with a certain amount of faith; so Post put a copy of *The Road to Wellville* in each package. By 1901, C.W. Post was netting a million dollars a year.

In 1904, C.W. Post [scandalized the religious community of Battle Creek when he] divorced his suspender-sewing wife and married his typist. He was in his fifties; she was in her twenties. He also introduced a new cereal called "Elijah's Manna." Actually, it was corn flakes, which he had appropriated from Kellogg. But the cereal was unsuccessful until he changed its name to "Post Toasties." Then it became the cornerstone of Post Cereals, and later, General Foods.

In 1914, having tried to build his own city in Texas, and having failed to make it flourish by setting off explosions to bring rain, C.W. Post became depressed. In his Santa Barbara, California, home, he fired one of his own fine rifles into his head.

UNRELATED ASIDE
When Harry Truman was told there were ghosts in the White House, he replied: "I'm sure they're here and I'm not half so alarmed at meeting up with any of them as I am at having to meet the live nuts I have to see every day."

The scissors was invented by Leonardo da Vinci.

WHAT'S THE BEEF?

What's the real difference between Burger King and McDonald's?
Not what you'd think. An examination by Mike Wilkins.

For years, Americans have watched as the world's two largest and most successful hamburger chains—Burger King and McDonald's—battled it out over supposed differences:
- Flame-broiling vs. frying
- *Doing It All For You* vs. *Having It Your Way*
- Whoppers vs. Big Macs.

And so on. To the uninitiated, these distinctions may seem like advertising hyperbole...But the fact is, the differences between McDonald's (10,000 restaurants, $13 billion in sales) and Burker King (4,500, $1.5 billion) are quite real.

BACKGROUND
McDonald's
The mythology of the birth of the McDonald's chain is fairly well known. In 1954, Ray Kroc, a fifty-year-old paper cup and milkshake-mixer salesman (actually owner of the company that made them), visited the McDonald Brothers' bustling restaurant in San Bernardino, California in 1954, after they placed a large order for his mixers. Impressed with their volume of business and the simplicity of their limited menu operation, he struck a deal for franchise rights, opened his first restaurant in Des Plaines, Illinois in 1955, and built McDonald's into the burger behemoth it is today.

Burger King
Surprisingly, Burger King also began with a visit to the original McDonald's. In 1952—two years before Kroc arrived—Keith Cramer, owner of a small Florida drive-in restaurant, made a pilgimage to watch the McDonald brothers in action. He was so impressed that he adapted their methods and began franchising his "Insta-Burger King" concept. A year later, the enterprise was taken over by franchisees Jim McLamore and David Edgerton. At first, Burger King was concentrated in the Southeast. But in 1967 it was acquired by Pillsbury, which began to expand the chain nationawide. With Pillsbury's economic muscle behind it, Burger King

---

63% of the Americans who earn minimum wage are women.

could challenge McDonald's in head-to-head competition. Their ad strategy: Burger King encouraged consumers to compare the "differences" between the two giants.

None of the ads, however, pinpointed the *real* differences.

WHAT'S THE DIFFERENCE?

The biggest difference between Burger King and McDonald's is this: McDonald's cooks their hamburgers using a batch process. Burger King cooks theirs using a machine-paced assembly process.

• Check it out: Next time you go into one of these restaurants, watch how the burgers are cooked. McDonald's fries their hamburgers on a large platen, in batches, or groups, of up to twelve. Two or more batches may be on the platen at one time, in various stages of cooking. When the guy in the back says "Quarter Pounders Up," a whole batch is ready at the same time.

• Burger King is built around its "continuous chain broiler." Raw hamburgers are placed at one end, and 80 seconds later they come out the other end, cooked. This machine-paced assembly process is common in most industrial manufacturing processes. It turns hamburger production into an assembly line, much like the type Henry Ford introduced to automobiles in the early 1900s.

IT'S BIGGER THAN IT LOOKS

As simple as this distinction (broiled vs. fried) seems, it is, in fact, at the core of each chain's operation, and is responsible for the corporate culture of each.

• For example: When hiring workers, McDonald's makes a big point about joining the McDonald's team, of the many incentives for doing good jobs, of its nonsalary benefits. Most McDonald's have a framed picture of the "Crew Member Of The Month" on a wall near the cash registers. McDonald's holds an Olympic-style competition to reward the best workers from around the country at each aspect of its food preparation. Not long ago, its advertising featured successful people who had once worked at McD's. When ordering, look at the McD uniforms. Many of the workers have pins or special nametags that signify profiency or accomplishment at a task.

• Go to Burger King and all you see is a "Help Wanted" sign. There are no incentives to join the "Burger King Pit Crew" and the

It's against the law to catch fish with your bare hands in Kansas.

non-salary benefits are much less than those offered by McDonald's. (Total compensation was nearly $1 per hour greater at McDonald's in 1984.)

TEAMWORK VS. ASSEMBLY LINE

How does this relate to production methods? In a batch process, the speed of delivery is dependent upon the worker. At McDonald's, 12 burgers are made at one time. They are hand-seared after 20 seconds on the grill, turned at 60 seconds, and pulled at 100. When they come off the grill, workers must quickly add condiments, wrap and shelve them. If there are two batches going in different stages of cooking, it means that speed is even more essential to keep the production moving. And this means that the crew must all be motivated, or the process gums up. People must be willing and able to help in another's area in case of backup. Teamwork and a sense of team must be present. Thus the motivational and non-salary rewards.

At Burger King, on the other hand, no matter how fast the burgers are prepared once they are cooked, the rate-limiting step is the cooking itself. One burger at a time comes off the chain broiler at the rate of eight per minute, maximum. The machine paces the process. (Again, in slow times this is not entirely accurate because at these points in the day, BK keeps an inventory of already cooked patties in a steam tray at the end of the broiler. That is why BK sometimes has to microwave its burgers.) As long as you can do your part of the assembly process in 7.5 seconds per burger (adding pickles and onions in 7 seconds is easy even if you're not very motivated—try it someday), that's all that is required. If you get excited and love your work, and can do it faster, so what? You still have to wait for the machine to spit out the next patty. This means that Burger King saves money on wages and hiring expense, by not paying for all the motivation-inspired cross-talk.

HAVE IT WHOSE WAY?

Batch processing also means less room for individual differences in members of the batch. Twelve burgers come up, 12 burgers are all done exactly the same. At Burger King, since one patty comes out at a time, each can be made to individual order. Thus the *Have It Your Way* point of difference (vs. *We Do It All For You*) harped on by Burger King stems directly from the difference in production methods.

Also, batch processing means that twelve burgers will be ready (or 10 Quarter Pounders, or 6 Macs, since 12 patties = 6 Macs), whether or not customers are ready for them. During rush hour this is not a problem, but at other times it can be—especially in a business that promises fresh food. McDonald's and Burger King throw old food out—after 10 minutes in McDonald's case. That is what those cards with the numbers are doing on the McDonald's food shelves. When the minute hand gets to that number, all food in front of the card gets pitched.

WASTE NOT...

Since a product may stay in the bin nine minutes, keeping it warm is a problem. That is why McDonald's uses those Styrofoam containers, especially for its larger sandwiches. Styrofoam is much more expensive (and less ecologically sound) than the cardboard Burger King uses. Burger King doesn't need to keep finished burgers warm as long, so it doesn't spend for the fancy packaging. A McDonald's restaurant spends about 1¢ per revenue dollar more on paper costs than does a Burger King. That adds up to a yearly $15 million savings systemwide for BK.

• As one might guess, McDonald's throws away much more food than Burger King does. In fact, in the seedy Tenderloin area of San Francisco, the derelicts paint stars on the wastecans of the nearby restaurants and stores. The only four-star can in the neighborhood? McDonald's.

BATCHES MEAN BUCKS

How can McDonald's stay on top—or even competitive—with its system? The answer is that, when it is running right, the batch process allows for much greater throughput and faster speed of service. And speed is one big reason for the popularity of fast food in the first place. If an item is waiting in a bin, it obviously takes less time to serve than one made "your way."

• The batch process can deliver 300 burgers an hour vs. 200 for the continuous chain broiler.

• Speed standards given to individual restaurants by each head-quarters bear this out. At side-by-side locations, the standard for a McDonald's is up to twice as fast as for a Burger King (a customer wait of, say, 90 seconds vs. three minutes).

• This difference may not be that noticeable per individual customer, but it means that McDonald's can do twice the dollar volume at peak than can a similarly sized Burger King.

Even customer flow is regulated by the speed of the broiler. Once the steam tray and bin reserves are gone, Burger King simply cannot serve more than eight burgers per minute. This accounts for at least some of the tremendous difference in the dollar volume per store between the two chains ($1.5 Billion over 4,500 stores, vs. $13 billion over 10,000). McDonald's is systemically better equipped to handle crowded areas. It is only during off-peak times when Burger King comes close in dollar volume, and is actually more efficient because of less waste, paper, and salary expenses.

So there you have it. An enormous "hidden" difference at the heart of the two chains. Next time you hear either of them make a claim about their service or products, check to see if it's based on their methods of production. Chances are, it will be.

UNRELATED INFO:

These were the #1 songs in America during the first week of each of the following years, according to *Billboard* magazine:

- 1958: "At the Hop," by Danny and the Juniors
- 1960: "El Paso," by Marty Robbins
- 1963: "Go Away Little Girl," by Steve Lawrence
- 1965: "Downtown," by Petula Clark
- 1966: "The Sounds of Silence," by Simon and Garfunkel
- 1967: "Kind of a Drag," by the Buckinghams
- 1969: "Crimson and Clover," by Tommy James & the Shondells
- 1971: "Knock Three Times," by Dawn
- 1972: "American Pie," by Don McLean
- 1973: "You're So Vain," by Carly Simon
- 1974: "The Joker," by the Steve Miller Band
- 1975: " Lucy In the Sky," by Elton John
- 1976: "Saturday Night," by the Bay City Rollers
- 1979: "Too Much Heaven," by the Bee Gees
- 1980: "Please Don't Go," by KC & the Sunshine Band
- 1982: "I Can't Go for That," by Hall & Oates
- 1983: "Down Under," by Men At Work

On the average: You can get about 6 glasses of wine from a standard-size bottle.

ELEMENTARY MY DEAR STEVE: SOLUTIONS

PAGE 16

1. A man with the hiccups was cured when the bartender scared him. The man—who happened to own a carnival—was very grateful, and when he died, he left the bartender his Funhouse.

2. If the nightwatchman had a dream that the 5:30 train crashed, that meant he was sleeping on the job. It turned out well for the night watchman; he was such a sound sleeper that he was able to get a job demonstrating mattresses for department stores.

PAGE 127-28

1. Remember, they had just come from Thomasville. All they had to do was reposition the signpost so that the "Thomasville" arrow was correct. That way, the road to Montez was obvious. They got their in time, and thwarted the evil son-in-law just as he was breaking into the wall-safe

2. No one shaves the barber—she's a woman. Good barber, too.

3. They're two of three triplets. Leslie made Steve promise never to see them again.

4. The poison was in the ice cubes. Arnie luckily saved his own life when he gulped down his drink and left before the ice melted. Mingo wasn't so lucky. The bartender, it turned out, was working for a used car dealer on the side, and wanted Mingo's '64 Mustang convertible.

PAGE 214

1. She dropped her ring into a bag of dry, ground coffee.

2. She quickly grabbed one of the pieces of paper, and ripped it up. Then she said, "I've chosen my fate. Let us see which one is left." The paper that was left said "death," which meant she'd chosen "freedom." Von Springmeyer was forced by the rest of the gang to let Leslie go.

3. Leslie had a sweet tooth, and always put sugar in her coffee. When she tasted the coffee, it was sweet.

"The Star Spangled Banner" became America's national anthem in 1931.

THE LAST PAGE

FELLOW BATHROOM READERS:
The fight for good bathroom reading should never be taken loosely—we must sit firmly for what we believe in, even while the rest of the world is taking pot shots at us.

Once we prove we're not simply a flush-in-the-pan, writers and publishers will find their resistance unrolling.

So we invite you to take the plunge—"Sit Down and Be Counted"—by joining The Bathroom Readers' Institute. Send a self-addressed, stamped envelope to: B.R.I., 1400 Shattuck Avenue, #25, Berkeley, CA 94709. You'll receive your free membership card, a copy of the B.R.I. newsletter whenever it's published, and earn a permanent spot on the B.R.I. honor roll.

☞ ☞ ☞

UNCLE JOHN'S THIRD
BATHROOM READER IS IN THE WORKS

Don't fret—there's more good reading on its way. In fact, there are a few ways you can contribute to the next volume:

1) Is there a subject you'd like to see us cover? Write and let us know. We aim to please.

2) Got a neat idea for a couple of pages in the new *Reader*? If you're the first to suggest it, and we use it, we'll send you a free copy of the book.

3) Have you seen or read an article you'd recommend as quintessential bathroom reading? Or is there a passage in a book that you want to share with other B.R.I. members? Tell us where to find it, or send a copy. If you're the first to suggest it and we publish it in the next volume, there's a free book in it for you.

Well, we're out of space, and when you've gotta go, you've gotta go. Hope to hear from you soon. Meanwhile, remember:
Go With the Flow.